W9-ADM-961

LIBRARY

Name	Symbol	Atomic number	Atomic weight
Mercury	Hg	80	200·59
Molybdenum	Mo	42	95·94
Neon	Ne	10	20·18
Nickel	Ni	28	58·71
Niobium	Nb	41	92·91
Nitrogen	N	7	14·01
Osmium	Os	76	190·20
Oxygen	O	8	16·00
Palladium	Pd	46	106·40
Phosphorus	P	15	30·97
Platinum	Pt	78	195·09
Potassium	K	19	39·10
Rhenium	Re	75	186·20
Rhodium	Rh	45	102·91
Rubidium	Rb	37	85·47
Ruthenium	Ru	44	101·07
Scandium	Sc	21	44·96
Selenium	Se	34	78·96
Silicon	Si	14	28·09
Silver	Ag	47	107·87
Sodium	Na	11	22·99
Strontium	Sr	38	87·62
Sulphur	S	16	32·06
Tantalum	Ta	73	180·95
Tellurium	Te	52	127·60
Thallium	Tl	81	204·37
Tin	Sn	50	118·69
Titanium	Ti	22	47·90
Tungsten	W	74	183·85
Vanadium	V	23	50·94
Zinc	Zn	30	65·37
Zirconium	Zr	40	91·22

546.028
P26p

78329

DATE DUE			

Practical Inorganic Chemistry

Preparations, reactions and instrumental methods

Practical
Inorganic Chemistry

Preparations, reactions and instrumental methods

GEOFFREY PASS, B.Sc., Ph.D.
and
HAYDN SUTCLIFFE, B.Sc., Ph.D.
Lecturers in Chemistry, University of Salford

CHAPMAN AND HALL LTD
11 NEW FETTER LANE · LONDON EC4

CARL A. RUDISILL LIBRARY
LENOIR RHYNE COLLEGE

546.028
P26P
78329
apu.1972

First published 1968
Reprinted 1969
© 1968 *Geoffrey Pass and Haydn Sutcliffe*
Printed in Great Britain by
Fletcher & Son Limited, Norwich
SBN 412 08890 8

Distributed in the U.S.A.
by Barnes & Noble, Inc.

Preface

The student of inorganic chemistry is fortunate in having a wide choice of textbooks covering the descriptive and theoretical aspects of the subject. There is no comparable choice of textbooks covering practical inorganic chemistry. Moreover, there is a tendency for many students to draw an unfortunate distinction between chemistry taught in the lecture room, and laboratory work. Consideration of these points prompted the preparation of this book, in which we have attempted to emphasize the relationship between theory and practice.

The experimental work described in this text has been selected with a view to covering most of the principles of inorganic chemistry discussed in an undergraduate course. Each chapter or section is preceded by a theoretical discussion which, it is hoped, will provide a thread of continuity between lecture room and laboratory. This discussion is in outline only and amplification through lectures and standard textbooks is necessary. Much of the experimental work described is of a preparative nature. Each preparation is followed by a set of complementary exercises which must be completed in order to gain maximum benefit from the work. The complementary work includes questions and practical exercises.

Analytical chemistry is seen in correct perspective when used on real, rather than artificial systems. Consequently, the complementary work frequently requires the student to analyse the compound which he has prepared. This may involve the techniques of volumetric or gravimetric analysis, and a student can develop his knowledge of analytical chemistry by devising an analytical method for a particular purpose. Alternatively, more sophisticated instrumental methods of analysis may be used, details of which are given in the later chapters of the book. Satisfactory answers to the complementary questions can often only be given after a certain amount of library work. This study will lead the student back to the theoretical introduction or to some related topic. In this way it is hoped to emphasize the unity between theory and practice. References are provided at the end of an experiment to assist with this library work. The bibliographies at the end of the chapters and the General Bibliography at the end of the book will provide background reading. The connexion between theory and practice may be more fully emphasized if the theoretical introduction, preparation, and complementary work are taken as headings for an essay.

In addition to illustrating theoretical aspects of the subject, an attempt has been made to demonstrate the diversity of techniques used in inorganic chemistry. Such diversity of method is inevitable in a subject which covers the whole of the periodic table. A representative selection of techniques has been included, but an exhaustive coverage has not been attempted. Some preparations and techniques have been omitted because they present a potential hazard in student hands. Where experiments do involve a possible hazard, suitable safety precautions are given.

The book is suitable for use parallel to a lecture course for an honours degree in chemistry, or its equivalent. The material is arranged in an approximate order of increasing complexity, but it is not suggested that this order must be rigidly followed. A selection of material dependent on the students' current lecture course is advocated. Suitable selection will also enable the text to be used for chemistry courses at a lower level. Some experiments could well be included in more than one chapter, but to avoid duplication of the text, while allowing full correlation of such experiments, cross-references have been given to other sections of the book.

The experimental details have been drawn from a wide range of sources and all have been used in the form in which they are described. Some are from original papers, some we have devised, and some have been adapted from *Inorganic Syntheses, Experimental Inorganic Chemistry* by W. G. Palmer, *Inorganic Preparations* by H. F. Walton, *Handbook of Preparative Inorganic Chemistry* by G. Brauer, and *Inorganic Preparations* by A. King.

Finally, our thanks are due to colleagues with whom we have discussed chapters of the book, and in particular to those who have read the manuscript and made many useful suggestions.

G.P.
H.S.

Contents

1 Typical elements

These elements have by definition no incompletely filled d or f orbitals, and the valence electrons are located in s and p orbitals. The reactions included are designed to illustrate points in the chemistry of a given subgroup of the periodic table and to demonstrate more general theoretical considerations.

Ion size effects

The preparation of caesium dichloroiodide

The formation of polyhalides AB_n^- depends on the combination of a central halide ion with a halogen or interhalogen molecule, where the atomic weight of $A \geqslant$ atomic weight of B. No polyhalides are known where fluorine acts as the central atom. The oxidation state of A depends on the halogen B with which it is combined; increasing oxidation states occur with decreasing atomic weight of B and increasing atomic weight of A. Only large cations with low charge give a stable ionic lattice with the large polyhalide ions. With a small cation, such as sodium, polarization of the polyhalide ion would occur, resulting in the formation of a more stable sodium halide lattice.

The preparation of caesium dichloroiodide

Materials required: Caesium chloride
Iodine
Chlorine

1

This experiment must be carried out in a fume cupboard.
Dissolve caesium chloride (3·5 g) in 35 ml of water and add iodine
(2·6 g). Heat to just below the boiling point and bubble chlorine into
the hot solution until the iodine just dissolves. The solution is conveniently contained in a boiling tube. Avoid excess chlorine, otherwise caesium tetrachloroiodide may be formed. Cool and filter the
precipitated caesium dichloroiodide. Record the yield.

Complementary work:

(1) What is the structure of the ICl_2^- ion? How does this compare
with the structure of xenon difluoride?

(2) Study the effect of heat on the dry product and compare this
with the effect of heat on potassium iodide. Identify the volatile
product and comment.

The preparation of barium peroxide

Within the subgroups of alkali metals, and alkaline-earth metals
there is a decreasing tendency with increasing cation size for the
oxide M_2^IO or $M^{II}O$ to be formed by direct combination of the
elements. As described on p. 3, the small Li^+ cation will form a more
stable crystal lattice with a small anion than will a larger alkali metal
cation. With increasing size of the cation a more stable crystal structure is obtained by expanding the lattice, and increasing the separation of the cations. This may be achieved by replacing the oxide ion
O^{2-} by a larger anion such as peroxide, O_2^{2-} or superoxide O_2^- ions.
The peroxide ion O_2^{2-} is larger than the oxide ion, O^{2-}. It should
be noted that for lithium the most stable lattice is achieved with a
small ion, as in Li_2O. For a larger cation such as Ba^{2+} or K^+ the
most stable lattice is achieved with the larger anion, O_2^{2-} as in
BaO_2 or K_2O_2.

The experimental details for the preparation of barium peroxide
are given on p. 34.

Lattice energy effects

The preparation of lithium nitride

One of the reactions in which lithium differs from the other alkali
metals, but resembles magnesium, is the formation of a nitride Li_3N,

an example of the so-called 'diagonal relationship' in the periodic table. The reaction

$$3M + \tfrac{1}{2}N_2 = M_3N$$

may be represented in terms of a Born–Haber cycle

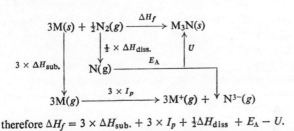

therefore $\Delta H_f = 3 \times \Delta H_{sub.} + 3 \times I_p + \tfrac{1}{2}\Delta H_{diss} + E_A - U$.

The dissociation energy of nitrogen ($\Delta H_{diss.}$) and the electron affinity E_A for the formation of N^{3-} are both endothermic terms, and are independent of the alkali metal M. The ionization energy (I_p) and the sublimation energy ($\Delta H_{sub.}$) are also endothermic and decrease down the group from Li → Cs. The only energetically favourable term in the cycle is the lattice energy (U). The fact that lithium forms a nitride, while sodium does not, demonstrates that the lattice energy of lithium nitride is greater than the lattice energy of the hypothetical sodium nitride. This decrease in lattice energy with increasing size of the cation is a general effect, but is more pronounced with a small highly charged anion e.g. N^{3-}, O^{2-}. The effect is readily noticed in the case of the nitride since it results in the distinct change from compound formation to no compound formation.

The experimental details for the preparation of lithium nitride are given on p. 33 under High temperature reactions.

Ionization energy

The preparation of a cationic iodine compound

Across any period in the periodic table the ionization potential required to form a given cation M^{n+} generally increases. Within a given group in the periodic table the ionization potential generally decreases with increasing atomic weight. As a consequence there is little tendency for the halogens to form M^{n+} cations, but within the group the maximum tendency to form such cations is found with iodine. Astatine should have the greatest tendency to form M^{n+} cations. However, a knowledge of the chemistry of astatine is limited because the longest lived isotope has a half-life of only 8·3 hours. In practice, a limited number of cationic compounds (as opposed to compounds, such as potassium iodate, in which iodine has a formal positive oxidation state), of iodine have been prepared. The number of cationic bromine and chlorine compounds is even more restricted.

The preparation of dipyridineiodine(I) nitrate

Materials required: Iodine
Silver nitrate
Pyridine

Dissolve silver nitrate (1·7g) in 5 ml of pyridine, and iodine (2·5g) in 50 ml of chloroform. Add the chloroform solution slowly to the pyridine solution, stirring well. Allow to stand, and filter off the yellow precipitate, which can be discarded. To the filtrate add 50 ml of diethyl ether, shake, and allow to stand. Filter off the yellow crystals with suction, wash with ether, and suck dry.

Complementary work:
(1) Dissolve a portion of the product in dilute hydrochloric acid and record your observations.
(2) Dissolve a portion of the product in dilute sodium hydroxide and record your observations.
(3) To each of the above solutions add a solution of potassium iodide. Comment on your observations.
(4) Devise a method for the quantitative determination of iodine in the compound.
(5) Dissolve a portion of the product in 4M sodium hydroxide solution, and boil until no more volatile material can be detected. Now add a little zinc dust to the solution and boil. Comment on the reactions which have occurred.

Reference
Arotsky, J. and Symons, M. C. R., *Quart. Rev.*, (1962), **16**, 282.

Electronegativity effects

The preparation of silicon tetrachloride

The elements of the first short period have considerable differences in chemistry when compared with the element of the same group in the second short period (cf. Li_3N p. 3). This difference is probably most pronounced between carbon and silicon. Some reference to the M(IV) halides is instructive.

Carbon tetrachloride is thermodynamically unstable with regard to hydrolysis at 25°C,

$$CCl_4 + 2H_2O = CO_2 + 4HCl \qquad \Delta G^0 = -55 \cdot 5 \text{ kcal.}$$

The absence of any vacant orbitals of suitable energy on the carbon atom prevents coordination of the attacking group and so hydrolysis of carbon tetrachloride does not occur. The sharp decrease in electronegativity from carbon to silicon means that the Si—Cl bond will have more polar character than a C—Cl bond, and will be more susceptible to attack by hydroxyl ion. Furthermore, the silicon atom has available $3d$ orbitals through which the attacking group may initially coordinate. Silicon tetrachloride is therefore readily hydrolysed. This discontinuity in chemical properties between group elements of the first and second short periods is a general effect, and may often be attributed to the availability of $3d$ orbitals in the second short period element.

The elements from Si → Pb will all have available d orbitals through which coordination of the attacking group may occur. The hydrolysis of the M(IV) halides from Si → Pb shows some correlation with the change in electronegativity within the group, a change which is not smoothly continuous. The changes in electronegativity will result in changes in the polarity of the M—X bond with a subsequent change in its resistance to attack by hydroxyl ion.

The experimental details for the preparation of silicon tetrachloride are given on p. 35 under High Temperature Reactions.

Reference
Payne, D. A. and Fink, F. H., *J. Chem. Educ.*, (1966), **43**, 654.

Variation of bond character with oxidation state

The preparation of tin(II) chloride, and tin(IV) chloride

If the compounds tin(II) chloride and tin(IV) chloride were both purely covalent in character then it might be expected that the higher molecular weight compound, tin(IV) chloride, would have the higher melting and boiling point. The reverse is in fact the case. This is due to a greater ionic character of an Sn—Cl bond in tin(II) chloride and it may be considered in two ways.

The Sn^{2+} ion has a lower charge/radius ratio than Sn^{4+}. Thus in tin(IV) chloride, which may be considered initially to contain Sn^{4+} ions and Cl^- ions, the polarization of the Cl^- by the Sn^{4+} is greater than the polarization of Cl^- by Sn^{2+} in tin(II) chloride. Consequently tin(IV) chloride would have a more covalent character.

An alternative approach is to consider the values of the ionization potentials. The third and fourth ionization potentials are so high that the total energy required to produce Sn^{4+} is greater than that made available by the formation of an ionic lattice. Thus there is little probability of electron loss to form Sn^{4+}, little ionic contribution to the overall bond type, and any Sn(IV) compounds formed are essentially covalent. The lower values of the first and second ionization potentials imply a greater probability of the formation of Sn^{2+}, with a consequent increase in the ionic contribution to the overall bond type.

The preparation of tin(II) chloride

Materials required:　　Tin foil
　　　　　　　　　　　　Hydrochloric acid (S.G. 1.18)
　　　　　　　　　　　　Acetic anhydride

Dissolve tin foil (5 g) in concentrated hydrochloric acid and warm the reaction mixture to complete the reaction. Transfer the solution to an evaporating basin, and reduce the volume of solution until crystallization occurs on cooling. Filter off the crystals and dry over calcium chloride. Record the yield. The product of the reaction is the compound $SnCl_2.2H_2O$, and this may be readily converted to the anhydrous salt by reaction with a readily hydrolysed material, such as acetic anhydride.

Add the crystalline dihydrate (5 g) to acetic anhydride (10 ml) in a beaker. The reaction is vigorous and requires no heating. *Carry out the reaction in a fume cupboard.* The anhydrous salt precipitates from the solution. Filter, wash with a little ether, and dry on the filter. Record the yield.

Complementary work:
(1) Place a little of the product in a test tube and add water slowly, dropwise. Comment on your observations.
(2) Place a little of the anhydrous salt in a test tube, and slowly add 2M sodium hydroxide. Comment on your observations.
(3) Test the solubility of the anhydrous salt in acetone, ether, and alcohol.
(4) Determine the melting point of the anhydrous product. Comment on your result together with your results from (3). How does the melting point of tin(II) chloride compare with the corresponding value for tin(IV) chloride? Explain.
(5) To a mixed solution of iron(III) chloride and potassium hexacyanoferrate(III) add a freshly prepared solution of tin(II) chloride. Comment on your observations.

The preparation of tin(IV) chloride

Materials required: Tin foil
Chlorosulphuric acid

The experiment must be carried out in a fume cupboard. Wear protective gloves when handling chlorosulphuric acid.
The procedure adopted follows that of Heumann and Kochlin, who demonstrated the use of chlorosulphuric acid as a chlorinating agent for a number of metalloids, and for tin.

Place tin foil (10 g) in a two-necked 100 ml round-bottomed flask, which is fitted with a dropping funnel, and a still-head connected to a condenser. Place chlorosulphuric acid (50 ml) in the dropping funnel, and add the acid dropwise to the tin in the flask. The reaction is vigorous and the rate is controlled by regulating the addition of the chlorosulphuric acid. Do not heat the flask since the reaction will become too vigorous. The reaction proceeds more smoothly if the round-bottomed flask is shielded from draughts by being placed in an empty beaker. (See Figure 1.)

The product of the reaction, tin(IV) chloride has a lower boiling point (b.p. 114°C) than the chlorosulphuric acid (b.p. 158°C) and may be distilled from the reaction mixture using the heat of reaction. The product may be further purified by fractionally distilling the liquid in the receiver and collecting the fraction boiling between 112–115°C.

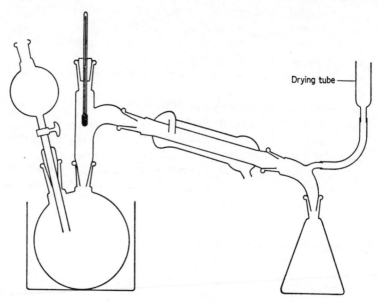

Figure 1. Apparatus for the preparation of tin(IV) chloride.

Complementary work:

(1) Place about 1 ml of tin(IV) chloride in a test tube and carefully add excess 2M sodium hydroxide solution. Comment on your observations. Repeat the procedure using 4M hydrochloric acid.

(2) Place about 2 ml of water in a test tube, and carefully add 1 ml of tin(IV) chloride. Cool to 0°C. What is the product of the reaction? How do these reactions compare with the corresponding reactions of carbon tetrachloride and silicon tetrachloride?

(3) Dissolve ammonium chloride (2 g) in the minimum of water and carefully add tin(IV) chloride (1 ml). Cool, and identify the crystalline product.

Reference

Heumann, K. and Kochlin, P., *Ber.*, (1882), **15**, 416.

Charge transfer effects

The preparation of tin(IV) iodide

One of the more obvious physical differences between tin(IV) chloride and tin(IV) iodide is the intense colour of the latter. The trend in intensity of colour can be compared with a similar colour trend in the two series AgCl, AgBr, AgI; and Cl_2, Br_2, I_2. The occurrence of these colours in compounds of transition and non-transition elements should be distinguished from the generally less intense colour produced by a *d–d* transition. See p. 170 under Electronic Spectra.

Consider a molecule MA; the colour is produced as a result of the transition

$$M^+A^- \xrightarrow{\ h\nu\ } M^{\cdot} A^{\cdot}$$

The transfer of an electron from A^- to M^+ corresponds to an internal oxidation—reduction reaction. Usually the electron returns to its original position so that there is no net chemical reaction, but in some cases free radicals can be detected

$$Fe^{3+} Cl^- \xrightarrow{\ h\nu\ } Fe^{2+} + Cl^{\cdot}$$

On a simple model the energy of the transition ΔE will depend on the ionization potential (I_p) of A^-, and on the electron affinity (E_A) of M^+, and a third quantity δ which depends on the change in electrostatic energy due to charge transfer. This can be written as

$$E = h\nu = I_p - E_A + \delta.$$

Therefore, for a given metal ion the electron affinity remains constant, but from $Cl^- \to I^-$ the ionization potential of the halide ion will decrease, that is the anion is more readily oxidized. The frequency at which absorption takes place decreases and changes from the ultraviolet to the visible region of the spectrum. The fact that absorption occurs in the visible region means that the energy required to transfer an electron from the anion is small. If the given anion is replaced by a more readily oxidizable anion, then irreversible oxidation may occur, e.g. the reaction of Fe^{3+} with SCN^- and I^-, p. 45.

The intense colours of some transition metal compounds are due to charge transfer bands. See the reactions of titanium, chromium, manganese, and iron, p. 40.

The preparation of tin(IV) iodide

Materials required: Iodine
                       Tin foil
                       Acetic acid
                       Acetic anhydride

Prepare the solvent for the reaction by adding acetic anhydride (25 ml) to acetic acid (25 ml) in a 100 ml round-bottomed flask. Add tin (0·5 g) cut into small fragments, and iodine (2 g). Fit the round-bottomed flask with a condenser and reflux the mixture until no tin remains, and there is no observable violet colour of iodine vapour. If any tin remains, add a few crystals of iodine and reflux again. Cool the mixture, filter off the tin(IV) iodide with suction and recrystallize from chloroform. Record the weight of product and calculate the percentage yield based on tin.

Complementary work:
(1) Prepare a solution of tin(IV) iodide in acetone (~5 ml) and divide it into two portions A, and B. To A add a few drops of water. To B add a similar quantity of saturated potassium iodide solution. Comment on your observations.
(2) Determine the percentage of iodine in the product by titration in concentrated hydrochloric acid with standard potassium iodate.
(3) Could lead(IV) iodide be prepared in a similar manner? Comment.

Coordination compounds of non-transition elements

The preparation of chelate complexes of aluminium

The formation of metal complex compounds is by no means confined to the transition elements, and examples can be found in all the metal groups of the periodic table. For example, elements of the subgroup Al → Tl form complex compounds with a coordination number of 4 or 6. Probably the most important octahedral complexes are formed with chelating ligands. The reaction of aluminium with acetylacetone produces a neutral complex while reaction with the oxalate ion gives the complex anion, $[Al(C_2O_4)_3]^{3-}$. This complex ion has similar crystallographic properties to the trioxalato complex ions of iron(III), cobalt(III) and chromium(III), and is prepared in a similar manner.

The preparation of potassium trioxalatoaluminate

Materials required: Aluminium sulphate
Potassium oxalate
Oxalic acid
Sodium hydroxide

Dissolve aluminium sulphate (7 g of the hexadecahydrate) in 100 ml of water and add to this, with stirring, a solution of sodium hydroxide (2·5 g in 20 ml of water). Filter off the freshly precipitated aluminium hydroxide, and wash with water. Prepare a solution of oxalic acid (4 g of the dihydrate) and potassium oxalate (6 g of the monohydrate) in 100 ml of water, and boil this with the aluminium hydroxide. Filter off any unreacted aluminium hydroxide and evaporate the filtrate to crystallization. Dry and record the yield.

Complementary work:
(1) Investigate the effect of the following reagents on a solution of the product; 4M sodium hydroxide, sodium acetate solution (boil), sodium carbonate solution, and sodium orthophosphate solution. Compare the results with those obtained when a simple aluminium salt is treated with the same reagents.
(2) Note the effect of potassium permanganate in acid solution on the product, and use this reaction to determine the percentage of oxalate in the product.
(3) What is the structure of the product? Can it be resolved into optical isomers? Comment.

References
Burrows, G. J. and Lauder, K. H., *J. Amer. Chem. Soc.*, (1931), **53**, 3600.
Johnson, C. H., *Trans. Faraday Soc.*, (1935), **31**, 1612.
Dwyer, F. P. and Sorgeson, A. M., *J. Phys. Chem.*, (1956), **60**, 1331.

The preparation of tris(acetylacetonato)aluminium

Materials required: Aluminium nitrate
Acetylacetone
2M aqueous ammonia

Dissolve aluminium nitrate (8 g of the nonahydrate) in water (50 ml) and add acetylacetone (2·5 ml). To the well stirred solution add dropwise 2M aqueous ammonia until the solution is just alkaline. Cool the resultant solution in ice, filter by suction and dry in a warm oven, (about 70°C). To remove any aluminium hydroxide impurity take up the product in chloroform, filter, and evaporate off the chloroform to leave the tris(acetylacetonato)aluminium. Record the yield and measure the m.p.

Complementary work:
(1) Dissolve a sample of the complex in 4M hydrochloric acid, and add 4M aqueous ammonia until the solution is basic. Boil a sample of the complex with 4M hydrochloric acid, cool and add 4M aqueous ammonia as before. Comment on your observations.
(2) Observe the effect of heat on a sample of the complex.
(3) Comment on the effect of 4M sodium hydroxide on the complex.
(4) Investigate the solubility of the product in alcohol, ether, and acetone.

2 Oxo-acids and oxo-acid salts

Introduction

The oxo-acids and oxo-acid salts of boron and the elements of groups IV–VII of the periodic table, from the second short period onwards, contain anions which can be considered as based on MO_x units, where M is the group element and x can have values from 1–6.

The simple oxo-acids, that is acids in which discrete MO_x^{n-} units are present, contain at least one —OH group. With certain hypothetical oxo-acids elimination of water occurs with the precipitation of hydrated oxides. The —OH group may be replaced by one of a number of alternative functional groups, e.g. —Cl, —NH$_2$, or —OOH. The replacement of one —OH group in sulphuric acid by chlorine gives chlorosulphuric acid, $Cl.SO_3.H$, see p. 7, while replacement of both —OH groups gives sulphuryl chloride SO_2Cl_2. Even when the free acid is unknown, or at best occurs under very limited conditions, the chlorosubstituted acid may be prepared. Thus potassium monochlorochromate and chromyl chloride which are respectively mono- and di-substituted chloro-derivatives of chromic acid, H_2CrO_4 are known and their preparation is described below.

The replacement of one —OH group in sulphuric acid by —NH$_2$ gives amidosulphuric acid NH_2SO_3H while replacement of both —OH groups gives sulphamide $SO_2(NH_2)_2$. These amine substituted acids may polymerize in an analogous manner to unsubstituted oxo-anions but elimination of ammonia occurs instead of elimination of water.

Reaction of hydrogen peroxide with some oxo-acids or substituted oxo-acids will give anions which contain either the —OOH group as in peroxomonosulphuric acid, or the —O—O— bridging group, as

13

in peroxodisulphuric acid. Potassium peroxodisulphate is prepared by electrochemical oxidation as described on p. 82. However, with other oxo-acid salts the product of the reaction with hydrogen peroxide apparently does not contain a peroxo-anion but hydrogen peroxide of crystallization is present in the solid product. The distinction between the true peroxo-salts and the peroxo-hydrates is by no means clear cut. Some compounds apparently contain both a peroxo-anion and hydrogen peroxide of crystallization, e.g. peroxocarbonates such as $K_2CO_4.H_2O_2.1\frac{1}{2}H_2O$. Other compounds have been formulated as isomeric forms; one form contains the peroxoanion, the other form is the peroxo-hydrate. Such a compound is sodium peroxoborate, but the presence of the structural unit

in the compound and the conclusion that a similar pair of apparently isomeric salts $Na_2CO_4.1\frac{1}{2}H_2O$ and $Na_2CO_3.H_2O_2.\frac{1}{2}H_2O$ are in fact identical may well mean that sodium peroxoborate exists only as the peroxo-salt. The formation of peroxo-anions of the transition elements should be noted in view of their use in quantitative and qualitative analysis.

The increasing acidity of the oxo-acids from group IV–VII is accompanied by a decreasing tendency for the MO_4^{n-} tetrahedral anion, where it occurs, to form polymeric anions. This is most apparent in the second short period where a number of polymeric anions based on SiO_4, and PO_4 occur. Consider the oxo-anions of elements in a given group. The acidity of such oxo-anions decreases with increasing atomic weight of the group element. Consequently, in certain groups of the periodic table, although oxo-anions containing the lighter elements do not polymerize appreciably, the heavier elements may now form oxo-anions which are sufficiently weakly acidic to polymerize, e.g. tellurium.

The polymerization reaction may be written in general terms as

$$MO_4^{n-} + MO_4^{n-} = M_2O_7^{(2n-2)} + O^{2-}$$

$$O^{2-} + 2H^+ = H_2O.$$

This polymerization should occur most readily with anions having the greatest tendency to lose oxygen ions. Such anions will be those with a high negative charge on the oxygen in the M—O bond, that is with the group elements having low electronegativities. These are the group elements which form weak oxo-acids. If the oxide ion eliminated in the polymerization step reacts as shown above to give water, then the polymerization reaction should be favoured in acid solution. The polymeric anions are formed from two or more MO_4 tetrahedra which are linked together through common oxygen atoms. This polymerization can result in the formation of either cyclic or chain anions. The condensation may be brought about in a number of ways: by changing the pH of a solution of the simple anion, by increasing the concentration of the simple anion in solution, or by the action of heat on an oxo-acid salt or mixture of oxo-acid salts.

In the case of the phosphorus(V) oxo-acid salts the condensation is effected by heating a suitable mixture of sodium hydrogen orthophosphates. The degree of polymerization is a function of the acidity of the original solid or mixture of solids, i.e. on the initial $H^+:PO_4^{3-}$ ratio. This is illustrated by the following examples:

$$2Na_2HPO_4 = Na_4P_2O_7 + H_2O$$

where

$$H^+:PO_4^{3-} = 1:1$$

and

$$x\,NaH_2PO_4 = x\,H_2O + (NaPO_3)_x$$

where

$$H^+:PO_4^{3-} = 2:1.$$

The polymeric anions may be depolymerized by hydrolysis, either by acid or base. The ultimate product of the hydrolysis is the orthophosphate ion but by suitable adjustment of reaction conditions the hydrolysis may be stopped at an intermediate stage.

Elements which form catenated compounds, that is compounds containing element to element bonds, also form catenated oxo-acids. These differ from the polyacids in that the chain is built up of element to element bonds—M—M— and not from element—oxygen —element bonds —M—O—M—. Examples of catenated oxo-acids are found, as might be expected, with oxo-acids of carbon and sulphur and the preparation of salts of thionic acids illustrates this point.

The preparation of chloric acid

A general method for the preparation of solutions of acids, particularly useful when the acid has only a limited stability, is the reaction of a suitable metal salt of the required acid with a mineral acid. The metal ion and the anion of the mineral acid form an insoluble salt which is filtered off leaving a solution of the required acid. Barium and silver salts are obviously suitable for such a reaction.

Materials required: Barium chlorate
Sulphuric acid

Dissolve barium chlorate (30 g) in water (35 ml) and add slowly, with stirring, the calculated amount of hot 3M sulphuric acid. It is necessary to have a slight excess of barium chlorate to ensure that no free sulphuric acid is present in the solution. Therefore, test the solution for the presence of Ba^{2+} and SO_4^{2-} ions. Filter off the barium sulphate. The prepared solution of chloric acid should be about 20% w/w.

Complementary work:
(1) Determine the concentration of the chloric acid solution, by titration with a base, or with a reducing agent.
Dilute to 20% w/w if necessary and carry out the next preparation.

The preparation of iodine pentoxide

Iodine can be oxidized by a variety of oxidizing agents to iodic acid, which may be dehydrated to iodine pentoxide. Two methods are described below so that a comparison may be made of their relative merits.

Materials required: Iodine
Chloric acid, see the previous experiment.

Place sublimed iodine (7·5 g) in a two-necked flask and add 24 ml of 20% chloric acid (5% excess). Fit the flask with an air inlet leading below the surface of the liquid, and connect to the exit side of the flask two wash bottles containing 20% sodium hydroxide solution. Draw a slow current of air through the solution and warm the flask gently to start the reaction. When only a faint colour of iodine remains in the solution warm the flask again to produce a colourless solution. The reaction should be complete in about 20 minutes. Cool the solution, filter to remove any barium iodate or other solid material, transfer the filtrate to a large evaporating basin, and evaporate just to dryness with frequent stirring. If during the evaporation a brown colour appears it can be removed by immediate addition of a little chloric acid solution. Place the solid in a smaller dish, heat in an oven at 150–160°C for 3 hours, and finally heat in the oven for 3 hours at 240°C.

The product should be white or faintly pink. The intensity of the colour is a measure of the purity of the product. Weigh the product and record the percentage yield based on iodine.

If the chloric acid contains any sulphuric acid then the dehydration process leads to fairly extensive decomposition of the product. Hence the need to test the chloric acid for the presence of sulphate. If sulphate is present it should be precipitated by the addition of a slight excess of barium ions.

Complementary work:

(1) Chlorate ion will oxidize iodine to iodate ion in acid solution. Can bromine be oxidized to bromate ion using chlorate ion in acid solution? Explain the answer in terms of electrode potentials.

(2) Dissolve a portion of the iodine pentoxide in water. Acidify and add potassium iodide solution. Comment.

(3) Determine the percentage of iodine in a sample of iodine pentoxide.

Reference

Lamb, A. B., Bray, W. C., and Geldard, W. J., *J. Amer. Chem. Soc.*, (1920), **42**, 1636.

The preparation of iodine pentoxide

Materials required: Iodine
                        Nitric acid (S.G. 1·5)

This experiment must be carried out in a fume cupboard.

Place iodine (5 g) in a round-bottomed flask, fitted with a reflux condenser, and add fuming nitric acid (50 ml). Concentrated nitric acid does not oxidize iodine under these conditions. Reflux for 20–30 minutes, cool, and decant the acid solution. Dissolve the yellow solid in the minimum of distilled water and filter to remove unreacted iodine. Transfer the solution to a large evaporating basin and evaporate just to dryness with frequent stirring. Transfer the solid to a smaller basin, heat in an oven for 3 hours at 150–160°C, and then for 3 hours at 240°C. Weigh the product and calculate the percentage yield based on iodine.

Complementary work:
    (1) Carry out tests (2) and (3) listed under the alternative preparation of iodine pentoxide.
    (2) Compare the two methods for the preparation of iodine pentoxide in terms of yield, smoothness of oxidation, and purity of product.

The preparation of tellurium dioxide

Materials required: Tellurium powder
                            Concentrated nitric acid (S.G. 1·4)

Carry out this reaction in a fume cupboard.
Add slowly concentrated nitric acid (32 ml) to a suspension of tellurium powder (3·0 g) in 40 ml of water in a 250 ml beaker. Heat the mixture to 70°C, cool, allow to stand for ten minutes, and then filter off any insoluble material. Evaporate the filtrate in a small evaporating dish on a water bath to about one tenth of its original volume. Cool, and filter the solid at the pump. Wash the product with water and dry between filter papers. Record the weight of product. Heat the solid product in an oven at 400–430°C for two hours and record the weight loss. The product should be pure white.

Complementary work:
    (1) What is the nature of the product which crystallizes from the nitric acid solution? How does the loss in weight on heating agree with this? What does this indicate about the acidic or basic character of tellurium dioxide? Comment.
    (2) Test the solubility of the oxide in water, 4M hydrochloric acid, and 4M sodium hydroxide. Comment.

(3) Prepare a solution of tellurium dioxide in sodium hydroxide solution and to two separate portions add:
    (*a*) barium chloride solution and acidify with dilute hydrochloric acid,
    (*b*) sulphur dioxide. Comment.
(4) Determine the percentage of tellurium in tellurium dioxide using cerium(IV) sulphate solution.

The preparation of chromyl chloride

Materials required: Chromium(VI) oxide
                      Concentrated hydrochloric acid
                      Concentrated sulphuric acid

Wear protective gloves when handling chromyl chloride.
Dissolve chromium(VI) oxide (7·5 g) in 5 ml of water and 15 ml of concentrated hydrochloric acid. Place the solution in a 100 ml two-necked flask fitted with a dropping funnel, a reflux condenser, and a thermometer. Connect a tube to the top of the condenser to remove the exhaust gases to the sink, see Figure 2. It is advisable to fit all the ground glass joints with polytetrafluorethylene (p.t.f.e.) sleeves to prevent their sticking together. *Place the apparatus in a fume cupboard* and cool the solution in ice. To the solution add 25 ml of concentrated sulphuric acid from a dropping funnel. Adjust the rate of addition so that the temperature does not rise above 10°C. Stir the solution continuously with a magnetic stirrer during the addition of the sulphuric acid. When the reaction is complete, remove the dropping funnel and thermometer, and connect the 100 ml flask for distillation. Again protect the ground glass joints with p.t.f.e. sleeves. Collect the fraction boiling in the range 110–116°C. Record the weight of product. Store the product in a stoppered flask, using a p.t.f.e. sleeve on the stopper.

Complementary work:
    (1) Add a few drops of chromyl chloride to ∼5 ml of water. Then add a little lead nitrate solution. Comment on your observations.
    (2) Compare the properties of chromyl chloride and sulphuryl chloride. What other similarities occur in the chemistry of chromium and sulphur?

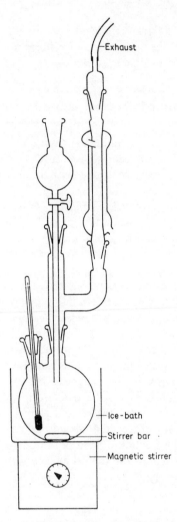

Exhaust

Ice-bath

Stirrer bar

Magnetic stirrer

Figure 2. Apparatus for the preparation of chromyl chloride.

The preparation of potassium monochlorochromate

Materials required: Chromyl chloride, see previous experiment.
                        Potassium chloride

Wear protective gloves when handling chromyl chloride.
Add slowly chromyl chloride (2·7 g) to a saturated solution of
potassium chloride (1·5 g). Keep the solution cool during the addition
of the chromyl chloride. Filter the red crystals, wash with a little
ice-cold water, and dry in air. Weigh the product and record the
yield.

Complementary work:
(1) Heat a small portion of the product in an ignition tube.
Identify the volatile products.
(2) Carry out the following tests on 1 ml portions of a solution of
the product and comment on your observations.
    (*a*) Add barium chloride solution,
    (*b*) test the pH of the solution,
    (*c*) add a few drops of 6 % hydrogen peroxide solution and 2 ml
of diethyl ether.
(3) Determine the percentage of chromium in the product by a
volumetric method.

The preparation of sodium peroxoborate

Materials required: Sodium tetraborate decahydrate (borax)
                        Sodium hydroxide 3·3 %
                        Hydrogen peroxide 6 %

Dissolve sodium tetraborate decahydrate (6 g) in 40 ml of 3·3 %
sodium hydroxide solution. Cool the solution in ice and add slowly
40 ml of 6 % hydrogen peroxide solution. Stir thoroughly for about
20 minutes, or until crystallization is complete. Filter at the pump,
wash first with alcohol, then ether, and dry on the filter.

Complementary work:
Use 5 ml aliquots of a freshly prepared aqueous solution of the
product for reactions (1)–(3).

(1) Add 2M sulphuric acid and 0·02M potassium permanganate solution.

(2) Add 2M sulphuric acid and 10% w/v potassium iodide solution.

(3) Add approximately 1 ml of 1% titanium(IV) sulphate solution, followed by excess sodium fluoride solution. Comment on your observations in these three reactions.

(4) Prepare a small fused bead of the product on the end of a platinum wire. Dip the cooled bead into chrome alum solution and heat in a bunsen flame. Comment.

(5) Determine the percentage of peroxide in the product.

The preparation of sodium polymetaphosphate

Materials required: Sodium dihydrogen phosphate
                        Platinum crucible

Place sodium dihydrogen phosphate (5 g) in a platinum crucible and heat in an electric furnace at 800°C for two hours. Pour the clear mobile melt quickly on to a metal sheet (nickel or copper). When the bead has cooled on the metal sheet transfer it to a mortar and grind to a fine powder. *Wear a face shield or goggles while pouring the melt and while grinding the product in the mortar.*

Complementary work:

(1) Prepare a solution of the sodium polymetaphosphate. To separate portions of this solution add a few drops of a solution of (*a*) calcium chloride, (*b*) barium chloride, (*c*) zinc chloride, (*d*) magnesium chloride, and (*e*) silver nitrate. To each of the mixed solutions add a few drops of sodium carbonate solution. Comment on your observations.

(2) What is the probable structure of sodium polymetaphosphate?

(3) What possible application is there for sodium polymetaphosphate?

The preparation of sodium tripolyphosphate

Materials required: Sodium dihydrogen phosphate
                        Disodium hydrogen phosphate
                        Platinum crucible

Prepare 10 g of a mixture of sodium dihydrogen phosphate and disodium hydrogen phosphate in the molar ratio 1:2. Grind the materials in a mortar, place the mixture in a platinum crucible and heat the crucible and contents to 580°C for 2 hours in an electric furnace. Allow to cool in the furnace. Grind the product to a powder in a mortar.

Complementary work:
(1) Carry out the reactions listed under (1) for sodium polymetaphosphate. Compare the results with those obtained for sodium polymetaphosphate.
(2) What is the structure of sodium tripolyphosphate?
(3) Determine the tripolyphosphate content of the product b potentiometric titration, see p. 211.

The preparation of sodium trimetaphosphate

Materials required: Sodium dihydrogen phosphate
Platinum crucible

Place sodium dihydrogen phosphate (5 g) in a platinum crucible and heat in an electric furnace at 550°C for 5 hours. Allow the crucible and contents to cool in the furnace. Transfer the product to a mortar and grind to a fine powder.

Complementary work:
(1) Prepare a solution of sodium trimetaphosphate and repeat the reactions listed under (1) in the preparation of sodium polymetaphosphate. Compare and contrast the results obtained with those obtained for sodium polymetaphosphate.
(2) What is the structure of sodium trimetaphosphate?
(3) Dissolve sodium trimetaphosphate (3 g) and sodium hydroxide (1 g) in 20 ml of water. Heat to 100°C and maintain at this temperature for about 10 minutes. Cool, and filter the white crystalline product. Wash with a little cold water and dry on the filter. Weigh the product. Prepare a solution of the product and carry out the tests under (1) above. What can you deduce as to the nature of the product?

The preparation of zinc dithionite

Materials required: Zinc dust
                        Ethanol
                        Sulphur dioxide

This reaction must be carried out in a fume cupboard.
Prepare a suspension of zinc dust (2 g) in 5 ml of ethanol and 5 ml
of water. Pass in sulphur dioxide from a storage cylinder. An
exothermic reaction soon begins and in a short time crystalline zinc
dithionite separates out. When the reaction is complete, cool the
mixture and filter off the crystals *rapidly* by suction. Wash the product with alcohol and dry it in a desiccator over calcium chloride.
Record the yield.

Complementary work:
(1) What is the structure of the dithionite ion?
(2) Add a sample of the product to potassium permanganate solution. Comment.
(3) Analyse the product for dithionite ion by the following procedure:
Pipette 25 ml of 0·1M silver nitrate into a 250 ml beaker, add
dilute aqueous ammonia until the hydrated silver oxide first precipitated dissolves, add another 5 ml of aqueous ammonia. Add
directly 0·2 g of zinc dithionite to this solution and allow it to stand
for ten minutes but do not warm. Filter off the precipitated silver and
any zinc hydroxide. Wash the precipitate with ammonia to which a
little ammonium nitrate has been added to avoid peptising the
precipitate. Dissolve the precipitate in hot nitric acid, boil the solution for five minutes to remove oxides of nitrogen. Titrate the silver
with 0·1M ammonium thiocyanate which should be standardized
against the silver nitrate used initially. Use 5 ml of 10% ferric alum as
indicator.
  Calculate the percentage dithionite in your product from the
equation

$$S_2O_4^{2-} + 2[Ag(NH_3)_2]^+ + 2OH^- = 2Ag + 2HSO_3^- + 4NH_3.$$

The preparation of barium dithionate

Materials required: Manganese dioxide
                       Sulphur dioxide
                       Barium hydroxide

This reaction must be carried out in a fume cupboard.
Make up a suspension of manganese dioxide (8 g) in water (50 ml),
cool in ice, and pass sulphur dioxide into the solution until all the
manganese dioxide has reacted. Do not allow the temperature to rise
above 10°C. At this stage of the reaction both dithionate and sulphate
ions are in solution

$$MnO_2 + 2SO_2 \rightleftharpoons MnS_2O_6$$
$$MnO_2 + SO_2 \rightleftharpoons MnSO_4.$$

When all the manganese dioxide has reacted, add hot saturated
barium hydroxide solution until all the manganese is precipitated as
manganese hydroxide, and the sulphate as barium sulphate. Filter,
and wash the precipitate with hot water. Pass carbon dioxide into the
filtrate to precipitate any excess barium hydroxide, filter off the
carbonate and evaporate the filtrate until crystals of barium dithionate dihydrate begin to separate; filter off the product, press dry
on filter paper, and complete the drying in a desiccator.

Complementary work:
(1) Boil a solution of the product.
(2) To a solution of the product add a few drops of potassium
permanganate solution.
(3) To a solution of the product add dilute hydrochloric acid and
warm.
  Compare the results with the behaviour of other sulphur-
containing oxo-anions under similar conditions.

The preparation of sodium thiosulphate

Materials required: Sodium sulphite
                       Flowers of sulphur

Dissolve sodium sulphite (6 g) in hot water (30 ml) and add sulphur

(2 g). Boil the suspension until nearly all the sulphur has reacted. Filter hot and evaporate the filtrate until crystallization commences. Cool, and filter the crystals by suction. Dry the product in a warm oven (40–50°C). Record the yield.

Complementary work:
    (1) Determine the degree of hydration of the product by titrating an accurately weighed sample with standard iodine solution. What sulphur containing anion is produced in this reaction and what is its structure?
    (2) Add dilute acid to a sample of the product and note what happens. Identify the gas evolved.
    (3) What is the structure of the thiosulphate ion?

Bibliography

Lister, M. W., *Oxyacids and Oxyacid Salts*, Oldbourne, (1965).

3 High temperature reactions

Introduction

The general type of reaction considered here involves heating an element or compound in a gas stream. The solid material, in a suitably inert container, is placed in a reaction tube which is heated by a tube furnace, and a measured flow of gas is passed through the tube. A gas absorption system may be incorporated on the inlet side of the reaction tube in which undesirable impurities in the gas stream can be removed by absorption in suitable solutions. A smaller absorption system may also be placed on the exit side of the tube to prevent any back absorption of air. This system also provides a useful visual check on the flow of gas from the reaction tube. It is also advisable to have a mercury-sealed lute on the inlet side of the reaction tube to release any pressure build-up should the gas flow be blocked in any way. This will eliminate the possibility of sealed joints being forced open, with subsequent spraying out of the contents of the Drechsel bottles, see Figure 4, p. 34.

In the reactions described below a silica-alumina tube has been found to be quite satisfactory as the reaction tube. The exit line from this tube was attached either by a ground glass socket to a cone, which had been cemented with 'Araldite' to the furnace tube, or through a rubber stopper, when the end of the reaction tube was fitted with a water cooled copper coil, as shown in Figure 3.

High temperature reactions may also occur in which no external application of heat is required. Such reactions have a large negative enthalpy. Any limitations on the occurrence of these reactions will be primarily kinetic. Once a temperature has been reached at which the

27

reaction rate is appreciable then the heat of reaction will maintain, and possibly increase, the high reaction temperature.

The reduction of certain metal oxides with aluminium powder is a good example of such a high temperature reaction, a reaction often

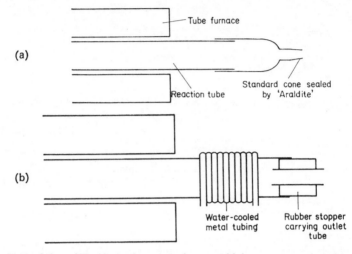

(a)

Tube furnace

Standard cone sealed by 'Araldite'

Reaction tube

(b)

Water-cooled metal tubing

Rubber stopper carrying outlet tube

Figure 3 (a and b). Alternative connexions to a high-temperature reaction tube.

known as the thermite or Goldschmidt reaction. The reaction between aluminium and chromium(III) oxide is described below. Again it should be noted that although this reaction is thermodynamically favourable at room temperature the kinetic rate is imperceptible. The high temperature at which the reaction rate is appreciable, is achieved initially by the use of an ignition charge, but is subsequently maintained by the heat of the reaction.

Thermodynamic considerations

A measure of whether a given reaction may proceed is the change in Gibbs Free Energy, ΔG. Although the absolute value of the Gibbs Free Energy, (G), for a given system is not known, the change in Gibbs Free Energy, ΔG, which occurs when one system (i.e. reactants) is converted into another system (i.e. products), can be measured or calculated. For any chemical reaction to occur at constant temperature and pressure ΔG must be negative, indicating a decrease in free energy in the system. The change in Gibbs Free Energy has a temperature dependence as shown by the equation

$$\left(\frac{\partial(\Delta G)}{\partial T}\right)_P = -\Delta S$$

where ΔS = (entropy of products)—(entropy of reactants). Therefore the change in ΔG with temperature will be governed by the sign and numerical value of ΔS. If the sign of ΔS remains constant over the temperature range under consideration, then ΔG becomes more negative or more positive depending on whether ΔS is positive or negative. The sign of ΔS should remain constant provided that there are no phase changes in the reactants or products over the given temperature range and the value of ΔS is not close to zero. A useful approximate order of magnitude for the effect of phase changes on ΔS, in the absence of any published data is: entropy of a gas > entropy of a liquid > entropy of a solid. Remember that the phase to be considered will be the phase which exists at the reaction temperature.

For a reaction in which ΔG is negative at a given temperature and the entropy of the products > the entropy of the reactants then an increase in temperature will result in a more negative value of ΔG. However, in a large number of synthetic reactions there is a decrease in the number of species in the products compared with the reactants, that is the overall randomness or entropy of the system decreases. For example:

$$Si(s) + 2Cl_2(g) = SiCl_4(g)$$

Entropy at
25°C and 1 atm
in cal. deg. $^{-1}$

$$\qquad 4{\cdot}47 \quad 2 \times 53{\cdot}29 \qquad 79{\cdot}2$$

$$\Delta S = 79{\cdot}2 - (4{\cdot}47 + 2 \times 53{\cdot}29)$$

$$= -31{\cdot}85 \text{ cal. deg. }^{-1}.$$

The change in ΔG with temperature will therefore be positive and the reaction becomes less favourable from a thermodynamic viewpoint. It should be noted that although ΔG is being altered unfavourably it is still negative at the reaction temperature. It follows that although the synthesis of silicon tetrachloride is carried out at an elevated temperature the reason does not lie in the thermodynamics of the reaction.

A somewhat different situation is found in the case of pyrolysis or thermal decomposition reactions. Here the value of ΔG and ΔH for the reaction may be positive at low temperatures but the increase in the number of species in the products compared with the reactants results in a positive value for ΔS. Consider the decomposition of calcium carbonate

$$CaCO_3(s) = CaO(s) + CO_2(g)$$

Entropy at
25°C and 1 atm.
in cal. deg. $^{-1}$

$$21 \cdot 2 \qquad 9 \cdot 5 \qquad 51 \cdot 06$$

$$\Delta S = (9 \cdot 5 + 51 \cdot 06) - 21 \cdot 2$$

$$= 39 \cdot 36 \text{ cal. deg.}^{-1}.$$

From the equation

$$\left(\frac{\partial (\Delta G)}{\partial T} \right)_p = -\Delta S$$

it follows that for this reaction ΔG becomes more negative with increasing temperature. Starting with a positive value of ΔG at room temperature, a temperature will be reached eventually at which $\Delta G = 0$, and above this temperature ΔG has an increasing negative value. The lower temperature limit for the reaction, i.e. the temperature at which $\Delta G = 0$, can be calculated from the equation

$$\Delta G = \Delta H - T\Delta S.$$

Satisfactory values of ΔG with increasing temperature can be calculated from this equation, since the effects of temperature on ΔH and ΔS are partly self-compensating. If required, a more rigorous calculation can be made using an expression of the form

$$\Delta G_T = \Delta H_0 + 2 \cdot 303 a T \log T + b \times 10^{-3} T^2 + c \times 10^5 T^{-1} + I.T$$

where a, b, and c are derived from the variation with temperature of the heat capacities of products and reactants. The appropriate values for the coefficients a, b, c and I may be substituted from tables [1]. The preceding calculations of the variation of the change in Gibbs Free Energy apply irrespective of whether reactants and products are in standard states, i.e. at unit activity. The values of enthalpy and entropy given in tables of thermodynamic data are for elements and compounds in their standard states. The value for the change in Gibbs Free Energy that is calculated using this data, will be the value for reactants and products in their standard states.

The change in Gibbs Free Energy in a reaction is related to the equilibrium constant for the reaction at constant pressure by the equation

$$\Delta G^0 = -RT \ln K_p$$

where the superscript ^{0} specifies reactants and products in their standard states, viz. unit activity. Thus from the change in Gibbs Free Energy when reactants in their standard states are converted into products also in their standard states, an equilibrium constant for the reaction can be calculated. For any arbitrary concentration of reactants giving some arbitrary concentration of products the following equations are used,

$$\Delta G = \Delta G^0 + RT \ln J_p \qquad (3.1)$$

or $$\Delta G = -RT \ln K_p + RT \ln J_p \qquad (3.2)$$

where J_p is of the same form as the equilibrium constant, and is a function of the activities (or more approximately a function of the partial pressures or concentrations) of the products and reactants. When the arbitrary activities are equal to the equilibrium activities then $J_p = K_p$ and hence $\Delta G = 0$. No further reaction will occur. When the arbitrary activities are equal to those of the standard states of the reactants and products, then $J = 1$ and therefore $\Delta G = \Delta G^0$. It should also be apparent that an unfavourable, i.e. positive value of ΔG^0, might be overcome by suitably adjusting the partial pressures or concentrations of the components in the reaction system, giving a negative value for $RT \ln J_p$. This may be achieved by increasing the concentration of the reactants, decreasing the concentration of the products or both. Consider the reaction

$$CO(g) + H_2O(g) = CO_2(g) + H_2(g).$$

At $700°C$ $\Delta G^0 = +0.66$ kcal. If the reactants are each added at a pressure of 3 atm and products removed each at a partial pressure of 1 atm, then

$$J_p = \frac{1 \times 1}{3 \times 3} = 0.1111$$

therefore $RT \ln J_p = 1.987 \times 973 \times 2.303 \times (-0.9643)$

$$= -4250 \text{ cal.} = -4.25 \text{ kcal.}$$

$$\Delta G = 0.66 - 4.25 = -3.59 \text{ kcal.}$$

By adjustment of the concentration of the reactants the reaction now becomes feasible. Note that a change of 10^{-4} in J_p will give only a fourfold change in $RT \ln J_p$ so that there are obvious limits to the size of a positive ΔG^0 which can be overcome in this way. Therefore from values of ΔG^0 for a reaction it can be seen whether a reaction is feasible, i.e. ΔG^0 is negative, or whether it cannot take place under the stated conditions, i.e. ΔG^0 is positive. If the value of ΔG^0 is only small but positive then the general equation (3.2) can be used to see whether values of J_p can be obtained which will overcome the positive ΔG^0.

There are thus two possible methods for altering the change in Gibbs Free Energy for a given reaction; adjustment of temperature, and adjustment of activities by changes in pressure. The first method is the simplest and most effective. Should a negative value for the change in Gibbs Free Energy be obtained under a given set of reaction conditions, this indicates that the reaction is feasible but provides no information as to the rate of the reaction.

Reaction rates

The effect of temperature on the reaction rate is given by the Arrhenius equation

$$k = A\mathrm{e}^{-E/RT}$$

where
k = the rate constant

A = the frequency factor

E = the activation energy

T = the temperature in $°K$

Since E is always $\geqslant 0$, increase in temperature will always lead to an increase in reaction rate. Reaction rates approximately double or treble for a ten degree rise in temperature. Temperature increase will also favour the transport processes, such as diffusion or convection to and from the reaction interface, which might otherwise slow the overall reaction rate. Consider again the silicon tetrachloride preparation. The increased temperature has an unfavourable effect on the position of equilibrium but this is more than compensated by the increased rate at which equilibrium would be reached. This principle is not confined to small-scale preparations but is applied in large-scale syntheses. For example, ammonia is synthesized at elevated temperature and pressure, although a lower temperature would give a higher equilibrium concentration of ammonia. For the equilibrium

$N_2 + 3H_2 \rightleftharpoons 2NH_3$ the approximate equilibrium concentrations of ammonia are,

Temperature	Pressure	% NH$_3$
500°C	400 atm	~34
300°C	400 atm	~78.

However, at the higher temperature the rate of ammonia formation will be increased. Therefore a lower equilibrium concentration is accepted in order to obtain some product in a reasonable period of time.

A chemical reaction is governed by temperature in two ways: through the change in ΔG and the change in reaction rate. It should now be apparent that instead of finding the conditions for a given reaction in a purely empirical way, it is possible to calculate approximate conditions under which a reaction will proceed.

The preparation of lithium nitride

Materials required: Lithium
Nitrogen
Tube Furnace
Iron or Nickel boats
Silica-alumina tube

Assemble the apparatus as shown in Figure 4, replacing items G, H, J with two Drechsel bottles. The inlet absorption train should contain one wash bottle filled with concentrated sulphuric acid, and one empty wash bottle to collect any spray. The exit absorption train should contain an empty wash bottle to protect the reaction tube against sucking back, and a wash bottle filled with concentrated sulphuric acid.

Wash a small piece of lithium in light petroleum to remove the oil in which it has been stored. Slice off the outer crust and then cut it into four or five pieces, with a total weight of approximately 0·75 g. Place the pieces of lithium in iron or nickel combustion boats and place these at the centre of the reaction tube in the tube furnace. Purge the reaction system for half an hour with a nitrogen flow of 5–10 litres/hour. See p. 113 for a description of a soap film flowmeter. Raise the temperature of the furnace to 400°C and maintain this temperature for one hour. Allow the tube to cool in a slow stream of nitrogen. The product will be a hard, red-purple material, con-

taminated with unreacted lithium. Remove as much of the product
from the boats as possible.

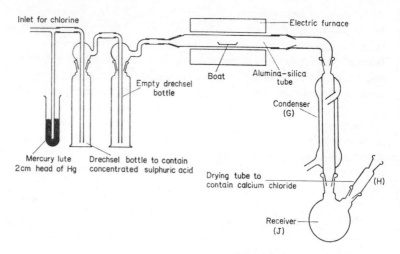

Figure 4. Apparatus for the preparation of silicon tetrachloride.

Complementary work:

(1) Add a small portion of the product to water. Identify the products.

(2) Determine the percentage of lithium and nitrogen in the product. Take the lithium as equal to the total alkalinity after boiling off the ammonia. Determine ammonia by Kjehldahl's method. Find the ratio of Li:N in the product. Given that the product is Li_3N, calculate the percentage of lithium converted to nitride.

(3) What other elements form ionic nitrides? Explain in terms of a Born–Haber cycle the ability of these elements to form nitrides. See also p. 3.

The preparation of barium peroxide

Materials required: Barium
Oxygen
Nickel boats
Tube furnace
Silica-alumina tube

Wash the barium free from paraffin oil with light petroleum and dry on a filter paper. Weigh 1·5–2·0 g of the metal and divide this into three or more pieces. Place the pieces in nickel boats in the furnace tube. Connect the oxygen cylinder directly to the furnace tube. No purification or drying train is required, but a mercury lute should be included. A Drechsel bottle containing concentrated sulphuric acid is included on the exit side of the furnace as a ready method of checking the gas flow rate. The gas flow is measured and set using a soap film flowmeter attached to the exit of the Drechsel bottle. See p. 113 for a description of a soap film flowmeter. Heat the furnace tube to 500–550°C in an oxygen flow of 15–20 litres/hour for about one hour. Cool the tube while maintaining the oxygen flow. Remove the product and break into smaller pieces with a pestle and mortar.

Complementary work:
(1) Add a small amount of the product to ∼2 ml of 1% titanium(IV) sulphate solution. Comment.
(2) Determine the percentage purity of the barium peroxide using potassium permanganate solution.
(3) What would be the product of the reaction between calcium or strontium, and oxygen under similar conditions?
See also p. 2.

The preparation of silicon tetrachloride

Materials required: Silicon
Chlorine
Refractory, non-metallic boat
Silica-alumina tube
Electric furnace

This experiment must be carried out in a fume cupboard.
The apparatus is assembled as shown in Figure 4. The first Drechsel bottle is half-filled with concentrated sulphuric acid to dry the incoming chlorine, the second one is empty to prevent any spray being carried into the reaction tube. A mercury lute is also incorporated into the entry side of the reaction tube in case of excessive pressure build-up within the tube. The exit of the reaction tube is attached to

a condenser and a previously weighed two-necked flask. The exit of the flask is fitted with a calcium chloride drying tube.

Place silicon (5–10 g) in the boat and insert this into the centre of the reaction tube. Heat the furnace to 400°C, attach a cylinder of chlorine to the Drechsel bottle and pass chlorine over the heated silicon. Adjust the rate of flow of chlorine so that only a very small amount escapes from the two-necked flask. The crude silicon tetra-chloride soon begins to distill over and collects in the receiving flask. The product may be purified by fractional distillation using a 6 in. column packed with Fenski glass helices. Collect the fraction boiling

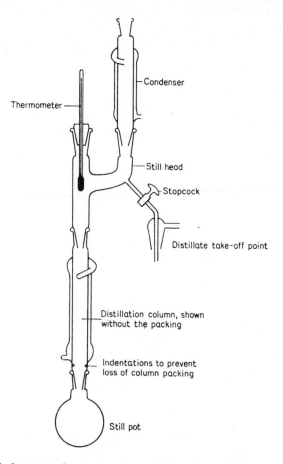

Figure 5. Apparatus for the fractional distillation of silicon tetrachloride.

over the range 56–59°C. A typical distillation apparatus is shown in Figure 5. An efficient column may be constructed from a condenser in the following way: Make four indentations into the condenser near the standard cone joint, seal off one of the water connexions and to the other connexion attach a small length of glass tubing. Clean and silver [1] the internal surface of the water jacket. Thoroughly evacuate the silvered jacket and seal off. To pack the column fill it with acetone and drop in the Fenski helices a few at a time, tapping the column from time to time to ensure even packing of the helices. Drain out the acetone and air dry the column, taking care not to disturb the helices.

Complementary work:
Add the product drop-wise to (*a*) concentrated hydrochloric acid, (b) water. Compare the results and comment.
See also p. 5.

Reference
[1] *Handbook of Chemistry and Physics*, Chemical Rubber Publishing Company.

The preparation of chromium metal

Materials required: Chromium(III) oxide
Potassium dichromate
Aluminium powder
Calcium fluoride

Fuse potassium dichromate (1 g) in a porcelain crucible. Cool, and grind to a fine powder. Ignite hydrated chromium(III) oxide (4 g), (note that the bottle may be labelled chromic hydroxide), in a porcelain crucible until the green anhydrous chromium(III) oxide is obtained. Prepare a mixture containing chromium(III) oxide (2 g), fused potassium dichromate (0.5 g), and aluminium powder (1 g). The reaction will proceed without the potassium dichromate but the temperature may not be sufficiently high to fuse the chromium metal produced. This makes recovery more difficult.

Fill a crucible (4 × 7 cm o.d.) to within 1 cm of the rim with powdered calcium fluoride, and make an indentation about 2 cm in depth in the centre of the powder with the end of a boiling tube. Place the prepared mixture in this indentation in the calcium fluoride. Prepare an ignition charge of barium peroxide (1 g) and aluminium powder (0·1 g) and place this on the surface of the reaction mixture. Insert a short length of magnesium ribbon into the ignition charge to act as a fuse. *Place the crucible in a fume cupboard,* surround it vertically on four sides with asbestos board and fasten another asbestos board horizontally above the asbestos 'walls'. *During the firing of the charge wear safety goggles or a face mask.* Ignite the magnesium ribbon using a micro burner. There will be some sparking initially but this will quickly cease and the charge will continue to react quite smoothly. Allow the product to cool, and carefully transfer it to a mortar. Grind the product and remove the bead (or beads) of chromium metal. Weigh the chromium and calculate the yield. Break the chromium bead into smaller pieces in a mortar.

Complementary work:

(1) Estimate the minimum temperature in the above reaction.

(2) Calculate the free energy change for the reaction at 500°, 1000°, and 1500°C,

$$2Al + Cr_2O_3 = Al_2O_3 + 2Cr.$$

Repeat the calculations for the reactions of aluminium with zirconium(IV) oxide and magnesium oxide [1]. Comment.

(3) Investigate the reaction of chromium metal with sulphuric acid, hydrochloric acid, and nitric acid. Comment.

(4) Treat the sulphuric acid solution with a portion of ammonium peroxodisulphate and heat. Comment.

(5) Carry out reaction (10), p. 43 unless this work has already been done.

Reference

[1] *Handbook of Chemistry and Physics*, Chemical Rubber Publishing Company.

Bibliography

Rossini, F. D., *Chemical Thermodynamics*, Wiley, New York, (1951).
Coulson, E. A. and Herington, E. F. G., *Laboratory Distillation Practice*, Newnes, (1958).

4 The elements of the first transition series

Introduction

The reactions described below are designed to illustrate some of the chemistry of the elements of the first transition series. The majority of the reactions selected can be carried out on a test tube scale. The relative stabilities of the different oxidation states for a given element in aqueous solution open to the atmosphere are demonstrated and the changes in the stability of the oxidation states for each element. The reactions of a number of the elements with a given anion are included to illustrate differences which occur in the products of the reaction. Reactions in which complex ions are produced are included, but the use of complexes to stabilize the less common oxidation states is not described at this stage (see page 68). Reactions which can be considered as characteristic of a given metal ion are also included.

Although trends in the chemistry of the elements across the series can be discerned, discontinuities do occur. For example, nickel(II) hydroxide does not dissolve in concentrated alkali to give a nickelate, whereas both cobalt(II) and copper(II) hydroxides dissolve fairly readily to give cobaltates, and cuprates, respectively. Consequently it is informative not only to study the reaction of a given metal ion with a given anion, but also to see the reaction in the context of the first transition series. In this way a greater appreciation of the similarities, and apparent anomalies, in the chemistry of these elements will be obtained.

Reactions of titanium

The reactions are conveniently studied using a solution of titanium(IV) chloride (15% w/v). Concentrated solutions are not recommended since they tend to fume vigorously. The solution of titanium(IV) chloride is made up in hydrochloric acid.

(1) What are the species present in the solution?

(2) Add ~5 ml of 4M sodium hydroxide solution to ~2 ml of the titanium(IV) chloride solution. What is the product of the reaction?

(3) Add ~5 ml of 4M aqueous ammonia to ~2 ml of the titanium(IV) chloride solution. Is there any difference in the product of this reaction compared with reaction (2) above?

(4) Pass a stream of sulphur dioxide through ~2 ml of titanium(IV) chloride solution. *(Fume cupboard)*. Comment on your observations.

(5) Add a little zinc dust to ~1 ml of the titanium(IV) chloride solution. Comment and compare with reaction (4).

(6) Add a few drops of titanium(IV) chloride solution to ~2 ml of water and then add one drop of 6% hydrogen peroxide. Now add a little solid sodium fluoride and shake. Comment and indicate the nature of the products of the reactions.

(7) Prepare a solution of selenous acid and add ~1 ml of this solution to ~1 ml of titanium(IV) chloride solution. What is the nature of the product?

For the following reactions use a solution of titanium(III) chloride (15% w/v) or prepare a solution of titanium(III) chloride from titanium(IV) chloride *in situ*.

(8) Add ~5 ml of 4M sodium hydroxide to ~2 ml of a solution of titanium(III) chloride.

(9) Add ~5 ml of 4M aqueous ammonia to ~2 ml of titanium(III) chloride. Compare the results with reaction (7) above.

(10) Prepare a concentrated solution of sodium perchlorate. Warm, and add a few drops of titanium(III) chloride. Comment on the reaction.

Which of the above reactions could be used for the quantitative or qualitative determination of titanium?

See also Electrochemical reductions p. 86 and spectroscopy p. 174.

Reactions of vanadium

Ammonium metavanadate is a suitable starting compound for use in this study of the reactions of vanadium.

(1) Heat gently a sample of ammonium metavanadate ($\sim$2 g) in a nickel crucible. What are the products of the reaction?

(2) Dissolve vanadium pentoxide in 4M sodium hydroxide. Add slowly 4M hydrochloric acid until precipitation occurs. Comment on the colour changes which occur and the species present in solution.

(3) Add a little vanadium pentoxide to concentrated hydrochloric acid and warm. Identify the products of the reaction.

(4) Dissolve a little vanadium pentoxide in concentrated sulphuric acid ($\sim$2 ml) and add the solution to an equal volume of water. Divide this solution into three equal parts, (a), (b) and (c).

(a) Pass sulphur dioxide through the solution *(fume cupboard)*.

(b) Add zinc dust to the solution.

(c) Add an equal volume of 4M hydrochloric acid to the solution and then add magnesium turnings. Comment on the colour changes which occur, and suggest the possible final oxidation state of the vanadium in each solution.

(5) Prepare a mixture of 1 part of ammonium metavanadate and 3 parts of oxalic acid. Carefully fuse this mixture in a nickel crucible. Extract the cooled solid product with 2M sulphuric acid. To this solution add slowly excess 4M sodium hydroxide solution. Comment on the reactions occurring.

(6) *This reaction must be carried out in a fume cupboard.*
Prepare a mixture of equal parts of vanadium pentoxide and carbon. Place the mixture in the two necked flask in the apparatus shown in Figure 6. Gently warm the flask while passing a stream of chlorine gas. Collect the yellow liquid product. Add a few drops of water to a few drops of the product. What are the products of the reactions? How does ΔG^0 vary with temperature for the reaction $2C + O = 2CO$, compared with the majority of reactions of the type $M + \frac{n}{4}O_2 = M^{n+}O_{n/2}^{2-}$? Indicate why. Use this comparison to show why carbon finds wide use in the reduction of metal oxides.

Which compounds of vanadium have been used for its quantitative and qualitative determination? Which oxidation states of vanadium are present in these compounds?

Reactions of chromium

Use solutions of chrome alum and chromium(III) chloride. The chrome alum solutions are suitable under strong oxidizing conditions, while in some reactions chromium(III) chloride is preferable since the colour changes are more distinct.

(1) To a solution of chrome alum ($\sim$2 ml) add slowly excess 4M sodium hydroxide. Then add $\sim$2 ml of 6% hydrogen peroxide and warm. Comment on the reactions which are occurring.

(2) Add slowly 4M aqueous ammonia in excess to ~2 ml of chrome alum solution. Comment on your observations.

(3) Add excess sodium carbonate solution to ~2 ml of chrome alum solution. Compare the result with reaction (1).

(4) Acidify ~2 ml chromium(III) chloride solution with ~2 ml 4M hydrochloric acid and add a little zinc dust. Warm the solution until it is effervescing vigorously. Note any colour change. Quickly decant the liquid into a saturated solution of sodium acetate. Comment on the reactions which are occurring.

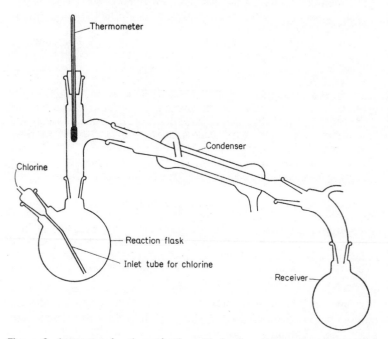

Figure 6. Apparatus for the reductive chlorination of vanadium pentoxide.

(5) Again to a hydrochloric acid solution of chromium(III) chloride add a little zinc dust and warm until the solution effervesces vigorously. Cool the solution and rotate the tube while the solution spreads in a thin layer over the wall. Note the colour changes which occur. Comment.

(6) To a solution of chrome alum (~2 ml) add a little solid ammonium peroxodisulphate and boil. Comment on your observations.

(7) To a solution of potassium dichromate (~2 ml) add 1 ml of diethyl ether. Then add a few drops of 6% hydrogen peroxide and acidify with 2M sulphuric acid. Shake the tube and comment on your observations.

(8) Prepare a solution of potassium dichromate and adjust the pH to ~4 with 2M sulphuric acid, add slowly 4M sodium hydroxide until the

pH is ~9. Then add slowly 2M sulphuric acid until the pH is again ~4. Comment on the colour changes.

(9) To an acid solution of potassium dichromate (~1 ml) add a few drops of barium chloride solution. What is the precipitate and how does it arise?

(10) *This reaction must be done in a fume cupboard.*
Place a small quantity of chromium metal powder in a Pyrex test tube. Flush the tube with a slow stream of chlorine gas. Gently warm the tube and remove the flame when reaction starts. What is the product of the reaction? Test the solubility of the product in water. Add one drop of concentrated hydrochloric acid and a small piece of zinc. Comment on your observations.

What compounds of chromium have been used in its quantitative and qualitative determination?

Potassium dichromate solution has considerable application as an oxidizing agent in quantitative analysis. One advantage is that it can be prepared as a primary standard, although it may be standardized if required. Alternatively, a solution containing a chromium salt may be oxidized to dichromate, and the dichromate present titrated against a standard reducing agent. For examples of the use of potassium dichromate as a titrant see pp. 21, 56, 93.

The chemistry of chromium is further illustrated by the preparation of chromium(II) salts, p. 205; chromium(III) complexes, p. 91; and the preparation of chromium metal, p. 37.

Reactions of manganese

Use a solution of manganese(II) chloride or manganese(II) sulphate.

(1) Add 4M sodium hydroxide slowly until in excess, to ~2 ml of manganese(II) chloride solution. Then allow the tube to stand, preferably on the slope, so that a large surface of liquid is exposed to the air. Comment on your observations.

(2) Dissolve a little ammonium chloride in ~5 ml of 4M aqueous ammonia and add this solution to ~2 ml of manganese(II) chloride solution. Allow to stand. Comment on the reactions which have occurred.

(3) Add excess sodium carbonate solution to ~2 ml of manganese(II) chloride solution. Boil the solution and allow to stand. Wash the precipitate several times by decantation, and then add 2M hydrochloric acid to the precipitate. Comment on your observations.

(4) Acidify ~2 ml of manganese(II) sulphate solution with an equal

volume of 4M sulphuric acid. Add ~0·5 g of ammonium peroxodisulphate and boil. Then add a drop of silver nitrate solution to the hot solution. Comment on the reactions which have occurred.

(5) Add ~1 g of manganese dioxide to ~5 ml of 4M hydrochloric acid and warm the suspension. Identify the products of the reaction.

(6) Add freshly prepared iron(II) sulphate solution in excess to ~1 ml of dilute potassium permanganate solution acidified with 2M sulphuric acid. Compare this reaction with the reaction which occurs when excess iron(II) sulphate solution is added to ~1 ml of potassium permanganate solution, to which one drop of 4M sodium hydroxide has been added.

(7) Add excess potassium iodide solution to ~1 ml of potassium permanganate solution acidified with 2M sulphuric acid. Compare this reaction with the reactions which occur when excess potassium iodide solution is added; (a) to ~1 ml of potassium permanganate solution to which one drop of 4M sodium hydroxide has been added, and (b) to ~1 ml of potassium permanganate solution to which an equal volume of 4M sodium hydroxide has been added.

See also the preparation of manganese(II) chloride, manganese(III) phosphate, potassium manganate and potassium permanganate, p. 49.

Potassium permanganate finds wide application in volumetric analysis, especially in acid solution. A standard solution of potassium permanganate may be used to determine the amount of oxidizable ion in a given solution, e.g. iron(II). Alternatively, it may be used to determine the amount of manganese present in a given solution. The manganese is oxidized to the manganese(VII) oxidation state by a suitable oxidizing agent, and the permanganate produced is titrated against a standard reducing agent. Examples of the use of potassium permanganate in volumetric analysis are given on p. 54.

Reactions of iron

Use a freshly prepared solution of ammonium iron(II) sulphate for the reactions of iron(II). Iron(III) nitrate solution is suitable for studying the reactions of iron(III).

(1) Add excess 4M sodium hydroxide solution to ~2 ml of ammonium iron(II) sulphate solution. Iron(II) hydroxide is white. Comment on your result.

(2) Add excess 4M aqueous ammonia to ~2 ml of ammonium iron(II) sulphate solution. Compare your result with reaction (1) above.

(3) Add excess sodium carbonate solution to ~2 ml of ammonium iron(II) sulphate solution. Compare this reaction with reaction (1) above.

(4) Repeat reactions (1), (2) and (3) but use iron(III) nitrate solution instead of ammonium iron(II) sulphate solution. Comment on your obervations.

(5) Add excess ammonium thiocyanate solution to separate $\sim$1 ml samples of iron(II) ammonium sulphate solution and iron(III) nitrate solutions. Compare the two reactions.

(6) Add excess potassium iodide solution to $\sim$1 ml of iron(III) nitrate solution, followed by sodium thiosulphate solution until the mixture is colourless. Now add a drop of ammonium thiocyanate solution. Comment on the reactions which are occurring.

(7) Add excess potassium iodide solution to $\sim$1 ml of ammonium iron(II) sulphate solution. Add a few drops of copper(II) sulphate solution. Compare this reaction with reaction (6) above.

(8) Add excess potassium iodide solution to $\sim$1 ml of potassium hexacyanoferrate(III) solution. Then add $\sim$1 ml of zinc sulphate solution. Comment on the reactions which have occurred.

(9) Bubble hydrogen sulphide through a solution of iron(III) nitrate. Comment on the reaction which has occurred, referring to any expected reaction which does not occur.

(10) Prepare fresh solutions of potassium hexacyanoferrate(II) and potassium hexacyanoferrate(III). To $\sim$1 ml of each solution add $\sim$1 ml of ammonium iron(II) sulphate solution. Repeat using iron(III) nitrate solution instead of ammonium iron(II) sulphate solution. Compare the reactions which occur.

(11) Add a drop of bromine water to $\sim$1 ml of ammonium iron(II) sulphate solution. Then add a drop of ammonium thiocyanate solution. From reactions (6) and (11) estimate the range within which the oxidation potential for $Fe^{2+} \rightarrow Fe^{3+}$ must lie.

Which compounds of iron have been used in its quantitative and qualitative estimation. Indicate the reactions in which there is a change of oxidation state of the iron during the reaction.

See also the preparation of iron(II) oxalate, p. 57.

Reactions of cobalt

Use a solution of cobalt(II) chloride or cobalt(II) nitrate.

(1) Add slowly a concentrated solution of sodium hydroxide ($\sim$50%) to $\sim$2 ml of the cobalt(II) solution. Comment on the reactions which occur.

(2) Add excess 4M sodium hydroxide solution to $\sim$2 ml of the cobalt(II) solution. Compare the reactions which occur with reaction (1) above.

(3) Add excess sodium carbonate solution to $\sim$2 ml of the cobalt(II) solution. Compare your observations with reaction (2).

(4) Add excess 4M aqueous ammonia to ~2 ml of the cobalt(II) solution. Compare with reaction (2). Now add a few drops of 6% hydrogen peroxide and boil the solution with excess 4M sodium hydroxide. Comment on the reactions which have occurred.

(5) Add 1 drop of 2M hydrochloric acid to a solution of the cobalt(II) salt. Bubble hydrogen sulphide through the solution. Now add a few drops of 4M aqueous ammonia solution. Comment on your observations.

(6) Add concentrated potassium thiocyanate solution to ~2 ml of the cobalt(II) solution. Then add a few drops of pyridine. Comment.

(7) Add a concentrated solution of potassium thiocyanate to ~2 ml of the cobalt(II) solution. Then add ~2 ml of diethyl ether, and acidify the solution with 4M hydrochloric acid. Comment on your observations.

(8) Acidify ~1 ml of the cobalt(II) solution with acetic acid and add a little solid potassium nitrite, Comment on the reactions which occur.

Which compounds of cobalt have been used in its quantitative and qualitative estimation? Which oxidation states of cobalt are involved in quantitative oxidation—reduction reactions?

Reactions of nickel

Use a solution of nickel(II) chloride or nickel(II) sulphate.

(1) Add excess 4M sodium hydroxide to ~2 ml of the nickel(II) solution. Boil the solution. Cool, and add a little solid potassium peroxodisulphate. Comment on the reactions.

(2) Add excess 4M aqueous ammonia to ~2 ml of the nickel(II) solution. Compare this reaction with the first part of reaction (1). Add a few drops of 6% hydrogen peroxide to the solution. Then add excess 4M sodium hydroxide and boil. Compare with reaction (4) under cobalt.

(3) Add excess sodium carbonate solution to ~2 ml of the nickel(II) solution. Compare the result with the first part of reaction 1. Comment.

(4) Add ~2 ml of potassium thiocyanate solution to ~2 ml of the nickel(II) solution. Now add a few drops of pyridine. Comment.

(5) *This reaction must be performed in a fume cupboard. Wash the test tubes and your hands thoroughly after the reaction.* Add slowly excess potassium cyanide solution to ~2 ml of the nickel(II) solution. Comment on the reaction, and compare with reaction (5) under copper.

(6) Add a drop of 2M hydrochloric acid to ~2 ml of the nickel(II) solution. Bubble hydrogen sulphide through the solution. Add a few drops of 4M aqueous ammonia. Comment.

(7) *This reaction must be done in a fume cupboard.* Add excess 4M potassium hydroxide to ~2 ml of the nickel(II) solution. Bubble chlorine through the suspension in the cold. Wash the precipitate four

or five times by decantation. This is the same product as formed in reaction (1). Add potassium iodide solution to the precipitate and acidify with 4M hydrochloric acid. Comment on your observations.

What reactions are used for the quantitative and qualitative estimation of nickel. Are oxidation-reduction reactions used in the quantitative determination of nickel?

Reactions of copper

The reactions of the copper(II) ion are conveniently studied using a solution of copper(II) sulphate.

(1) Add slowly excess 4M sodium hydroxide to ~1 ml of copper(II) sulphate solution. Warm the solution. Comment on your observations.
(2) Add slowly excess 50% sodium hydroxide solution to ~1 ml of copper(II) sulphate solution. Comment on the reactions which occur.
(3) Add a little tartaric acid to ~1 ml of copper(II) sulphate solution. Then add excess 4M sodium hydroxide. Add ~1 ml of acetaldehyde to this solution and warm the mixture. Comment on your observations.
(4) Add slowly excess 4M aqueous ammonia to ~1 ml of copper(II) sulphate solution. Compare with reaction (1).
(5) Add excess sodium carbonate solution to ~2 ml of copper(II) sulphate solution. Boil the solution. Compare your observations with reaction (1).
(6) *This reaction must be done in a fume cupboard.* Do *not* test the product by smell! Carefully wash the tubes which have contained potassium cyanide. Wash your hands well. Add slowly excess potassium cyanide solution to ~2 ml of copper(II) sulphate solution. Bubble hydrogen sulphide through the solution. Comment on your observations.
(7) Add slowly excess potassium thiocyanate solution to ~1 ml of copper(II) sulphate solution. Bubble sulphur dioxide through the solution. Comment on the reactions which are occurring.
(8) Add excess potassium iodide to ~1 ml of copper(II) sulphate solution. Compare this reaction with reaction (6). (Cf. reaction (6) under reactions of iron).

What reactions of copper are used in its quantitative and qualitative estimation? Again note any oxidation-reduction reactions, and the oxidation states of copper which occur.

See also the preparation of copper(I) chloride, and the experiments described in the chapter on the stabilization of oxidation states, p. 68.

General questions on the first transition series

(1) To what extent does the formation of polyanions containing first transition series elements occur?

(2) How do the commonly occurring oxidation states, as represented by the compounds you have prepared and used, change across the first transition series?

(3) Comment on the acidic and basic properties of the oxides of the first transition series elements.

(4) To what extent is the reaction of chromium with chlorine typical of the reactions of the first series transition elements with halogens?

Bibliography

Larson, E. M., *Transitional Elements*, Benjamin, New York, (1965).

5 The preparation of some manganese compounds

Introduction

A characteristic property of the transition elements is the ability of an element to exist in a number of different oxidation states. Manganese has oxidation states from $-$III to $+$VII. The lower oxidation states are only formed with π-bonding molecules (see p. 70). For the change from one oxidation state to another, the oxidation potentials when available, give some information as to the type of oxidizing or reducing agent which will bring about the required reaction. By suitable adjustment of reaction conditions a transition element in one oxidation state may be converted to a different oxidation state.

Manganese(IV) oxide is a suitable starting material for the preparation of manganese compounds in other oxidation states. It is the most important manganese(IV) compound, and owes its stability primarily to its insolubility. With hydrochloric acid it functions as an oxidizing agent liberating chlorine and producing manganese(II) chloride.

The preparation of manganese(II) chloride

Materials required: Manganese(IV) oxide
Hydrochloric acid
Manganese(II) carbonate

This preparation must be carried out in a fume cupboard. Add slowly manganese(IV) oxide (8 g) to hot hydrochloric acid (33 ml of concentrated acid and 10 ml of water). Maintain the hydrochloric acid at such a temperature that reaction proceeds smoothly. Allow the reaction to subside between the addition of each portion of manganese(IV) oxide. When the reaction is complete, filter, and to the filtrate add manganese carbonate to precipitate iron as iron(III) hydroxide. Filter off the iron(III) hydroxide and evaporate the filtrate until crystallization of manganese(II) chloride commences. Record the weight of product and calculate the yield.

Complementary work:

(1) Write an equation for the reaction between manganese(IV) oxide and hydrochloric acid.

(2) Compare the intensity of colour of a manganese(II) chloride solution with an equimolar solution of chromium(III) chloride. Explain.

(3) Measure the paramagnetic susceptibility of manganese(II) chloride and calculate the magnetic moment. Comment on the degree of agreement with the spin-only formula. The measurement of magnetic susceptibility is described on p. 201.

Compounds containing manganese(III) are readily reduced in solution. In the absence of reducing agents disproportionation occurs,

$$2Mn^{3+} + 2H_2O = Mn^{2+} + MnO_2 + 4H^+ \qquad (K = 10^9)$$

Some increase in stability can be achieved in the presence of excess acid, as expected from the above equation, but the only really stable compounds of manganese(III) are produced by precipitation or coordination, see p. 68.

The preparation of manganese(III) phosphate

Materials required: Ammonium manganese(II) phosphate
Concentrated orthophosphoric acid

Dissolve ammonium manganese(II) phosphate (4 g) in dilute nitric acid (5 ml of concentrated nitric acid: 20 ml of water). Add this solution to 30 ml of orthophosphoric acid contained in a conical flask. Close the flask loosely with a small funnel and heat; maintain the temperature at 110–120°C (critical) for 1 hour. Note any colour changes. Pour the contents of the flask into about 100 ml of hot water and dislodge any phosphate adhering to the flask. Filter by suction, wash well with hot water, and with acetone to assist the drying. Record the yield and quote this as a percentage based on ammonium manganese(II) phosphate.

Complementary work:
(1) Investigate the effect of acids and bases on the product.
(2) Determine the degree of hydration of the product by pyrolysis. Weigh accurately 0·3–0·4 g of the product into a small, previously ignited crucible. Heat the sample until no further colour change is observed. Cool in a desiccator and reweigh. On ignition, manganese(III) phosphate is converted into manganese(II) pyrophosphate

$$2MnPO_4xH_2O = Mn_2P_2O_7 + \tfrac{1}{2}O_2 + 2xH_2O$$

The preparation of tris(acetylacetonato)manganese(III)

Materials required: Manganese(II) chloride tetrahydrate
Sodium acetate trihydrate
Acetylacetone

Dissolve manganese(II) chloride tetrahydrate (5 g) and sodium acetate trihydrate (13 g) in water (200 ml), and to the stirred solution add slowly acetylacetone (21 ml). Treat the resultant two-phase system with potassium permanganate solution (1 g in 50 ml of water); after a few minutes add, in small amounts with stirring, sodium acetate solution (13 g of the trihydrate dissolved in 50 ml of water). Heat the solution to about 60°C for 10 minutes, cool in ice-cold water and filter at the pump. Wash the product with ice-cold water and *small* quantities of acetone to facilitate drying. Dry at the pump.

Complementary work:
(1) Measure the paramagnetic susceptibility of the compound and hence determine whether it is a high-spin complex or a low-spin complex. See p. 201 for experimental details.
(2) Dissolve a small amount of the complex in water and allow to stand for a few minutes. Note what happens and comment.

(3) Prepare a solution of the complex in water which has been saturated with acetylacetone. Add a few drops of 4M sulphuric acid, followed by a few drops of 4M sodium hydroxide. Note any colour changes which take place during the addition of acid and base, and comment on your observations.

Reference
Cartledge, G. H., *J. Amer. Chem. Soc.*, (1951), **73**, 4416.

The higher oxidation states of manganese are produced under strong oxidizing conditions. The oxidation state VI is found only in the manganate ion, MnO_4^{2-}, and since this ion is stable only in strongly basic solution the conditions under which it can be prepared are limited.

The preparation of potassium manganate

Materials required: Potassium hydroxide
                         Potassium permanganate

Dissolve potassium hydroxide (6 g) in water (~5 ml) and add potassium permanganate (2g). Heat the solution carefully on an electric hotplate to 120–140°C. Use a hotplate in preference to a bunsen burner in order to minimize the formation of potassium carbonate. Continue the heating, with stirring, until the purple colour of permanganate has been replaced with the green of manganate. Solid potassium manganate separates out during the course of the reaction. *Spurting of the strongly alkaline solution may occur. This can be confined by covering the reaction vessel with a short stemmed funnel, and placing the stirrer through the neck of the funnel.*
When the reaction is complete, cool the reaction vessel and contents, add potassium hydroxide solution (10 g of potassium hydroxide in 10 ml of water), cool in ice, and filter on sintered glass. Dry the product in a vacuum desiccator over potassium hydroxide. Record the yield.

Complementary work:
(1) Dissolve a small amount of the product in water, acidify the

solution, and note what happens. Interpret your observations in the form of an equation.

(2) Add a small amount of the product to acidified potassium iodide solution and note what happens. Devise a method for the volumetric analysis of potassium manganate.

The highest oxidation state of manganese, as with titanium, vanadium, and chromium, corresponds to the removal of all the $4s$ and $3d$ electrons from the metal atom. The succeeding elements of the first transition series do not achieve the corresponding high oxidation state, in fact there is a marked increase in the importance of the lower oxidation states, see p. 44. Although potassium permanganate is produced on a large scale by the electrolytic oxidation of potassium manganate an oxidative fusion reaction can be used for a small-scale preparation.

The preparation of potassium permanganate

Materials required: Manganese(IV) oxide
Potassium hydroxide
Potassium chlorate

Protect the hands and eyes when handling the melt.
Fuse together potassium hydroxide (5 g) and potassium chlorate (2·5 g) in a nickel crucible. Add slowly, with stirring, the manganese(IV) oxide (2 g). As the addition proceeds, the melt thickens; at this stage a few more pellets of potassium hydroxide may be added to keep the melt mobile. When the addition of manganese(IV) oxide is complete, allow the melt to cool and extract it with two 100 ml portions of boiling water. Place a drop of the solution on a filter paper and note if any green colour is apparent; if so, pass carbon dioxide into the solution until a similar colour test shows only the purple of permanganate. Filter through a sintered glass crucible and evaporate the filtrate until crystallization commences. Cool, filter off the potassium permanganate and dry it in an oven at about 100°C. Record the yield.

Complementary work:

(1) Determine the percentage purity of the product by a suitable volumetric procedure.

(2) What would be the effect of omitting the potassium chlorate from the experiment?

The preparation of the above-mentioned compounds demonstrates the interconvertibility of the oxidation states of manganese under suitable conditions, starting with manganese(IV) oxide. The cycle is completed by reducing potassium permanganate in weakly alkaline solution when manganese(IV) oxide is precipitated, or in acid solution when manganese(II) is formed (the usual conditions for using potassium permanganate as a titrant, see p. 44). Manganese(VII) in potassium permanganate can be reduced under appropriate conditions to give manganese(VI), manganese(IV), or manganese(II) compounds. See p. 44.

The following experiments, which occur in the text as indicated, give products suitable for analysis using potassium permanganate,

The preparation of tetrapyridinesilver(II) peroxodisulphate	p. 77
The preparation of potassium peroxodisulphate	p. 82
The preparation of titanium(III) chloride	p. 86
The preparation of potassium permanganate	p. 53
The preparation of potassium trioxalatochromate(III)	p. 56
The preparation of iron(II) oxalate	p. 57
The preparation of cis- and trans-potassium dioxalato-diaquochromate(III)	p. 91
The preparation of barium peroxide	p. 34

6 Coordination chemistry I: typical compounds

Introduction

The reaction between two or more independently stable molecules to give a stable product with its own characteristic properties has been known for many years. The ammine complexes formed between ammonia and cobalt(II) chloride are typical examples. In many instances the complex does not give reactions in solution characteristic of the uncomplexed metal ion or ligand. However, thermodynamic and kinetic stabilities vary so widely that this is not a general criterion of the formation of a coordination compound. The development of the ideas as to the nature of these compounds should be known to the student.

Central to the ideas of the structure of coordination compounds is that transfer of electrons takes place between the ligands and a molecule or metal ion. In its simplest form a coordinate bond is formed by transfer of a pair of electrons from the ligand to the molecule or metal ion. Molecules or ions which act as ligands should therefore have lone pairs of electrons for donation, e.g. NH_3, Cl^-, $C_2O_4^{2-}$. The simplest type of coordination compound will thus be formed by a σ-bond between a ligand and a molecule or metal ion. This is demonstrated by the formation of the boron trifluoride-ammonia adduct described on p. 143, and by the preparation of the cobalt ammines described on p. 77.

A similar boron trifluoride adduct formed with trimethylamine is much more stable than the corresponding adduct with trimethylphosphine. The converse is true in complexes with transition metal ions where trimethylphosphine forms the more stable complexes.

Both ligands possess a lone pair of electrons but in the phosphine suitable orbitals are available for π-bonding, and this results in an overall increase in bond strength. Many complexes are known in which both σ- and π-bonding can occur, in fact this applies to the majority of ligands. Complexes formed by the oxalate ion $C_2O_4^{2-}$ described below are of this type, with the possibility of π-bonding from the $2p$ orbitals on the oxygen making some contribution to the overall bond. In other ligands the contribution from the π-bonding orbitals plays a more significant part in the overall bonding, and may result in the formation of complexes in which the metal ion is in a less common oxidation state. See the chapter on the stabilization of oxidation states, p. 68.

In another group of complex compounds there is no lone pair, as such, on the ligand molecule to form a conventional σ-bond. All bonding probably occurs through the use of π-orbitals on the ligands. The complex $(C_2H_4PdCl_2)_2$ described on p. 114 is an example of such a compound. Similarly the preparation of ferrocene illustrates bonding between the ligand and the metal ion in which no localized σ-bonds are present.

The preparation of potassium trioxalatochromate(III)

Materials required: Potassium oxalate
Oxalic acid
Potassium dichromate

Dissolve potassium oxalate (6 g of the monohydrate) and oxalic acid (14 g of the dihydrate) in water (200 ml), and add potassium dichromate (5 g) slowly with continuous stirring. When the reaction is complete, evaporate the solution nearly to dryness and allow the product to crystallize. Isolate the product by filtration, wash with acetone, and dry in a warm oven. Record the yield.

Complementary work:
(1) Boil a small amount of the product with alkali and identify the solution and solid so formed.
(2) Devise methods for the analysis of potassium trioxalatochromate(III) for chromium and oxalate.

(3) What is the structure of the trioxalatochromate(III) ion? Can this be resolved into optical isomers?

Reference
Bushra, E. and Johnson, C. H., *J. Chem. Soc.*, (1939), 1937.

The preparation of iron(II) oxalate

Materials required: Ammonium iron(II) sulphate
                       Oxalic acid

Dissolve ammonium iron(II) sulphate (8 g) in water (25 ml) which has been acidified with about 1 ml of 2M sulphuric acid. Add a solution of oxalic acid (5 g in 30 ml of water) and boil. Filter the yellow precipitate on a Buchner funnel and wash well with hot water. Finally, wash with acetone and dry at the pump. Record the yield.

Complementary work:
(1) Determine the composition of the product by the following procedure. Dissolve 0·2–0·3 g (accurately weighed) of the product in 2M sulphuric acid and titrate with standard potassium permanganate solution. When the colour of the permanganate is slow to fade, heat the solution to about 60°C and continue the titration until the usual permanganate end-point is reached. Boil the solution with zinc dust (2.0 g) for 20 minutes when the solution will be colourless. Test a drop of the solution with thiocyanate solution; if there is no immediate pink colour the rest of the titration may be carried out. If there is a pink colour continue the boiling for a further 10 minutes. This test is very sensitive and a very faint colour can be tolerated without any serious effect on the subsequent titration. Filter the solution through glass wool and wash the residual zinc and the flask thoroughly with 2M sulphuric acid. Titrate the combined filtrate and washings with the standard permanganate solution. From the results determine the iron, oxalate, and water content of the product. Derive an empirical formula. Explain the chemistry of the stages in the determination.
(2) What are the possible structural formulae of iron(II) oxalate?

The preparation of ferrocene

Materials required: Anhydrous iron(III) chloride
Iron powder
Dicyclopentadiene
Diethylamine
Tetrahydrofuran

Equip a 250 ml three-necked flask with a stirrer, a reflux condenser, and an inlet for nitrogen. Purify the tetrahydrofuran by refluxing over solid potassium hydroxide followed by distillation from lithium aluminium hydride. *Do not distil to dryness. Destroy the remaining lithium aluminium hydride by carefully adding a dry ester to the cold residue. Treat any spillage immediately with an ester.* Place pure, dry, tetrahydrofuran (100 ml) in the 250 ml flask and to this add, in portions, with stirring, anhydrous iron(III) chloride (27 g) and 300 mesh iron powder (4·5 g). The particle size of the iron powder is important since a coarser grade of iron will lower the yield of ferrocene. Flush the flask with nitrogen and maintain a steady stream of nitrogen while the mixture is refluxed for about $4\frac{1}{2}$ hours.

During this period the dicyclopentadiene is distilled to convert it to the monomer. Equip a 100 ml flask with a 12 in. × $\frac{3}{4}$ in. glass column packed with glass helices and surmounted by a distillation head and double-surface condenser. Collect the freshly distilled cyclopentadiene in a container cooled to −78°C in a solid carbon dioxide-acetone bath, taking precautions to exclude moisture. Store the cyclopentadiene at −78°C until required.

When the $4\frac{1}{2}$ hr reflux period mentioned above is complete, remove the tetrahydrofuran under reduced pressure until the residue is almost dry. Maintain an atmosphere of nitrogen. Cool the flask in ice, and to the residue add cyclopentadiene (45 ml) and diethylamine (100 ml). Stir the mixture vigorously for 8 hours, or overnight, maintaining an atmosphere of nitrogen. Remove the excess amine under reduced pressure and extract the residue with several portions of refluxing petrol. Filter the extracts hot and evaporate the solvent to leave a residue of ferrocene. Purify the product by recrystallization from pentane or cyclohexane. Measure the m.p. and record the yield.

Complementary work:

(1) Heat a sample of ferrocene in a dry test tube and note what happens.

(2) What is the structure of ferrocene?

(3) What other methods can be used for the synthesis of ferrocene and related compounds.

(4) The aromatic character of the cyclopentadienyl ring in ferrocene may be demonstrated by acetylation using a Friedel Craft's technique [3].

Prepare a solution of ferrocene (5 g) in 80 ml of methylene chloride in a three-necked flask and add acetic anhydride (10 g). Fit the flask with a stirrer, a dropping funnel, and a drying tube. Cool the flask in ice and water. Add dropwise, with stirring 25 ml of boron trifluoride etherate over 30 minutes, and stir the solution for a further 3 hours. Transfer the solution to a separating funnel, add excess sodium acetate solution, and shake the funnel vigorously. Separate the organic layer and dry it over anhydrous sodium sulphate. Filter, remove the solvent, and recrystallize the product twice from benzene —60/80°C petrol. Record the yield. Measure the melting point of the acetyl ferrocene.

References

[1] Wilkinson, G., *Org. Synth.*, Coll. vol. **4**, 476.

[2] Pauson, P. L., *Quart. Revs.*, (1955), **9**, 391.

[3] Triggle, D. J., Unpublished work.

Bibliography

Basolo, F. and Johnson, R. C., *Coordination Chemistry*, Benjamin, New York, (1964).

Murmann, R. K., *Inorganic Complex Compounds*, Reinhold, New York, (1965).

Jones, M. M., *Elementary Coordination Chemistry*, Prentice-Hall, New York, (1964).

7 Clathrate compounds

Introduction

A distinction should be drawn between the reaction of two or more independently stable molecules to form a third stable molecule in which a coordination complex is produced, and apparently similar reactions in which double salts and clathrates are produced.

In a clathrate compound the stoichiometry may be variable, depending on the proportion of suitable sites in the 'host' lattice which are occupied by 'guest' molecules. The proportion which is occupied varies with the method of preparation, and also with the different guest molecules in the same 'host' lattice. The process may be considered a physical trapping of the guest molecule in the host lattice, with interactions between the 'guest' and 'host' molecules limited to Van der Waals forces. For instance, in the sulphur dioxide-quinol clathrate the quinol host assumes a β-quinol lattice, which if produced in the absence of a guest molecule changes spontaneously into α-quinol, but which is stable indefinitely in the clathrate compound. Consequently any physical process which involves breakdown of the crystal lattice of the host, e.g. melting or dissolution, should liberate the trapped molecules. Dissolution of the sulphur dioxide-quinol clathrate in acetone should liberate the sulphur dioxide and this can be readily determined by gas-liquid chromatography.

The clathration of a given molecule in a host lattice is dependent on its size. Compounds of similar chemical and physical properties will therefore differ in their ability to form clathrate compounds primarily because of differences in molecular size. The lattice of the complex compound which crystallizes from an ammoniacal solution of nickel cyanide has dimensions suitable for the inclusion of a variety of aromatic molecules.

The example given below illustrates the change in clathrating ability of the host lattice, due to the addition of a small side chain to a benzene molecule, with consequent increase in molecular size.

The preparation of a sulphur dioxide-quinol clathrate

Materials required: Quinol
Sulphur dioxide

This reaction must be carried out in a fume cupboard.
Dissolve quinol (5 g) in water (50 ml) at 50°C. Pass a slow stream of sulphur dioxide through the solution at 50°C, and continue the flow while allowing the solution to cool. After 30 minutes the sulphur dioxide flow may be stopped, the yellow crystals filtered with suction, without washing, and dried over sulphuric acid. Record the yield.

Complementary work:
(1) Dissolve a portion of the product in water, warm and identify the gas evolved.
(2) Dissolve a portion of the product in a little starch/iodine solution. Comment on your observations.
(3) Devise a volumetric method for the quantitative determination of sulphur dioxide in the product.
(4) Sketch the quinol lattice indicating how the cavities for sulphur dioxide inclusion are formed[1]. What would be the stoichiometry of the clathrate if all the cavities were filled?
(5) Calculate the percentage of cavities filled in your product.
(6) *The detection of sulphur dioxide by gas-liquid chromatography.*
Place a sample of the yellow product (0·1–0·2 g) in a test-tube, add acetone (5 ml) and quickly seal the end of the test tube with a serum cap. Shake the tube until all the solid has dissolved. Observe the evolution of gas bubbles. Now insert the needle of a hypodermic syringe through the serum cap and withdraw a sample of the gas. Inject a 5 ml sample on to a gas-liquid chromatographic column and compare the retention volumes of the peaks with those obtained

by injecting sulphur dioxide, and acetone separately on to the column. See p. 192.

Water is not recommended as a solvent in this part of the exercise since a considerable time will elapse before it will be eluted from the column. Satisfactory results have been obtained using a 6 ft. column packed with 5% polyethylene glycol adipate and 7% bentone 34 at room temperature. Nitrogen was used as a carrier gas with a flow rate of 50 ml/minute.

Reference
[1] Palin, D. E. and Powell, H. M., *J. Chem.Soc.*, (1947), 208.

The preparation of a dicyanoamminenickel(II) clathrate

Materials required: Ammonia solution (S.G.0·88)
Potassium cyanide
Acetic acid
Nickel(II) sulphate or ammonium nickel(II) sulphate
Benzene
p-Xylene

Exercise caution when using potassium cyanide. Wash your hands and the apparatus thoroughly after completing the reaction. Clean up any spillage immediately.

To a solution of nickel(II) sulphate (2·0 g) or ammonium nickel(II) sulphate (2·8 g) in 8 ml of water, add 8 ml of ammonia solution. Then add 4 ml of a 25% solution of potassium cyanide, cool in ice and allow to stand for a few minutes. Filter off the crystals of potassium sulphate which precipitate and divide the solution into two parts, A and B.

Solution A
To solution A add slowly 10 ml of acetic acid (6 ml of glacial acetic acid diluted with 4 ml of water), shaking the liquid thoroughly until a slight turbidity is produced. Add 2 ml of a prepared mixture containing equal volumes of benzene and *p*-xylene, and shake the

mixture vigorously. Keep a little of the benzene—*p*-xylene mixture for comparative analysis. Allow to stand for a few minutes and filter with suction. Wash thoroughly with water, alcohol, and ether, and dry on the filter. Weigh the product and record the yield.

Solution B

Take solution B and repeat the procedure described for solution A but this time do not add any benzene-*p*-xylene mixture. Cork the tube and shake vigorously for a few seconds. Allow to stand and if the precipitate is slow to form add another drop of acetic acid. Repeat the shaking and allow the solution to stand until the precipitate settles. Filter, wash, and dry as described above. Weigh the product and calculate the yield.

Complementary work:

(1) Dissolve each sample in ammonia solution. Comment.

(2) Ignite a small quantity of each sample. Comment.

(3) Draw the lattice of the complex compound, indicating how the aromatic molecule is included [1]. What would be the stoichiometry of the clathrate compound if all the available sites were occupied.

(4) Measure the infrared spectrum of each product, as a 'Nujol' mull, see p. 161. Note that the intensity of the spectrum of product A decreases with time in the infrared beam.

(5) Dissolve 0·5 g of product A in concentrated aqueous ammonia (10 ml) at 40°C. Cool, extract this solution with ether (2 ml), and separate. Inject ∼0·5 μl of this ether extract on to a gas-liquid chromatographic column. Compare the bands obtained with the bands produced by injecting separately ether, benzene, and *p*-xylene on to the column. Also compare the chromatogram of the ether extract with the chromatogram of the prepared *p*-xylene-benzene mixture. Identify the aromatic molecule which has formed the clathrate compound. See p. 192.

A satisfactory separation of the organic components was achieved using a 5ft column packed with 5% 'Apiezon' on 'Celite' and a nitrogen carrier flow rate of 50 ml/min.

Reference

[1] Rayner, J. H. and Powell, H. M., *J. Chem. Soc.*, (1952), 319.

[2] Drago, R. S., Kwon, J. T. and Archer, R. D., *J. Amer. Chem. Soc.*, (1958), **80**, 2667.

Bibliography

Madelcorn, L., 'Clathrate compounds', *Chem. Rev.*, (1959), **59**, 827.

Hagen, M., *Clathrate Inclusion Compounds*, Reinhold, New York, (1962).

8 Double salts

Introduction

A double salt, unlike a clathrate compound, will have a definite stoichiometry. Provided the starting proportions of the separate salts comprising the double salt are kept within certain limits, the compound which first crystallizes will be the double salt. This can be more easily understood by reference to the appropriate phase diagram, see Figure 7. A double salt is formed from a three-component

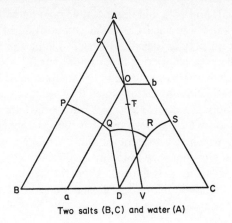

Two salts (B,C) and water (A)

Figure 7. Phase diagram of a three-component system.

system, comprising two separate salts and water, and at a given temperature this may be represented by a triangular diagram. The properties of such a phase diagram are fully described in standard

65

physical chemistry texts and the student is referred to any of these for amplification of the selected points given below.

The percentage composition of the system at any point O is proportional to the length of the three lines drawn from O parallel to the sides of the triangle. At O, the composition is Oa parts of A, Ob parts of B, and Oc parts of C. Take the line $AOTV$, at point O the composition of the system will be as given. Continuing towards T the proportion of water in the system continues to decrease but the ratio of component B to component C remains constant. Such a line represents the change in the system during evaporation at constant temperature. When the curve QR is reached, further evaporation will lead to crystallization and the solid which crystallizes will be double salt. As evaporation is continued more double salt will crystallize and the composition of the remaining solution will change along QR towards R. When the composition of the solution in contact with the double salt reaches the point R, then further evaporation will lead to crystallization of component C and double salt. If the solution were evaporated completely to dryness the total composition of the dry solid would be given by V, with DV parts of C and VC parts of double salt. Therefore, when preparing a double salt it is advisable to limit the amount of double salt which is crystallized out, and so avoid any possible contamination by either of the single salts. Provided the initial composition of the solution lies in the region AQR then double salt will be the first solid to crystallize when the solution is evaporated, but for maximum yield it is obviously advisable to have an initial solution in which the single salts are in a ratio close to that in which they occur in the double salt.

The formation of a double salt does not involve the formation of any complex ion which is not present in the component salts. The crystal units, which are present in the component salts, are re-assembled in the proportions found in the double salt so that a more stable crystal structure is produced. Thus, the free energy of formation of a crystalline double salt is greater than the sum of the free energies of formation of the component salts.

The preparation of ammonium nickel(II) sulphate

Materials required: Nickel(II) sulphate hexahydrate
                        Ammonium sulphate

Dissolve nickel(II) sulphate (4·5 g) and ammonium sulphate (2·0 g) in 15 ml of hot water. Allow the solution to cool and filter the crystals at the pump. Dry the crystals by pressing between a pad of filter papers. The filtrate may be concentrated to about half its original volume to obtain a second crop of crystals. Filter, and dry these in the same way as the first crop. Record the total weight of product but keep the two samples separate.

Complementary work:
   (1) On which of the component salts would you base your percentage yield?
   (2) Dissolve a little of the product in water. Test for nickel, sulphate, and ammonium ions.
   (3) Determine by a gravimetric method the percentage of nickel in the two samples of product. Comment.

The preparation of ammonium copper(II) sulphate

Materials required: Copper(II) sulphate pentahydrate
                        Ammonium sulphate

Dissolve copper(II) sulphate pentahydrate (4 g) and ammonium sulphate (2 g) in hot water (10 ml). Cool the solution, and filter the crystals at the pump. Dry between a pad of filter papers. Evaporate the solution to about 5 ml, cool, filter, and dry the second crop of crystals. Record the total weight of product but keep the two samples separate. Calculate the percentage yield.

Complementary work:
   (1) Dissolve a little of the product in water and add potassium iodide solution.
   (2) Determine by an iodimetric method the percentage of copper in the two samples of product.
   (3) Measure the absorption spectrum over the range 350–750 mμ of a solution of the double salt, see p. 170. Compare this with the spectra of equimolar solutions of copper(II) sulphate pentahydrate and tetramminecopper(II) sulphate. Comment.

9 The stabilization of oxidation states

Introduction

When an element can exist in more than one oxidation state in aqueous solution each oxidation state will have a different thermodynamic stability. The relative stability of two oxidation states in aqueous solution is most conveniently expressed in terms of the electrode potential for the reaction

$$M^{a+} + (a - b)e^- \rightleftharpoons M^{b+} \quad \text{where b} < \text{a.}$$

The electrode potential for a solution containing the ions M^{b+} and M^{a+} is given by the equation,

$$E = E^0 + \frac{RT}{zF} \ln \frac{[M^{a+}]}{[M^{b+}]}$$

where z = the number of electrons per ion transferred at the electrode

F = the Faraday = 96,500 coulombs

E = the electrode potential of the solution

E^0 = the standard electrode potential

$[M^{a+}]$ = the activity of M^{a+} ions in the solution

$[M^{b+}]$ = the activity of M^{b+} ions in the solution.

Therefore any species added to the solution which reduces the concentration of either M^{a+} or M^{b+} and so alters the ratio $[M^{a+}]/[M^{b+}]$ will cause an observable change in the electrode potential. If $[M^{a+}]$ is reduced then the observable potential will become less

68

positive, that is the higher oxidation state will become more stable. Alternatively, if $[M^{b+}]$ is reduced the observed potential will become more positive and the lower oxidation state will become more stable. The electrode potential for a given reaction indicates whether the stability of the higher oxidation state has been increased or decreased by the formation of a given compound. It does not provide any information as to how that increase or decrease in stability has been produced. Examples of the stabilization of unusual oxidation states will now be considered.

The elements copper ($3d^{10} 4s^1$) and silver ($4d^{10} 5s^1$) have similar outer electron configurations but differ in the stability of the M^I and M^{II} oxidation states. For copper the 'normal' oxidation state in aqueous solution is Cu^{II} while for silver it is Ag^I. However, compounds in which the Cu^I oxidation state has been stabilized can be prepared in aqueous solution and compounds containing Ag^{II} can also be prepared.

Insoluble compounds

The standard electrode potentials using the IUPAC convention [1] for the reactions

$$Cu^+ + e^- = Cu^0 \qquad E^0 = 0.52V \qquad (9.1)$$

$$Cu^{2+} + e^- = Cu^+ \qquad E^0 = 0.153V \qquad (9.2)$$

show that Cu^+ ions in aqueous solution are unstable with respect to disproportionation into Cu^0 and Cu^{2+}

$$2Cu^+ = Cu^0 + Cu^{2+} \qquad E^0 = 0.367V.$$

Note that the IUPAC convention for electrode potentials differs from the convention used in a number of textbooks, where electrode potentials are written as oxidation potentials, e.g. $Cu^0 = Cu^+ + e^-$, $E^0 = -0.52V$. The numerical value of the electrode potential is the same but the sign is reversed. Consequently it is important to check which convention has been used for quoted values.

From the equation

$$E = E^0 + \frac{RT}{zF} \ln \frac{[Cu^{2+}]}{[Cu^+]}$$

any species added to the solution which reduces the concentration of Cu^+ but affects the concentration of Cu^{2+} to a lesser extent will cause an increase in the measured electrode potential. Such a reduction in concentration of Cu^+ can be brought about by addition of an ion which forms an insoluble salt with Cu^+ but not with Cu^{2+}. Thus copper(I) chloride is insoluble in aqueous solution and the increase in stability of Cu^+ is given by the electrode potential.

$$Cu^{2+} + Cl^- + e^- = CuCl \qquad E^0 = 0.566V \qquad (9.3)$$

There will be a similar effect on the electrode potential

$$Cu^+ + e^- = Cu^0 \qquad E^0 = 0.521V$$

in the presence of Cl^- due to the precipitation of copper(I) chloride

$$CuCl + e^- = Cu^0 + Cl^- \qquad E^0 = 0.124V \qquad (9.4)$$

Therefore by combination of eqns. (9.3) and (9.4) it follows that copper(I) chloride is stable with respect to the disproportionation,

$$2CuCl = Cu^0 + Cu^{2+} + 2Cl^- \qquad E^0 = -0.442V.$$

Soluble compounds

The increased stability of the lower oxidation state of copper by precipitation as the chloride can be readily understood in terms of the reduced concentration of the Cu^+ ion in solution. The reason for the stability of soluble copper(I) compounds is not immediately apparent. Stability can be achieved by complex formation. If the complex is sufficiently stable for the equilibrium $[ML_x]^+ \rightleftharpoons M^+ + xL$ to lie well to the left then the concentration of Cu^+ will be reduced. Ligands which, in addition to forming σ bonds with the metal ion, also function as π-electron acceptors are more likely to form stable complexes. When the metal ion has a high electron density it will more readily donate π-electrons to the ligand. The strength of the π-bonding and hence the stability of the complex will be increased. For a given metal the lower oxidation state has the higher electron density and participates more readily in π-bonding. Thiourea is a suitable ligand for the stabilization of Cu^+ ions in solution, with coordination occuring through the sulphur atom.

An indication of the stability of the tris(thiourea)copper(I) ion is given by the reaction between copper and hydrochloric acid. There is no reaction between copper and hydrochloric acid (see electrode potentials below) but on addition of thiourea hydrogen is liberated.

The electrode potentials of the half reactions are,

$$Cu^+ + e^- = Cu^0 \qquad E^0 = 0\cdot52V$$
$$H^+ + e^- = \tfrac{1}{2}H_2 \qquad E^0 = 0 \ (1 \ \text{Molar HCl}).$$

For the reaction $Cu^0 + H^+ = Cu^+ + \tfrac{1}{2}H_2$ to proceed, the electrode potential for $Cu^+ + e^- = Cu^0$ under the conditions of the reactions must be $\leqslant 0$. This can be achieved if the activity of Cu^+ ions in solution is greatly reduced. From the equation

$$E = 0 = E^0 + \frac{RT}{zF} \ln \frac{[Cu^+]}{[Cu^0]}$$

when

$$T = 25°C, [Cu^0] = 1, E^0 = 0\cdot52V.$$

Then

$$\log_{10}[Cu^+] = -\frac{0\cdot52}{0\cdot0591} = -8\cdot8.$$

Therefore the maximum concentration of Cu^+ ions in solution is $<10^{-8\cdot8}$ g. ions/l. This means that in the presence of thiourea the concentration of Cu^+ ions has been greatly reduced, due to complex formation.

When stabilization of a higher oxidation state occurs, e.g. Ag^{II}, then a ligand which can form π-bonds with the metal ion by donation of electrons to the metal ion may form a stable complex. When the metal ion has a high electronegativity it will more readily accept π-electrons from the ligand. The strength of the π-bonding and hence the stability of the complex will be increased. Electronegativity increases with increasing oxidation state of a given metal. Therefore metal ions of high oxidation state are more able to participate in this type of π-bonding. The increased stability of the complex again effectively reduces the concentration of metal ions in solution. The Ag^{II} oxidation state is unstable relative to Ag^{I}, but coordination with pyridine to form the tetrapyridine silver(II) ion results in the formation of a number of moderately stable compounds. See also p. 85.

The examples of soluble complexes referred to above have used π-bonding ligands in order to obtain stable complexes. However, it is possible to stabilize a given oxidation state by complex formation in which no π-bonding occurs. Thus the formation of hexammine complexes of cobalt results in an increased stability of the Co^{3+} ion compared with the hexaquo complex.

$$Co^{3+}(aq) + e^- = Co^{2+}(aq) \qquad E^0 = 1\cdot842V$$
$$[Co(NH_3)_6]^{3+} + e^- = [Co(NH_3)_6]^{2+} \qquad E^0 = 0\cdot1V.$$

The increased stability of the Co^{III} oxidation state in the cobalt hexammine complex compared with the cobalt hexaquo complex can be understood qualitatively, in terms of the crystal field stabilization energy. Assuming that the electron-pairing energy and the 3rd ionization potential of the Co(II) ion is approximately constant, then the gain in crystal field stabilization energy for Co^{II} in the hexammine compared with the hexaquo complex will be

$$-0.8 \; (\Delta_0'' - \Delta_0'), \text{ where } \Delta_0' = \text{crystal field splitting by } H_2O$$
$$\Delta_0'' = \text{crystal field splitting by } NH_3$$

and for Co^{III} will be $-2.4 \; (\Delta_0'' - \Delta_0')$. Higher values of Δ_0 will have a more marked effect on the stabilization of the Co^{III} oxidation state than on the Co^{II} oxidation state. Therefore a correlation would be expected between the stability of the Co^{III} oxidation state in a given complex and the position of the ligand in the spectrochemical series. For further information on the spectrochemical series see p. 173.

Any effective change in the free energy for the reaction $Co^{III} \rightarrow Co^{II}$ will result in a change in the electrode potential, and the equilibrium constant as shown by the expression

$$\Delta G^0 = -nFE^0 = -RT \ln K_p.$$

An increase in crystal field stabilization energy will be a contributory factor to a more positive ΔG^0 and hence a less positive electrode potential.

Note again, (see p. 32), that a distinction must be made between thermodynamic and kinetic stability. The above discussion has referred to the thermodynamic stability of a complex, that is its tendency to exist under equilibrium conditions. This is not necessarily a measure of the kinetic stability, i.e. lability, of the complex with regard to ligand replacement reactions.

Reference
[1] Christiansen, J. A., *J. Amer. Chem. Soc.*, (1960), **82**, 5518.

The preparation of copper(I) chloride

Materials required: Copper(II) chloride hydrate
                       Sodium sulphite
                       Glacial acetic acid

Copper(I) chloride is prepared by reducing copper(II) ions with sulphur dioxide or sulphite ions in the presence of chloride ions. The copper(I) ions once formed, react with chloride ions to form the insoluble copper(I) chloride.

Prepare three solutions:

(a) dissolve sodium sulphite (10 g) in 50 ml of water,

(b) dissolve copper(II) chloride (13 g) in 25 ml of water,

(c) prepare a sulphurous acid solution by dissolving sodium sulphite (1 g) in 1 litre of water and add 12 ml of 2M hydrochloric acid.

Add slowly, with constant stirring, the sodium sulphite solution to the copper(II) chloride solution. Dilute the suspension of copper(I) chloride so formed with about half the sulphurous acid solution, allow the precipitate to settle, and decant most of the supernatant solution. Filter the solid by suction on a sintered glass disc, wash the precipitate on to the sinter by means of sulphurous acid solution. Take care that the copper(I) chloride is always covered by a layer of solution. Finally wash the product with portions of glacial acetic acid, alcohol, and ether. Dry the product in a warm oven.

Copper(I) chloride is slowly oxidized by moist air to give the basic copper(II) chloride, $CuCl_2.3Cu(OH)_2$, so it must be stored in stoppered containers.

Complementary work:

(1) Prepare 10–20 ml of an aqueous solution of potassium chloride and to this add $\sim$1 g of copper(I) chloride. Note what happens and interpret your observations. Now add a few drops of ethylenediamine, identify the precipitate so formed, and comment.

(2) In what other ways may the copper(I) oxidation state be stabilized?

The preparation of copper(I) tetraiodomercurate(II)

Materials required: Mercury(II) iodide
Potassium iodide
Copper(II) sulphate pentahydrate
Sulphur dioxide

Suspend mercury(II) iodide (10 g) in about 50 ml of water add potassium iodide (8 g) and note that the mercury(II) iodide now dissolves. Add a concentrated solution of copper(II) sulphate penta-hydrate (10 g) and bubble a slow stream of sulphur dioxide through the resulting suspension until a bright scarlet precipitate is produced. *Carry out this part of the reaction in a fume cupboard.* Filter, wash with a little alcohol, and ether. Dry on the filter. Weigh the product and record the yield.

Complementary work:

(1) Use a melting point apparatus to determine the transition temperature between the red and black forms of the product. Compare this value with the transition temperature for mercury(II) iodide.

(2) Dissolve a little mercury(II) iodide in the minimum amount of potassium iodide solution. Make the solution alkaline with potassium hydroxide solution and add a drop of aqueous ammonia. Comment on your observations.

The preparation of tris(thiourea)copper(I) sulphate

Materials required: Thiourea
                        Copper(II) sulphate pentahydrate

Prepare a solution of thiourea (2·5 g) in 15 ml of water, and a solution of copper(II) sulphate pentahydrate (2·5 g) in 15 ml of water. Cool the two solutions. Add slowly the copper(II) sulphate solution to the thiourea solution, stirring the mixed solution con-tinuously, until all the copper(II) sulphate solution has been added. Allow the solution to stand. The product of the reaction may appear as white crystals or as oily drops on the side of the beaker. Prepare a cold solution of thiourea (1·0 g) in 10 ml of water and add this to the reaction mixture. Stir vigorously, allow to stand and filter the white crystals on a Hirsch funnel. Recrystallize the product by dissolving it in a solution of thiourea (0·15 g) in 30 ml of water containing a few drops of 1M sulphuric acid. The solution may be heated to a maximum of 75°C to dissolve the product. Cool the solution, and filter the crystals on a Hirsch funnel. Wash with 5 ml portions of cold water and then with 5 ml portions of alcohol. Dry on the filter.

Weigh the product and record the yield. The product is obtained as the dihydrate. Note that this is one of the general methods of preparing compounds containing a metal in a low oxidation state. The ligand, in this case thiourea, also functions as a reducing agent.

Complementary work:

(1) Sketch the ligand orbitals which are suitable for stabilizing the copper(I) oxidation state through π-bonding.

(2) Prepare a solution of thiourea (1 g) in 1M hydrochloric acid (10 ml). Add a little copper powder and warm gently. Repeat the experiment without thiourea. Comment.

(3) Determine the percentage of sulphate in the product. The complex must be decomposed before determining the sulphate content, otherwise on the addition of barium chloride a thiourea compound is also precipitated. The complex is readily destroyed by making use of its sensitivity to hydroxyl ion attack. Note that the product was recrystallized from acidified solution. Thiourea is also hydrolyzed by alkali.

$$NH_2CSNH_2 + 2H_2O = 2NH_3 + H_2S + CO_2.$$

Decompose a known weight of the complex (about 0·3 g) by boiling with 2M sodium hydroxide solution (40 ml) until no more ammonia is evolved. The copper precipitates as the sulphide, filter, and wash with cold water. Acidify the combined filtrate and washings with 2M hydrochloric acid and then proceed as for a standard sulphate gravimetric analysis.

(4) Determine the percentage of copper in the product iodimetrically. Decompose a known weight of the product (about 0·5 g) by boiling with 20 ml of 50% nitric acid. Carefully evaporate the solution to about 2 ml ensuring that no part of the solution is evaporated to dryness. Cool, and wash the sides of the flask and the bottom of the covering watch glass. Dilute the solution to about 50 ml and add 2M aqueous ammonia until there is a faint blue precipitate. Dissolve the precipitate in the minimum of 2M acetic acid and add 10 ml of 50% potassium iodide solution. Titrate the liberated iodine with standard sodium thiosulphate solution.

(5) What is the structure of the product? [1]

(6) For information on the infra red spectrum of the product see references [2] and [3].

References
[1] Okaya, Y. and Knobler, C. B., *Acta Cryst.*, (1964), **17**, 928.
[2] Quagliano, J. V., *et al.*, *J. Amer. Chem. Soc.*, (1958), **80**, 527.
[3] Swaminathan, K. and Irving, H. M. N., *J. Inorg. Nuclear Chem.*, (1964), **26**, 1291.

The preparation of tetrapyridinesilver(II) peroxodisulphate

Materials required: Ammonium peroxodisulphate
                         Silver nitrate
                         Pyridine

Prepare a solution of ammonium peroxodisulphate (2·5 g) in 25 ml of water. To this solution add slowly a solution of silver nitrate (0·5 g) in 10 ml of water and 5 ml of pyridine. Stir the mixed solution until all the silver nitrate has been added. Cool the solution and filter the precipitate on a Hirsch funnel. Wash the precipitate with two 10 ml portions of cold water and two 10 ml portions of alcohol. Dry on the filter paper. Weigh the product and record the yield.

Complementary work:
(1) Sketch the orbitals on the ligand which are suitable for stabilizing the silver(II) oxidation state through π-bonding.
(2) Determine the percentage of silver in the compound gravimetrically. Add a known weight of the product (about 0·4 g) to 5 ml of 2M sodium hydroxide solution in 20 ml of water. Stir the mixture well, filter, and retain the precipitate. Wash the precipitate with cold water and discard the filtrate and washings. For the gravimetric determination of silver, pierce a hole in the filter paper and wash the precipitate through with 2M aqueous ammonia. This reduces and dissolves the silver(II) oxide. Acidify the solution with 2M nitric acid and continue as for a standard gravimetric silver determination.
(3) Determine the oxidizing power of the silver in the compound.
The silver may be determined volumetrically using the decomposition procedure described above but now transfer the filter paper containing the silver(II) oxide to a conical flask containing 50 ml of acidified standard iron(II) sulphate solution. Dissolve the precipitate

and titrate the excess iron(II) sulphate with standard potassium permanganate solution.

Compare the results from (2) and (3).

An alternative preparation of a tetrapyridinesilver(II) complex is given on p. 85.

The preparation of hexamminecobalt(III) chloride

Materials required: Cobalt (II) chloride hexahydrate
                         Charcoal
                         6% Hydrogen peroxide (20 volume)
                         Ammonia solution (S.G. 0·88)
                         Ammonium chloride

Place decolorizing charcoal (1 g) in a conical flask and add a hot solution of cobalt(II) chloride (9 g) and ammonium chloride (6 g) in 10 ml of water. To this mixture add 20 ml of concentrated ammonia solution. Cool the mixture under the cold water tap and add slowly 20 ml of 6% hydrogen peroxide. When all the hydrogen peroxide has been added heat the mixture to 60°C and maintain this temperature for 15–20 minutes until the pinkish colour of the solution is removed. *Carry out this operation in a fume cupboard.* Cool the mixture under the cold tap and then in ice-cold water. Filter the solid on a Buchner funnel and transfer the precipitate to a beaker containing a boiling solution of 3 ml of concentrated hydrochloric acid and 80 ml of water. When all the solid, except the charcoal has dissolved, filter the hot suspension. Add 10 ml of concentrated hydrochloric acid to the filtrate and cool the solution in ice. Filter the crystals on a Buchner funnel and dry between filter papers. Record the weight of the product and calculate the yield. Note that the use of decolorizing charcoal has a number of applications in reactions involving Co—N bonds. In the absence of charcoal the chloropentamminecobalt(III) complex would be obtained, see p. 104.

Complementary work:

(1) Dissolve a little of the product in water, acidify with 4m hydrochloric acid, and boil the solution. Cool, and add about

1 ml of 50% potassium iodide solution. The reaction $[Co(NH_3)_6]^{3+}$ + $6H_3O^+$ = $[Co(H_2O)_6]^{3+}$ + $6NH_4^+$ has an equilibrium constant $K \sim 10^{25}$. Comment.

(2) Determine the magnetic moment of the complex and compare it with the magnetic moment of cobalt(II) chloride, see p. 199. From the crystal field energy level diagram show qualitatively in terms of crystal field stabilization energy why ammonia stabilizes the cobalt(III) oxidation state compared with water. Which oxidation state of cobalt would you expect to be stable in a complex with CN^- ?

(3) Determine the percentage of cobalt in the complex iodimetrically. Add a known weight of the product (about 0·15 g) to 25 ml of 4M sodium hydroxide solution and boil gently until all evolution of ammonia has ceased. Cool the suspension of cobalt(III) oxide, add about 1 g of potassium iodide, and then acidify the mixture with concentrated hydrochloric acid. Titrate the liberated iodine with standard sodium thiosulphate solution. Compare this reaction of cobalt(III) oxide in acid solution with reaction (1) above.

References

Blanchard, A. A., *Inorg. Synth.*, McGraw Hill, New York, vol. 2, p. 126.

Sen, D. and Fernelius, W. C., *J. Inorg. Nuclear Chem.*, (1959) **10**, 269.

Dwyer, F. P. and Sargeson, A. M., *Nature* (1960), **187**, 1022.

10 Electrochemical oxidation and reduction

The electrode reactions which occur when a solution of an ionic solute is electrolyzed involve the gain of electrons by an ion at the cathode, and the loss of electrons by an ion at the anode. The primary electrode reactions can be represented by the ionic equations

$$A^+ + e^- = A \qquad \text{at the cathode}$$
$$B^- - e^- = B \qquad \text{at the anode}$$

$$\overline{A^+B^- \qquad = A + B}$$

This allows the generalization that oxidation occurs at the anode and reduction occurs at the cathode. Transfer of electrons by electrolysis represents the most direct, although not necessarily the most convenient, method for oxidation or reduction.

Overpotential and discharge potential

Consider a metal electrode M in contact with a solution of its ions M^+. Then if the system is at equilibrium the reversible electrode potential is given by the equation

$$E = E^0 + \frac{RT}{zF} \ln \frac{[a_{ox}]}{[a_{red}]}$$

where E = the electrode potential

E^0 = the standard electrode potential

z = the number of electrons per ion transferred at the electrode

79

F = the Faraday = 96,500 coulombs

$[a_{ox}]$ = the activity of the oxidized form

$[a_{red}]$ = the activity of the reduced form.

If a slightly more negative potential than the reversible potential is applied to the electrode M then the rate of the electrode reaction will be sufficient to remove the excess electrons, and the electrode will maintain its reversible potential. However, when a much greater negative potential is applied to this electrode, a condition which applies in electrolysis, then the equilibrium will be disturbed and the rate of the electrode reaction $M^+ + e^- = M$ may be insufficient to reduce this more negative potential. Consequently the potential of this electrode, functioning as a cathode, will become more negative than the reversible potential. This change in potential is known as the overpotential, which is given by the equation

$$V_e = V_r - \eta$$

where V_e = the operating potential of the cathode

V_r = the reversible potential

η = the overpotential.

In practice the existence of overpotential can be used in selecting suitable electrode materials for a given electrolytic reaction. The discharge potential of a metal ion on to a variety of metal electrodes is very close to the reversible value. There is very little overpotential, i.e. there are no obviously slow steps in the electrode reaction. This is not the case for gas discharge at an electrode where there is a considerable variation of overpotential with the metal electrode being used. Thus hydrogen has a very small overpotential at a highly polished platinum electrode, but a large overpotential at a lead electrode. Since electrolytic reactions are frequently carried out in aqueous solution, discharge of oxygen at the anode and hydrogen at the cathode have to be considered as competitive reactions to the desired electrode reactions. The reaction which occurs first as the applied potential is gradually increased will be the electrode reaction with the least negative potential at the cathode and the least positive potential at the anode. Sodium with a large negative standard electrode potential, $-2\cdot71V$, will not be discharged at a cathode from an aqueous solution of its ions, but hydrogen is evolved. Copper, with a positive standard electrode potential, $+0\cdot34V$, would be discharged in preference to hydrogen from an aqueous solution of copper ions. However, with zinc the standard electrode potential, $-0 \cdot 76V$, is more negative than the hydrogen electrode potential in neutral solution, $-0 \cdot 4V$, so that at a platinum cathode, where the overpotential is low, hydrogen will be discharged in preference to zinc. If a lead cathode is used, at which there is a large hydrogen overpotential, it is now possible to discharge zinc only.

Selection of a suitable electrode material will therefore depend not only on the resistance of the electrode to attack by the solution or products, but also on avoidance of unwanted discharge reactions.

Cell construction

Separation of the anode and cathode solutions is necessary if the products at the two electrodes are capable of reacting together spontaneously. This separation can be achieved by placing a porous diaphragm around one of the electrodes. Similarly a cation M^+, which has been oxidized to M^{2+} at an anode, is separated from the cathode to prevent reduction and loss of product. When different solutions are used for the anolyte and catholyte these are joined through a porous diaphragm, or salt bridge. This provides a suitable arrangement when a metal ion is being oxidized and prevents the loss of metal ions from the solution due to deposition on the cathode. A diaphragm is not required when the anode products are not decomposed by the cathode nor when the desired electrolysis product is to be formed by the reaction of anode and cathode products.

Cell current and current density

The current flowing through the cell is related to the potential drop by Ohms Law,

$$I = V/R.$$

where I = the current

V = the potential drop

R = the resistance of the cell.

However, the voltage cannot be increased indefinitely to increase the current for the discharge of one ion, since this will possibly exceed the discharge potential for another ion, say from the solvent. This will lead to the discharge of two ions simultaneously. In order to increase the current without increasing the applied potential the area of the electrodes must be increased. There will be no change in the current density since the conductance of the cell $\propto (I/VA)$, where A = the surface area of the electrode. In reactions where a high current density is required this is usually achieved by reduction in size of one of the electrodes.

Apparatus

A simple circuit, as shown in Figure 8, is required. The variable resistance and voltmeter may not be essential for a given electrolysis. Adjustment of the separation of the electrodes provides an alternative method of varying the resistance. Current is conveniently obtained from two or three 2-volt accumulators connected in series. Measurement of the total duration of the electrolysis and the current flowing, enables a calculation of current efficiency for a given electrode reaction to be made from the expressions

$$\text{theoretical weight of product} = \frac{ItM}{zF}$$

where I = the current in amp.

t = the time in sec.

F = the Faraday = 96,500 coulombs

z = the number of electrons transferred per ion

M = the molecular weight of the product

and

$$\text{current efficiency} = \frac{\text{actual weight of product}}{\text{theoretical weight of product}} \times 100\%$$

The preparation of potassium peroxodisulphate

Materials required: Potassium hydrogen sulphate
Platinum electrodes
Ammeter reading 0–1 amp.
6 volt supply

The anode consists of a small coil of platinum wire, with a surface area ~ 0.75 cm. The cathode consists of a 5 cm length of platinum wire. Prepare a saturated solution of potassium hydrogen sulphate (17 g) by dissolving the salt in 50 ml of water. Cool the solution in ice for about half an hour and then filter off any solid which has

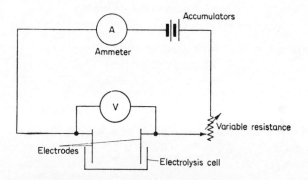

Figure 8. Circuit diagram of electrolysis apparatus.

precipitated. Transfer ~ 20 ml of this solution to a 30 ml beaker, cool in ice, and electrolyze. Adjust the separation of the anode and cathode in the solution so that with an applied potential of 6 volts a current of ~ 0.4 amp. is obtained. Record the current and the duration of the run. After about an hour switch off the current, filter the product on a sintered glass crucible, wash with alcohol, and ether, and dry in air. Record the weight of the product and calculate the current efficiency. The electrolysis may be repeated for a further period if more product is required.

Complementary work:

(1) Dissolve a little of the solid in the minimum of water and add 1 ml of a concentrated solution of silver nitrate. Now add excess aqueous ammonia. Comment on your observations.

(2) Treat a little of a freshly prepared solution of the product with barium chloride solution. Shake the solution and warm. Comment.

(3) Prepare a solution of manganese(II) sulphate, add a few drops of 0.1M silver nitrate, and 1 ml of a solution of the product. Warm. What is the purpose in adding silver nitrate solution?

(4) Prepare a solution of chrome alum, add a few drops of 0.1M

silver nitrate solution and then 1 ml of a solution of the product. Warm. Comment on the colour changes.

(5) Determine the percentage of peroxodisulphate in the product.

The preparation of potassium chlorate

Materials required: Potassium chloride
                        Platinum electrodes
                        Ammeter, 0–10 amp.
                        2 volt accumulators

This reaction must be carried out in a fume cupboard.

The electrolytic cell is made from a 150 ml beaker in which are placed a cathode of platinum foil (5 × 3 × 0·005 cm), semi-circular in shape, and a platinum anode (4 × 1 × 0·005 cm) in the mouth of the cathode. Prepare the electrolyte by dissolving potassium chloride (30 g) in 100 ml of water. Add potassium dichromate (0·2 g) to the electrolyte to regulate the hydrogen ion concentration and also to limit the reduction of the product at the cathode.

Warm the solution to 60°C, and pass a current of 1·5–2 amp. for 3–4 hours. Stir the solution to ensure adequate mixing. Check the pH of the solution at regular intervals since loss of chlorine will lead to increasing pH. If necessary add dilute hydrochloric acid to maintain pH 6–7. Allow the solution to cool and filter off the solid product. Dissolve the product in the minimum of hot water and allow the solution to cool slowly. Filter the crystals and dry in air. Weigh the product.

Complementary work:

(1) Dissolve a portion of the product in water, acidify with nitric acid, and add silver nitrate solution. Comment.

(2) Dissolve a portion of the product in water, acidify with dilute hydrochloric acid, and add potassium iodide solution. Comment.

(3) Determine the percentage purity of the sample of potassium chlorate.

(4) How does the reaction of the halogens with base depend on temperature?

The preparation of tetrapyridinesilver(II) nitrate

Materials required: Silver nitrate
                          Pyridine
                          2M sulphuric acid
                          Platinum crucible ($\sim$25 ml capacity)
                          Platinum electrode
                          6-volt supply
                          Ammeter reading 0–1 amp.

Prepare a solution containing silver nitrate (5 g), 20 ml of pyridine and 25 ml of water, and place $\sim$15 ml of this solution in the platinum crucible. Cool the crucible in an ice-bath. The use of an ice-bath is contrary to the original experimental procedure [1], but without it the yield of product proved to be very unsatisfactory. Place $\sim$5 ml of 2M sulphuric acid in a glass tube 10 × 2 cm diameter, the lower end of which has been plugged with cotton wool. To prevent the liquid running out of the tube, seal the open end with a cork. Now place the lower end of this glass tube in the solution in the platinum crucible and adjust its position until the liquid level in the tube is equal to the liquid level in the crucible. Remove the cork and place the platinum wire electrode in the sulphuric acid solution. The electrolytic cell has now been constructed with the platinum crucible to act as anode, and the platinum wire to act as cathode, see Figure 9. Connect the electrodes to the 6-volt supply and, if necessary adjust the position of the platinum cathode to give a cell current of $\sim$0·2 amp. An intense red-brown coloration will develop almost immediately in the anode solution and hydrogen will be evolved at the

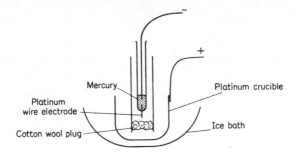

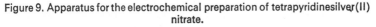

Figure 9. Apparatus for the electrochemical preparation of tetrapyridinesilver(II) nitrate.

cathode. After about thirty minutes disconnect the electrodes and filter the anode liquid. A crop of red-brown crystals will be obtained. If the product is contaminated with white crystals of tetrapyridine-silver(I) nitrate, which may precipitate when the anode liquid is cooled in the ice bath these may be removed by washing with a little pyridine. Wash the product with cold water, dry over potassium hydroxide pellets, and record the yield. Calculate the current efficiency.

Complementary work:
(1) Why are the contents of the anode and cathode compartments kept from mixing? Why is 2M sulphuric acid used as cathode liquid and not a portion of the silver nitrate solution?
(2) Determine the percentage of silver and the percentage of pyridine in the product.

Reference
[1] Barbieri, G. A., *Ber.*, (1927), **60**, 2424.
See also the alternative preparation of a tetrapyridinesilver(II) complex on p. 76.

The preparation of titanium(III) chloride

Materials required: 15% solution of titanium(IV) chloride
Lead electrode
Platinum electrode
Cylindrical porous pot
Ammeter, voltmeter, accumulators
Variable resistance

Place 100 ml of the titanium(IV) chloride solution in a 150 ml beaker. Place the cylindrical porous pot in this solution and fill it to the same level with dilute hydrochloric acid. Insert the platinum electrode (4 × 1 cm) in the dilute hydrochloric acid and the lead electrode (4 × 5 cm) in the titanium(IV) chloride solution. Cool the beaker in ice and water. Pass a current of about 0·5–1·0 amp. for 2–3 hours with the lead electrode as cathode and the platinum electrode as anode. Record the current flowing and the duration of the electrolysis. Transfer the purple solution to a stoppered vessel. It is advisable to fit the ground glass stopper with a polytetrafluoroethylene sleeve to prevent it becoming stuck fast.

Complementary work:
(1) Why is a lead cathode used? What would be the expected product at a platinum cathode?
(2) Measure the visible spectrum of the solution. See p. 170 for further details.
(3) Add a few drops of the titanium(III) chloride solution to solutions of (*a*) potassium iron(III) sulphate, (*b*) silver nitrate, (*c*) sodium selenate, and (*d*) hydrogen peroxide. Comment on your observations.
(4) Determine the quantity of titanium(III) chloride in the product using a volumetric method. Calculate the current efficiency for the electrolytic reduction.

Bibliography

Davies, C. W., *Principles of Electrolysis*, Royal Institute of Chemistry, Monographs for Teachers, No 1, (1959).

11 Coordination chemistry II: stereochemistry

Introduction

The study of isomerism in coordination compounds is of considerable interest since by determining the number and type of isomers for a variety of different compounds Werner was able to make his classic deductions regarding the shapes of such complexes. Subsequent work has shown Werner's conclusions to be essentially correct.

Isomerism in coordination compounds may be divided into a number of categories, of which the most important are:

(1) Geometrical isomerism
(2) Optical isomerism
(3) Ionization isomerism
(4) Hydrate isomerism
(5) Coordination isomerism
(6) Linkage isomerism.

The principle types of isomerism will be discussed briefly, mainly with reference to octahedral complexes. This is followed by a description of the synthesis of compounds which illustrates some of the isomeric types. The reader is referred to any of the standard texts on coordination chemistry for more detailed information.

Geometrical isomerism

Two types of geometrical isomerism may be recognized in octahedral complexes; these are the MA_4B_2 and the MA_3B_3 types, both of which can exist in *cis* and *trans* forms. M is a transition metal atom or ion and A and B are monodentate ligands.

(i) The MA_4B_2 type

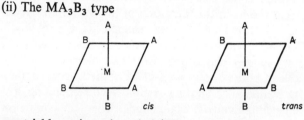

e.g. the dichlorotetramminecobalt(III) ion.

(ii) The MA_3B_3 type

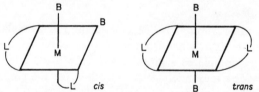

e.g. trichlorotriamminecobalt(III).

Similar isomeric types occur when monodentate liquids are replaced by multidentate ligands. For instance, a complex of the type ML_2B_2 where L is a bidentate ligand can also exist in *cis* and *trans* forms;

No general method is available for the synthesis of *cis* and *trans* isomers; specific methods must therefore be devised. These methods may utilize a complex of known configuration, or they may start from non-complex material and make use of differences in solubility in order to obtain the desired isomer. Thus, *trans*-dioxalatodiaquo-chromium(III) chloride may be obtained by a slow crystallization procedure from a solution which contains mainly the *cis* isomer. The equilibrium *cis* ⇌ *trans* is displaced to the right as the evaporation proceeds, due to the lower solubility of the *trans* isomer. *Cis* isomers may also be isolated by this technique. For example, the crystallization of dichlorobis(triethylstibine)palladium(II) from benzene solution gives only the *cis* isomer, despite the fact that there is only 6% of the *cis* isomer in solution [1].

The replacement of a chelating ligand by two monodentate ligands in a suitable complex might at first sight be expected to give an isomer having the *cis* configuration. In practice this is not necessarily the case and such replacement reactions may also give rise to *trans* isomers. This phenomenon is illustrated by the behaviour of carbonatotetramminecobalt(III) nitrate with hydrochloric acid; with cold concentrated hydrochloric acid the *cis*-dichlorotetramminecobalt(III) chloride is formed, whereas treatment with aqueous hydrochloric acid results in the formation of the *trans*-chloroaquotetramminecobalt(III) ion. A further example is the pyrolytic removal of a chelating ligand and entry of the associated anions into the coordination sphere. This is one of the best methods available for the synthesis of both *cis*- and *trans*-diacidobis(ethylenediamine)chromium(III) compounds, starting from the corresponding tris-(ethylenediamine)chromium(III) compounds. The temperature of decomposition varies with the nature of the anions, two of which enter the coordination sphere during the thermal decomposition. The pyrolysis is catalyzed by a trace of an ammonium salt which is conveniently introduced during recrystallization of the tris(ethylenediamine)chromium(III) compound.

The Trans *effect*

As mentioned previously, no general method is available for the preparation of *cis* or *trans* isomers of octahedral complexes. For square planar complexes a knowledge of the '*trans* effect' may be used to provide a reasonably general method for the preparation of the appropriate *cis* or *trans* isomer.

The study of ligand replacement reactions on square planar platinum complexes shows that certain ligands can labilize groups *trans* to themselves. The labilized ligand is then replaced preferentially by an incoming ligand.

Consider the reaction of nitrite ion with the tetrachloroplatinate(II) ion

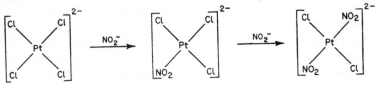

The second nitrite group enters *trans* to the first, hence nitrite has a greater *trans* directing effect than chloride. Extensive observations on reactions of this type have enabled ligands to be arranged in order of their ability to facilitate substitution *trans* to themselves. The order for a selection of ligands is:

$$H_2O < OH^- < NH_3 < Cl^- < Br^- < I^- \sim NO_2^- \sim PR_3 \ll CO \sim C_2H_4 \sim CN^-$$

The *trans* effect has proved useful in rationalizing known preparative methods and devising new ones. The preparation of *cis*-dichloro-dipyridineplatium(II), described below, demonstrates the greater *trans*-directing effect of chlorine relative to pyridine.

The preparation of *cis*- and *trans*-potassium dioxalato-diaquochromate(III)

(*a*) The *trans* isomer, $K[Cr(C_2O_4)_2(H_2O)_2]3H_2O$

Materials required: Oxalic acid
                       Potassium dichromate

Dissolve oxalic acid dihydrate (12 g) in the minimum amount of boiling water. It is advisable to use a beaker of not less than 300 ml capacity, since the ensuing reaction is rather vigorous. Add, in small portions, a solution of potassium dichromate (4 g) dissolved in the minimum quantity of hot water, covering the beaker while the violent reaction proceeds. Evaporate the solution to about one half of its original bulk and then allow spontaneous evaporation at room temperature to proceed until the solution is reduced to about one third of its original bulk. Filter off the crystals, wash with cold water, and alcohol. Record the yield, and express this as a percentage based on chromium. A high yield cannot be expected since only a part of the product is isolated.

Note that in solution there is an equilibrium between the *cis*- and *trans*-isomers, but the low solubility of the *trans* isomer results in its initial deposition. Excessive spontaneous evaporation should be avoided otherwise the product may become contaminated with the *cis* isomer.

(b) The *cis* isomer, $K[Cr(C_2O_4)_2(H_2O)_2]2H_2O$

Materials required: as in (*a*) plus ethanol.

Prepare an intimate mixture of finely ground potassium dichromate (4 g) and oxalic acid dihydrate (12 g) and heap the powder in a 6 in. diameter evaporating dish. Place one drop of water in a small depression in the mixture and cover the dish with a watch glass. After a short induction period the reaction commences and soon becomes vigorous with the evolution of steam and carbon dioxide. A solution of the product is avoided, and hence an equilibrium mixture of *cis*- and *trans*-isomers is not formed.

The product of this reaction is a purple viscous liquid over which is poured 20 ml of ethanol and the mixture stirred until the product of the reaction solidifies. If solidification is slow, decant the liquid and repeat the process with a second portion of alcohol until the product is entirely crystalline. Filter, dry at the pump, and record the yield.

Complementary work:

(1) What part does the oxalate ion play in these reactions other than that of a bidentate ligand?

(2) Use partial ionic equations to deduce an overall equation for complex formation.

(3) *Test for the purity of the isomers.* Place a few crystals of the complex on a filter paper and add a few drops of dilute aqueous ammonia. The *cis* isomer rapidly forms a deep green solution which spreads over the filter paper, and no solid remains. The *trans* isomer forms a light brown solid which remains undissolved. These changes are due to the formation of *cis* and *trans* dioxalato-hydroxoaquochromium(III) ions.

(4) What other method could be used to determine which of the two isomers is the *cis* form?

(5) Determine the composition of the *cis* or the *trans* isomer.

(*a*) Oxalate determination. Treat an accurately weighed sample of the complex ($\sim$ 0.3 g) with 20 ml of 5% potassium hydroxide and boil until no more hydrated chromium(III) oxide is precipitated. Filter off the precipitate, wash it well with hot water, and combine the filtrate and washings. The oxalate in solution may then be determined by any suitable volumetric or gravimetric procedure.

(*b*) Chromium determination. Almost any standard analytical procedure may be adopted; the following is a typical example. A known weight of the complex (0·2-0·3 g) is dissolved in dilute sulphuric acid (3 ml of concentrated sulphuric acid to 10 ml of water) and oxidized by boiling with potassium bromate (1·5 g) for 20 minutes. The excess potassium bromate is destroyed by adding ammonium sulphate (5 g in 10 ml of water) and boiling until nearly all the excess of bromine has been volatilized. Add 5 ml of 2M hydrochloric acid and boil until free halogen is no longer evolved. The resulting dichromate solution may now be determined by a standard iodimetric procedure.

(6) Determine the rate of isomerization of the *trans* to the *cis* isomer.

This experiment is for more advanced students who have had previous experience of instrumental work. The procedure is described on p. 179.

References
[1] Chatt, J., *J. Chem. Soc.*, (1951), 2532.
[2] Cunningham, G. E., Burley, R. W. and Friend, M. T., *Nature*, (1952), **169**, 1103.

The preparation of tris(ethylenediamine)chromium(III) chloride and the preparation of *cis*-dichlorobis(ethylenediamine)chromium(III) chloride

---

Materials required: Chromium(III) sulphate
Ethylenediamine (99%)
Hydrochloric acid

The first stage in this synthesis is the preparation of tris(ethylenediamine)chromium(III) sulphate, from which the chloride is obtained by treatment with hydrochloric acid.

Place chromium(III) sulphate (25 g), previously ground to a fine powder and dried at 110°C for a day, in a 250 ml flask, and add 99% ethylenediamine (25 ml). Fit the flask with an air condenser and heat on a steam bath. The chromium(III) sulphate soon begins to lose its bright green colour, usually within an hour or less. If this does not occur, a drop of water may be added to catalyse the reaction. Once the reaction is proceeding, the flask is shaken at intervals so that any unreacted sulphate becomes exposed to the amine. A brown mass is finally produced which is left on the steam bath for at least twelve hours. Grind the tris(ethylenediamine)-chromium(III) sulphate so produced to a powder, wash with alcohol, and air-dry. Reserve a sample of this compound for spectroscopic work, see p. 175.

To obtain the chloride from the sulphate, dissolve 16 g of the latter in dilute hydrochloric acid (15 ml of water to 3 ml of concentrated hydrochloric acid) at 60–65°C. Quickly filter the solution, and to the filtrate add an alcoholic solution of hydrochloric acid (14 ml of concentrated hydrochloric acid to 20 ml of ethanol), cool in ice. The crude tris(ethylenediamine)chromium(III) chloride separates as yellow crystals. The *cis*-dichlorobis(ethylenediamine)chromium(III) chloride is obtained by heating this product. The pyrolysis proceeds more smoothly in the presence of a trace of ammonium chloride. In order to introduce a catalytic amount of ammonium chloride recrystallize the complex from a 1% solution of ammonium chloride. Use 1 ml of this solution for every gram of crude complex to be recrystallized and do not allow the temperature to rise above 65°C. Cool the solution, filter off the product and dry it by washing with alcohol, and ether.

Carry out the pyrolysis in an oven, the temperature of which has been previously adjusted within the range 210°–215°C. Below 210°C the reaction is slow whereas above 215°C more extensive decomposition occurs. Spread the complex out in a thin layer on a watch glass or petri dish and place it in the oven. Decomposition soon begins and within one or two hours the colour changes to red-violet. The course of the reaction can be followed by observing the weight loss. Decomposition beyond 85% of the theoretical value is very slow and hardly practicable.

The purity of the product, *cis*-dichlorobis(ethylenediamine)-chromium(III) chloride is improved by washing with cold concentrated hydrochloric acid. Dry in an oven.

Complementary work:

(1) Analyse the product for ionic and total chloride content and hence establish that the ratio of coordinate to ionic chloride is 2:1.

(2) Resolve *cis*-dichlorobis(ethylenediamine)chromium(III) chloride into its optical isomers. See p. 213 for a description of this technique.

(3) The *cis* isomer is produced in this reaction. Which isomer is produced by the pyrolysis of tris(ethylenediamine)chromium(III) thiocyanate?

The preparation of tris(ethylenediamine)chromium(III) thiocyanate monohydrate and the preparation of *trans*-dithiocyanatobis (ethylenediamine) chromium (III) thiocyanate

---

Materials required: Tris(ethylenediamine)chromium(III) chloride
Ammonium thiocyanate

Add ammonium thiocyanate (7 g) with rapid stirring to a solution of tris(ethylenediamine)chromium(III) chloride (10 g in 30 ml of warm water). Cool the solution in ice, and filter the product by suction. Wash the crystals with alcohol, ether, and air-dry. The product so obained contains ammonium thiocyanate and is suitable for pyrolysis to *trans*-dithiocyanatobis(ethylenediamine)chromium(III) thiocyanate. The pyrolysis is carried out as described in the previous experiment but at a temperature of 130°C (not above 134°C). The theoretical weight loss is 18·4%. The product may be purified by quickly recrystallizing it from warm water.

Complementary work:
(1) Determine the ionic and total thiocyanate content of the pyrolysis product.
(2) Can the product be resolved into optical isomers?
(3) The *trans* isomer is produced in this experiment. Which isomer is produced by the pyrolysis of tris(ethylenediamine)chromium-(III) chloride?

References
Rollinson, C. L. and Bailar, J. C., *J. Amer. Chem. Soc.*, (1943), **65**, 252.
Rollinson, C. L. and Bailar, J. C., *J. Amer. Chem. Soc.*, (1944), **66**, 641.

The preparation of cis-dichlorodipyridineplatinum(II)

Materials required: Potassium tetrachloroplatinate(II)
Pyridine
Thiourea

Prepare a solution containing pyridine (2 ml in 25 ml of water). Add 1 ml of this solution from a burette to a solution of potassium tetrachloroplatinate(II) (0·2 g) in 2 ml of water. Stir the mixture and allow it to stand overnight. There is some variation in the rate at which the precipitate is formed but standing overnight is always a sufficient reaction period. Filter on a small Hirsch funnel, wash with ice-cold water, and dry in an oven at 100°C for one hour. Weigh the product, and record the yield.

Prepare a 10% solution of thiourea. To 1 ml of this solution at 80°C add slowly the solid product prepared above. Identify any volatile products. Cool the yellow solution and allow it to stand overnight. Filter the yellow crystals on a small Hirsch funnel, wash with a little ice-cold water and dry in an oven at 100°C. Weigh the product.

Complementary work:
(1) Ignite a known weight of the sample to constant weight in a small platinum crucible at 500°C. Calculate the percentage of platinum in the thiourea complex.
(2) Suggest a possible molecular formula for the thiourea complex.
(3) How would you prepare *trans*-dichlorodipyridineplatinum(II)? What would be the product of its reaction with thiourea?
(4) What can be deduced about the *trans*-directing properties of thiourea?
(5) Measure the infrared spectrum of the thiourea complex. Compare this with the spectrum of thiourea, and hence determine the coordinating atom in thiourea.

Reference
Quagliano, J. V., et al., J. Amer. Chem. Soc., (1958), **80**, 527.

Optical isomerism

The demonstration of optical activity in a coordination compound is often useful evidence when assigning a structure to a compound. *Cis* and *trans* isomers may be distinguished by this means, as also may planar structures be distinguished from tetrahedral ones. A complex molecule or ion exists in optically active isomeric forms when it possesses either axes of symmetry, in which case it is referred to as a dissymmetric molecule, or no symmetry elements at all, when the molecule is said to be asymmetric. Optical isomers are mirror images of each other and are not superimposable one upon the other. Isomers of this type are variously referred to as optical isomers, optical antipodes, or enantiomers. It should be noted that a molecule or ion need not possess an asymmetric atom in order to exhibit optical activity. Thus the *cis*-dichlorobis(ethylenediamine)chromium(III) ion exists as the two optical antipodes:

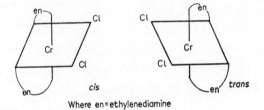

Where en = ethylenediamine

The *trans* isomer of this ion has a plane of symmetry and hence will not exist in optically active forms.

The chemical properties of optical antipodes are identical. However, optical antipodes, anionic or cationic, react with another optical antipode, cationic or anionic, to give diastereoisomers, which do not have identical properties. Diastereoisomer formation has been considerably exploited for the separation of optical antipodes; a process known as resolution. Most of the physical properties of optical antipodes are also identical. An exception to this generalization is the way in which optical antipodes interact with plane polarized light. When a beam of plane polarized light passes through a solution of an optical antipode, the plane of polarization is displaced in either a clockwise or an anticlockwise direction. When the displacement is in the clockwise direction the isomer in question is said to be dextrorotatory and the prefix D- is used before the name to indicate this property. Conversely, when the plane of polarization is rotated in an anticlockwise sense the isomer is said to be laevo-rotatary and the prefix L- is used. The prefixes d- and l- are reserved for describing optically active ligands in a coordination compound. The amount of rotation can be readily measured using a polarimeter; a full description of the construction and operation of a simple polarimeter is given on p. 214. Measurements are usually made at a specific wavelength. The sodium D line (5893 Å) is often used, although the mercury green line (5461 Å) may also be used to some advantage since the eye is more sensitive to green than to yellow light. The results of such measurements are usually expressed as the specific or molecular rotation and are given the symbols $[\alpha]_v^T$ and $[M]_v^T$ respectively.

The specific rotation of a solution is given by the expression

$$[\alpha]_v^T = \frac{100\alpha}{lc}$$

where α = the measured angular rotation

c = the concentration in g/100 ml of solution

l = the length of the column of solution in decimetres

v = the frequency of the light used for the measurement

T = the temperature of the sample, °C.

The specific rotation for a liquid is given by the expression

$$[\alpha]_v^T = \frac{\alpha}{ld}$$

where d = the density of the liquid at T°C and l, v, and α have the same significance as above.

The molecular rotation is given by

$$[M]_v^T = \frac{[\alpha]_v^T.M}{100}$$

where M = the molecular weight.

Optical rotation varies with wavelength, a phenomenon known as optical rotatory dispersion. Instruments have been devised for measuring this variation. Further discussion of optical rotatory dispersion is beyond the scope of this text, and the reader is referred to standard works on the subject. However, it should be noted that, as a result of optical rotatory dispersion studies it is known that an optical antipode may, at certain wavelengths, have a specific rotation of zero.

Resolution into optical isomers

Optical isomers, as ordinarily prepared in the laboratory, are obtained in the form of a racemic mixture which consists of equal amounts of dextro- and laevo- forms. A satisfactory resolution procedure should be capable of separating the two antipodes and giving a pure sample of each. The term resolution is also frequently used when only one optical antipode is obtained.

A variety of resolution procedures has been reported but by far the most important and most used is the formation of diastereoisomers which can be separated by fractional crystallization. Diastereoisomers are formed when a racemic mixture of ions is treated with a single enantiomer of an ion of opposite charge. An enantiomer used in this way is often referred to as the resolving agent, e.g.

$$\text{D-}[Cr(en)_2Cl_2]^+ + \text{L-}[Cr(en)_2Cl_2]^+ + 2\text{d-}C_{10}H_{14}OBrSO_3^- =$$
$$\text{D-}[Cr(en)_2Cl_2]\text{d-}C_{10}H_{14}OBrSO_3 + \text{L-}[Cr(en)_2Cl_2]\text{d-}C_{10}H_{14}OBrSO_3.$$

The two diastereoisomers which result are not mirror images of each other and so have different properties. Diastereoisomers can usually be separated by a simple physical technique such as distillation, crystallization, or chromatography. The most common method of separation is by fractional crystallization. The desired isomer is obtained from the diastereoisomer by displacing the resolving agent with a suitable ion, e.g.

$$\text{D-}[Cr(en)_2Cl_2]\text{d-}C_{10}H_{14}OBrSO_3 + HCl =$$
$$\text{D-}[Cr(en)_2Cl_2]Cl + \text{d-}C_{10}H_{14}OBrSO_3H$$

The resolution of cis-dichlorobis(ethylenediamine)-chromium(III) chloride into its optical isomers

---

Materials required: Ammonium d-α-bromocamphor-π-sulphonate
cis-dichlorobis(ethylenediamine)chromium(III) chloride (prepared as described on p. 93)

Dissolve cis-dichlorobis(ethylenediamine)chromium(III) chloride (1 g) in 15 ml of water and add ammonium d-α-bromocamphor-π-sulphonate (2 g) with vigorous stirring. Allow the solution to stand until the diastereoisomer of the L-form separates out. Filter the diasteroisomer and wash it with alcohol, and ether. Weigh the product. Dissolve the diastereoisomer in concentrated hydrochloric acid (use 4 ml of acid for every gram of diastereoisomer), and dilute the solution with twice its volume of alcohol. Dark red crystals of the L-form precipitate. Filter on a Hirsch funnel, wash with alcohol, ether, and dry in a desiccator. Calculate the percentage yield.

Complementary work:
(1) Measure the optical activity of a 0·075 % solution, and calculate the specific rotation. See p. 214 for a description of the measurement of optical activity.
(2) Is it possible to resolve the *trans* isomer of this complex into optical antipodes? Give reasons for your answer.

Reference
Selbin, J. and Bailar, J. C., *J. Amer. Chem. Soc.*, (1957), **79**, 4286.

The preparation and resolution of the tris(ethylene-diamine)cobalt(III) ion into its optical antipodes

---

Materials required: Cobalt(II) sulphate
Ethylenediamine
Barium d-tartrate
Activated charcoal

The preparation of barium d-tartrate
Dissolve d-tartaric acid (20 g) in 100 ml of water and add slowly, with stirring, barium carbonate (25 g). Warm and stir the resultant suspension for half an hour to ensure complete neutralization of the acid. Filter off the precipitate, wash with cold water and dry at 110°C.

Equip a Buchner flask with a rubber stopper carrying a glass tube which reaches almost to the bottom of the flask. Place in the flask 37 ml of a 24 % solution of ethylenediamine. To this solution add concentrated hydrochloric acid (5 ml), an aqueous solution of cobalt(II) sulphate (14 g of the heptahydrate in 25 ml of water), and activated charcoal (2 g). Pass a rapid current of air for four hours to oxidize the cobalt(II) to the cobalt(III) state. When the oxidation is complete, adjust the pH to 7·0–7·5 with either dilute hydrochloric acid or ethylenediamine as required. Heat the mixture on a steam bath for 15 minutes to complete the reaction, cool, and filter off the charcoal. To the resulting solution of tris(ethylenediamine)cobalt(III) ions add barium d-tartrate (14 g), stir well, and heat on a steam bath for half an hour. Filter off the barium sulphate, wash the precipitate with a little hot water, and evaporate the filtrate to about 25 ml. The diastereoisomer D-tris(ethylenediamine)cobalt(III) chloride d-tartrate crystallizes out on cooling the solution. Reserve the filtrate for the isolation of the L-isomer. Recrystallize the diastereoisomer from about 15 ml of water, wash the product with ethanol, and air dry.

The dextro isomer of the tris(ethylenediamine)cobalt(III) ion is obtained as the iodide by the following procedure. Dissolve the diastereoisomer in hot water (15 ml), add 0·5 ml of aqueous ammonia (S.G. 0·88), and a solution of sodium iodide (18 g of sodium iodide in 8 ml of hot water). Stir well during the addition of the sodium iodide solution. Cool the solution in ice, filter off the D-tris(ethylenediamine)cobalt(III) iodide, wash with 30% sodium iodide solution (20 ml), ethanol, and acetone; air dry. Record the yield.

Treat the filtrate containing the L-tris(ethylenediamine)cobalt(III) chloride d-tartrate with 0·5 ml of aqueous ammonia (S.G. 0·88), heat to 80°C, add sodium iodide (18 g), and cool in ice. Filter off the impure L-isomer, wash with ice-cold 30% sodium iodide (10 ml), alcohol, and air dry. The product so obtained contains some racemate which is removed by stirring the product with water (30 ml) at 50°C and filtering off the undissolved racemate. Add sodium iodide (5 g) to the warm filtrate (50°C), and cool in ice. Filter off the product, wash with ethanol, acetone, and air dry. Record the yield.

Complementary work:
(1) Determine the specific rotation of the two isomers, see p. 214 for experimental details.

Reference
Broomhead, J. A., Dwyer, F. P., and Hogarth, J. W., *Inorg. Synth.*, **6**, 183.

CARL A. RUDISILL LIBRARY
LENOIR RHYNE COLLEGE

Ionization and hydrate isomerism

Two or more coordination compounds are said to be ionization isomers if they have the same overall composition but differ in the composition of their coordination sphere. In other words a complex which has a coordinately bound anionic ligand X and an associated anion Y is isomeric with a complex having a coordinately bound anionic ligand Y and an associated anion X, e.g.

$$[Co(NH_3)_5NO_3]SO_4 \text{ and } [Co(NH_3)_5SO_4]NO_3$$

Such isomers will, of course, give different reactions in solution.

Hydrate isomerism may be regarded as a special case of ionization isomerism. Isomers arise depending upon whether water is held as coordinately bound water or as water of crystallization, provided that the overall composition of the compounds is the same, e.g.

$[Cr(H_2O)_6]Cl_3$	greyish blue
$[Cr(H_2O)_5Cl]Cl_2.H_2O$	light green
$[Cr(H_2O)_4Cl_2]Cl.2H_2O$	dark green

The preparation of the hydrate isomers of chromium(III) chloride hexahydrate

The dark green compound $[Cr(H_2O)_4Cl_2]Cl.2H_2O$ is readily available from laboratory suppliers as chromic chloride hydrated, and may be used for the preparation of the pentaquo isomer. Chrome alum or chromium(III) nitrate can be used for the preparation of hexaquochromium(III) chloride.

The preparation of chloropentaquochromium(III) chloride

Materials required: Hydrogen chloride
                              Dichlorotetraquochromium(III) chloride
                              Ether

This reaction must be carried out in a fume cupboard.
Cool 300 ml of ether in ice and saturate it with hydrogen chloride. Dissolve dichlorotetraquochromium(III) chloride (14 g) in water (20 ml), and reflux for ten minutes. Cool the solution in ice and

saturate with hydrogen chloride gas. Pour this solution into 200 ml of the ether saturated with hydrogen chloride, cool the mixture in ice, and stir mechanically for about 30 minutes. Filter off the precipitated salt and wash it with ether saturated with hydrogen chloride. Record the yield.

The preparation of hexaquochromium(III) chloride

Materials required: Potassium chromium(III) sulphate (chrome alum)
Hydrogen chloride

Prepare a saturated solution of chrome alum. Cool 25 ml of this solution in ice, and decant the supernatant liquid from the precipitated chrome alum. Cool the decanted liquid in ice, and saturate the solution with hydrogen chloride gas *(fume cupboard)*. Filter off the greyish-blue crystals so formed. Wash with acetone, ether, and dry in air.

Complementary work:
(1) Weigh accurately into separate weighing bottles a sample of each isomer. Place the three bottles, unstoppered, in a vacuum desiccator over concentrated sulphuric acid. Evacuate the desiccator and measure the weight loss of the three isomers over a period of a few days.
(2) Determine the amount of ionic chloride and the total chloride in each isomer.
(3) Explain qualitatively the differences in colour between the three isomers.
(4) Measure the spectrum of an aqueous solution of each isomer over the range 350–750 mμ. See p. 170 for a description of the measurement of such spectra. Interpret your results in terms of changes in Δ_0.

Linkage Isomerism

This type of isomerism occurs when a ligand can coordinate to a central metal using either of two atoms within the ligand. Both the nitrite ion and the thiocyanate ion have been shown to exhibit this type of isomerism. When the nitrite ion is attached to the central metal ion via the nitrogen atom it is referred to as a nitro ligand, whereas when one of the oxygen atoms is the donor the term nitrito is used. Nitro-nitrito linkage isomerism has been observed for the pentammines of cobalt(III), rhodium(III), iridium(III), and platinum (IV).

Linkage isomerism in the case of the thiocyanate ion is of more recent origin. The terms thiocyanato (where S is the donor atom) and isothiocyanato (where N is the donor atom) are used to describe the linkage isomers. Such isomerism has been observed for the compounds $[Pd\{As(C_6H_5)_3\}_2(SCN)_2]$ and $[Pd \ dipy(SCN)_2]$. In both cases the thiocyanato complex can be readily converted to the isothiocyanato complex by heating to 150°C for 30 minutes.

The preparation of chloropentamminecobalt(III) chloride

Materials required: Cobalt(II) carbonate
6% Hydrogen peroxide (20 volume)
Aqueous ammonia (S.G. 0·88)

Dissolve cobalt(II) carbonate (5 g) in concentrated hydrochloric acid (15 ml), add water (35 ml) and filter to remove any undissolved oxide which was present in the original carbonate. To this solution add ammonium chloride (5 g) and 50 ml of aqueous ammonia (S.G. 0·88). Cool the solution and add slowly, with stirring, 6% hydrogen peroxide (80 ml). When the oxidation is complete, as judged by the cessation of effervescence, draw air through the solution for about an hour to remove the excess ammonia. Neutralize the solution with concentrated hydrochloric acid. A precipitate of aquopentamminecobalt(III) chloride persists at the neutrality point. Add a further 20 ml of concentrated hydrochloric acid and heat the resulting suspension on a water bath for two hours. Filter off the product by suction, wash with water to remove any unreacted aquopentamminecobalt(III) chloride, wash with alcohol and dry at 110°C.

Complementary work:
Determine the total and ionic chloride in the product.

The preparation of nitro- and nitrito-pentamminecobalt (III) chloride

Materials required: Chloropentamminecobalt(III) chloride
Sodium nitrite
Aqueous ammonia (S.G. 0·88)

(1) Nitropentamminecobalt(III) chloride
Dissolve chloropentamminecobalt(III) chloride (1·5 g) in 20 ml of 2M aqueous ammonia. Warm on a water bath until the salt dissolves. Cool, and acidify with 4M hydrochloric acid to pH 4. Add sodium nitrite (2 g) and heat gently until the red precipitate first formed has dissolved. In some cases the red precipitate only appears transiently. Cool the solution, and add carefully, concentrated hydrochloric acid (20 ml). Cool in ice, filter off the yellow brown crystals, and wash with alcohol. Record the yield.

(2) Nitritopentamminecobalt(III) chloride.
Dissolve chloropentamminecobalt(III) chloride (1·5 g) in aqueous ammonia (25 ml of water to 5 ml of aqueous ammonia (S.G. 0·88)), warm if necessary to dissolve the salt. Neutralize the solution to litmus with 4M hydrochloric acid, and cool. Add sodium nitrite (1·5 g) and allow the solution to stand for 1–2 hours. Cool in ice, filter off the salmon-pink product, wash with ice-cold water, and alcohol. Dry at room temperature. Record the yield.

Complementary work:
(1) Measure the infrared spectra of the two isomers in the region 2·5–15μ. Use a freshly prepared sample in the case of the nitrito isomer. See p. 161 for a discussion of infrared spectroscopy and the treatment of samples. Compare the spectra and comment. (References [1]–[4].)
(2) Place a sample of the nitrito complex in an oven at 150°C for about 2 hours, note what happens and measure the infrared spectrum of the sample after this treatment. Comment on the results.

References
[1] Faust, J. P. and Quagliano, J. V., *J. Amer. Chem. Soc.*, (1954), **76**, 5346.

[2] Svatos, G. F., Curran, C. and Quagliano, J. V., *J. Amer. Chem. Soc.*, (1955), **77**, 6159.

[3] Penland, R. B., Lane, T. J. and Quagliano, J. V., *J. Amer. Chem. Soc.*, (1956), **78**, 887.

[4] Beattie, I. R. and Satchell, D. P. N., *Trans. Faraday Soc.*, (1956), **52**, 1590.

The preparation of dithiocyanatobis(triphenylarsine) palladium(II)

Materials required: Palladium(II) chloride
Triphenylarsine
Potassium thiocyanate
Absolute alchohol

Dissolve palladium(II) chloride (0·5 g) in 20 ml of warm water, and to the warm solution add potassium thiocyanate (2·0 g) dissolved in 5 ml of water. Evaporate the solution until about 5 ml of solution remains, cool in ice, and filter off the potassium tetrathiocyanato-palladate(II). Dissolve the precipitate in absolute ethanol (30 ml) to which water (0·5 ml) has been added, cool in ice. To this solution add an ice-cold solution of triphenylarsine (1·5 g) in absolute ethanol to which 0·5 ml of ether has been added. Stir the solution and add ice-cold water (50 ml) to precipitate the product. Continue stirring the suspension until the initially formed fine solid coagulates and can be filtered. Wash the product with ice-cold ethanol, and ether. Dry, record the yield, and measure the melting point.

Complementary work:
(1) Measure the infrared spectrum of the product in the region 2·5–15μ. See p. 161 for further details.
(2) Heat a sample of the product at 156°C for half an hour, note any colour change. Measure the infrared spectrum and the m.p. of the compound so formed. Comment on the two spectra.
(3) What is the product of the reaction between potassium tetrathiocyanatopalladate(II) and triphenylphosphine? Comment.

References
Burmeister, J. L. and Basolo, F., *Inorg. Chem.*, (1964), **3**, 1587.
Bertini, I. and Sabatini, A., *Inorg. Chem.*, (1966), **5**, 1025.
Raymond, K. N. and Basolo, F., *Inorg. Chem.*, (1966), **5**, 1632.

Bibliography

Jones, M. M., *Elementary Coordination Chemistry*, Prentice-Hall, New York, (1964).
Lewis, J. and Wilkins, R. G., *Modern Coordination Chemistry*, Interscience, New York, (1959).

12 Homogeneous catalysis

Introduction

Transition metal ions can be used to catalyse oxidation reactions. In such reactions the catalytic effect depends on the ability of the transition metal ion to exist in more than one oxidation state in solution. The ability to form a complex, although necessary for the reaction, is only a secondary consideration. The catalytic effect was recognized in connexion with the autoxidation of hydrocarbons, when the deterioration in the properties of edible oils and of lubricating oils was shown to be due to air oxidation of the oil, catalysed by the presence of traces of transition metals, such as iron, cobalt, nickel, or manganese. This catalytic oxidation can also be used synthetically, and the oxidation of *p*-xylene to terephthalic acid, using a cobalt(II) bromide catalyst and oxygen as the oxidizing agent, is described below.

A second type of catalytic action of a transition metal ion depends primarily on its ability to form a complex with one of the reactants. The transition metal ion is then reduced to a lower oxidation state. The olefin complexes of platinum and palladium can be used to show this aspect of catalysis, when an aldehyde or ketone is the final product of the oxidation of the olefin. The palladium(II) chloride catalysed oxidation of ethylene to acetaldehyde is now used on a large scale commercially, and the example given below illustrates the basis of this process.

Thirdly, complex formation may occur, and this complex may either react with another complex ion, or with uncomplexed reactant to give the product. The oxidation state of the metal ion need not change during the process, although it is difficult at times to assign unambiguously a definite oxidation state to a metal ion in a complex. A catalyst should be capable of acting specifically. Both these points are illustrated by the hydrogenation of buta-1,3-diene using the pentacyanocobaltate(II) ion as catalyst. Although three butene isomers are theoretically possible, more than 80% of the product is one isomer. It is also possible to effect reduction to a different butene isomer by changing the Co:CN ratio in the catalyst solution.

The change in Gibbs Free Energy for these reactions at the given temperature can be calculated from available data. From these calculations it will be seen that all the reactions are thermodynamically favourable, so that the catalyst is not required to alter ΔG^0 for the reaction. The catalyst affects the rate at which equilibrium is reached, and since ΔG^0, and hence the position of equilibrium is unaffected, the rates of the forward and back reactions must be affected equally. This represents a marked difference from the effect of temperature on a reaction when the position of equilibrium is altered, see p. 33.

The cobalt(II) bromide catalysed oxidation of p-xylene

Cobalt(II) bromide is the catalyst used for the oxidation of p-xylene to terephthalic acid. Both cobalt ions and bromide ions are necessary in this reaction system, and no oxidation will occur in the presence of cobalt ions alone. The bromide ion can be provided either as free bromine or as bromide ion. In the present example, a mixture of cobalt(II) acetate tetrahydrate and potassium bromide is used, such that the stoichiometric ratio of cobalt to bromide corresponds to cobalt(II) bromide. The action of the cobalt ions can be considered in terms of the oxidation of the hydrocarbon to aldehyde, which it has been suggested is the determining step in the overall oxidation of hydrocarbon to acid. The initiating step is considered to be a reaction between bromine atoms and the hydrocarbon to produce a free radical,

$$CH_3.C_6H_4.CH_3 + Br^{\cdot} = CH_3C_6H_4CH_2^{\cdot} + HBr \qquad (12.1)$$

and this is followed by reaction of the organic free radical with oxygen in solution

$$CH_3.C_6H_4.CH_2^{\cdot} + O_2 = CH_3.C_6H_4.CH_2O_2^{\cdot} \qquad (12.2)$$

The catalytic effect of the cobalt ion on the overall reaction can be shown in terms of its effect in decomposing the organic peroxide, $CH_3.C_6H_4.CH_2O_2'$,

$$CH_3.C_6H_4CH_2O_2' + Co^{2+} = Co^{3+} + CH_3.C_6H_4.CHO + OH^- \qquad (12.3)$$

This demonstrates the use of the multiple oxidation states of the transition metal ion, with some coordination probably occurring between the metal ion and the hydroperoxide. Regeneration of Co^{2+} from Co^{3+} occurs by reaction with the hydrogen bromide produced in stage 1; also producing bromine atoms which can now initiate further oxidation steps.

$$Co^{3+} + HBr = Co^{2+} + H^+ + Br^{\cdot} \qquad (12.4)$$

The sum of these four reaction steps is represented by the simple oxidation reaction,

$$CH_3.C_6H_4.CH_3 + O_2 = CH_3.C_6H_4.CHO + H_2O$$

Operation of further similar oxidation steps will eventually produce terephthalic acid.

Use of solvent
Reaction will occur if the catalyst and p-xylene are mixed, and oxygen gas bubbled through the mixture, but more satisfactory results are obtained when a suitable solvent is used. The general requirements for any solvent are that it will dissolve, but not react with, the starting materials and any intermediate products. It need not dissolve the final product of the reaction. The solvent must also be stable under the conditions of the reaction. In the cobalt(II) bromide catalysed oxidation of p-xylene these requirements are met by the aliphatic carboxylic acids, and since the final product of the oxidation of p-xylene is terephthalic acid, which is insoluble in this solvent, a ready method for the separation of the product is at once available.

Control of reaction temperature
A simple method of maintaining a reasonably constant reaction temperature is to use the steady reflux temperature of the solution. In the present example propionic acid has been chosen as solvent, since the solution will then reflux at a suitable reaction temperature at atmospheric pressure.

Stirring in gas-liquid reactions

The reaction system consists initially of two phases, the gaseous oxidizing agent and the *p*-xylene in solution. Before oxidation can take place the oxygen must dissolve in the solution, thus forming a homogeneous system. The amount of oxygen in solution will be small but as it reacts it will be constantly replaced by oxygen from the gas phase. It is important to ensure that there is maximum contact between the gas phase oxygen and the solution. In general for gas-liquid reactions satisfactory contact of the gas phase with the liquid phase can be achieved by high-speed stirring of the solution in a fluted flask. This stirring breaks up the bulk of the solution, and the gas phase is dispersed in the form of fine bubbles. In this way a rapid equilibrium is established between the gas phase and the dissolved gas.

The relative simplicity of this reaction system, the availability, and low cost of the starting materials makes it suitable for the large-scale preparation of aromatic carboxylic acids. Systems analogous to that used in the following example are now used commercially.

Materials required: Propionic acid.
                            p-Xylene
                            Cobalt(II) acetate tetrahydrate
                            Potassium bromide
                            Oxygen (or compressed air)

Place propionic acid (75 ml) and *p*-xylene (5 ml) in a 100 ml three-necked round-bottomed flask. Three equally spaced vertical indentations, approximately 4 cm long should have been made previously in the wall of the flask to facilitate efficient stirring of the reaction mixture. A diagram of the flask is shown in Figure 10. Prepare the cata-

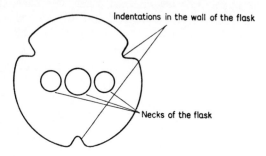

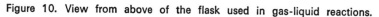

Figure 10. View from above of the flask used in gas-liquid reactions.

lyst by grinding together cobalt(II) acetate tetrahydrate (2·6 g) and potassium bromide (2·4 g). Add 0·5 g of this mixture to the solution in the round-bottomed flask. This corresponds to approximately 0·3% w/w of cobalt(II) bromide in solution. Fit the reaction flask with a high-speed paddle stirrer, a reflux condenser, a thermometer, and an inlet for oxygen gas to take the gas supply below the surface of the solution. Place the flask on an electrically heated mantle. Fit the oxygen inlet line with a mercury-sealed tube to release any pressure build-up, should the inlet tube become blocked. Adjust the oxygen flow (see below) to provide 3–4 litres/hour and start the rapid stirring of the solution. Heat the solution until it is refluxing steadily at about 130°C, and measure the duration of the reaction from this time. Adjustment of the stirring rate may be necessary while the solution is being heated and the solution viscosity is changing. A suitable stirring rate is one which maintains a continuous foam of solution above the bulk liquid. These reaction conditions should be maintained for about three hours. At the end of this reaction time switch off the heater, stirrer, and oxygen supply, A suspension of white solid should be present in the solution. Filter off the solid, wash with water, and dry at 110°C. This product can be identified as terephthalic acid by equivalent weight, melting point, and infrared spectroscopic measurements (see p. 161) without requiring any further purification. Record the yield and express it as a percentage based on initial p-xylene.

The filtrate contains p-toluic acid which can be precipitated by distilling off the bulk of the solvent, and then diluting the residue with water. Filter off the solid which, unlike the terephthalic acid, will require purification before analysis. Dissolve the solid in the minimum of 2M sodium hydroxide solution, and shake the solution with ether to remove any organic material other than carboxylic acid. Separate the aqueous layer, and reprecipitate the acid by addition of a slight excess of 4M hydrochloric acid. Filter off the solid, wash with water, and dry at 110°C. The product may be analysed in a similar manner to that used for the terephthalic acid. Record the yield and express it as a percentage based on p-xylene.

The reaction rate is a function of the oxygen concentration in solution, which in turn depends upon the partial pressure of oxygen above the solution. Thus compressed air may be used as an alternative oxidizing agent, at a flow rate of 7–8 litres/hour. In this case, with the other reaction conditions remaining constant, a greatly reduced yield of terephthalic acid is obtained, showing qualitatively the effect of oxygen partial pressure on the reaction. The need for the presence of a bromine-containing compound and a transition metal ion can be readily shown by carrying out the reaction in the absence of one or both of these. The effect of stirring on a gas-liquid reaction may be similarly demonstrated.

References

Burney, D. E., Weisemann, G. H. and Fragen, N., *Petrol. Refiner*, (1959), **38**, 186.

Ravens, D. A. S., *Trans. Faraday Soc.*, (1959), **55**, 1768.

A simple flow-meter

The experimental method described above requires a means of measuring the oxygen, or compressed air flow rate. The soap film flow-meter provides a very simple but reliable method of measuring a gas flow rate. The apparatus is illustrated in Figure 11. It consists of a piece of glass tubing 50 cm long × 1·5 cm o.d. on which two fixed points are marked. The tube is calibrated by adding 25 ml of water from a pipette to the tube already filled to the lower fixed

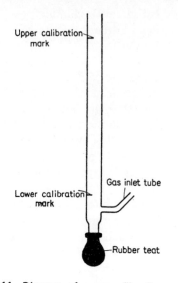

Figure 11. Diagram of a soap film flow-meter.

point. After the addition of the 25 ml of water the upper fixed point should be marked at the meniscus. Into the empty calibrated tube place a little soap solution to give a level just below the top of the side-arm entrance. Connect the gas flow to the side-arm and raise the liquid level by squeezing the rubber teat until two or three soap films are formed and start to rise up the tube. Measure with a stop watch the time taken for a particular soap film to travel from the lower to the upper mark. This will give a known volume of gas, i.e. the calibrated volume, flowing in a measured time and can be readily converted into litres/hour. Thus during the course of an experiment the flow rate can be checked regularly and rapidly.

The preparation of dichlorobis(benzonitrile)palladium(II) and the preparation of di-μ-chloro-dichlorodiethylene-dipalladium(II)

A simple route to the olefin complexes of palladium is through the dibenzonitrile complex, which is prepared by direct reaction of palladium(II) chloride and benzonitrile. The benzonitrile ligand can then be displaced by an olefin to give the olefin complex.

Materials required: Palladium(II) chloride
                             Benzonitrile
                             Ethylene

Place palladium(II) chloride (0·25 g) in a flask with 10 ml of benzonitrile. Heat on a steam bath until the bulk of the palladium(II) chloride has dissolved. Filter the hot solution to remove any insoluble material. Cool the filtrate and filter off the yellow crystals. A further crop of crystals will be produced by the addition of light petrol. Add these crystals to the first crop, wash with petrol and dry over calcium chloride. Record the weight and calculate the percentage yield of product.

Dissolve 0·3 g of dichlorobis(benzonitrile)palladium(II) in 15 ml of benzene and filter off any insoluble material. Pass a slow stream of ethylene through the solution for about 15 minutes. (*Fume cupboard.*) Filter off the crystals which precipitate, wash with petrol and dry over calcium chloride. Record the weight and calculate the percentage yield of product.

Complementary work:

(1) What is the structure of the olefin-metal complex. How is the olefin to metal bond formed?

(2) Place about half the olefin complex in a centrifuge tube and add about 1 ml of water. Shake the tube and comment on your observations. What possible application does the reaction have?

(3) Centrifuge the contents from the above reaction. Test the solution for pH and for chloride ion. Use the bulk of the solution to prepare a 2,4-dinitrophenylhydrazine derivative and identify the carbonyl compound in the solution.

(4) Show by an equation the overall stoichiometry of the hydrolysis of di-μ-chloro-dichlorodiethylenedipalladium(II).

(5) How could a continuous process for ethylene oxidation be developed?

References

Kharasch, M. S., Seyler, R. C. and Mays, F. R., *J. Amer. Chem. Soc.*, (1938), **63**, 882.

Smidt, J., *Chem. and Ind.*, (1962), 54.

Twigg, G. H., *Chem. and Ind.*, (1966), 479.

Aquito, A., *Advances in Organometallic Chemistry*, *Vol.* 5, Editors, Stone, F. G. A. and West, R., Academic Press, London and New York, (1967).

The pentacyanocobaltate(II) ion catalysed hydrogenation of buta-1,3-diene

---

This reaction is similar to the cobalt(II) bromide catalysed oxidation of *p*-xylene, in that maximum contact is needed between the gas phase and the solution. Consequently a well stirred reaction vessel is again required and a flask and stirrer should be used, similar to that shown in Figure 10.

Materials required: Buta-1,3-diene
  Hydrogen
  Potassium cyanide
  Cobalt(II) chloride

Fit the 100 ml flask with a stirrer, a gas inlet tube with a rubber tubing connexion sealed by a screw clip, and a flexible connexion leading to a 250 ml graduated vessel which is in turn connected to a levelling bulb, see Figure 12a. Measure the volume of the round-bottomed flask, connecting leads, and 'dead-space' above the calibration mark on the graduated vessel by filling the apparatus with water and emptying it into a measuring cylinder. Now fill all the apparatus with water, attach the cylinder of buta-1,3-diene to the round-bottomed flask by means of the rubber tubing connexion, open the screw clip and carefully displace the water from the flask and the connecting line to the graduated vessel with buta-1,3-diene, until a volume of ∼200 ml has been added. This calls for a little dexterity in manipulating the round-bottomed flask to ensure that all the water is displaced. *Since the gases used in this experiment are inflammable, all manipulation should be carried out well clear of any flame.* Adjust the position of the levelling bulb so that the gas is at atmospheric pressure. Close the valve on the cylinder, the screw clip on the gas inlet tubing and replace the buta-1,3-diene cylinder with a hydrogen cylinder. Add ∼200 ml of hydrogen, using the graduated vessel to measure the volume added. Adjust the pressure in the apparatus to atmospheric by means of the levelling bulb. Close the screw clip on the gas inlet tubing, remove the hydrogen cylinder, and attach a small dropping funnel to the inlet tube, see Figure 12b. Place 20 ml of ∼0·3M cobalt(II) chloride solution in the dropping funnel, open the screw clip, and add the cobalt(II) chloride solution to the flask. Place 20 ml of ∼1·5M potassium cyanide in the dropping funnel and add this to the cobalt(II) chloride solution. A light brown precipitate is formed, which dissolves to give a dark green solution, with a Co:CN ratio of ∼1:5. Remove the inlet tube and quickly seal this neck of the flask with a serum cap, see Figure 12c. *Wash thoroughly your hands and any apparatus which has contained potassium cyanide solution.*

Insert a hypodermic syringe through the serum cap, withdraw a 2 ml sample of the gas, and inject it on to a gas chromatographic column. Satisfactory results can be obtained using an 8 ft activated alumina column at 160°C with a hydrogen carrier gas at 50 ml/min. Stir the solution, and after about thirty minutes withdraw another 2 ml sample of gas and inject it on to the gas chromatographic column. Compare this chromatogram with that of the first sample. Note any additional peaks. Compare the retention volume of the product peak with that of n-butane, but-l-ene, and *cis-* and *trans-*

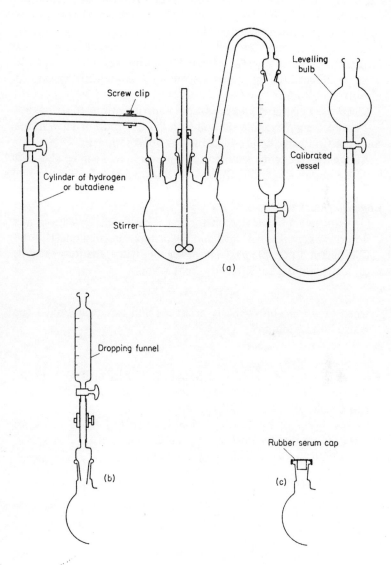

Figure 12. Apparatus used for the pentacyanocobaltate(II) ion catalysed
(a, b & c)   hydrogenation of butadiene.

but-2-ene. Follow the course of the reaction over about a two-hour period by regularly injecting gas samples on to the chromatographic column. The infrared spectrum of the product can now be measured. Connect an evacuated gas cell, (see p. 169), to the reaction vessel through a short drying tube, and fill it with gas at atmospheric pressure. Record the infrared spectrum and use standard spectra to identify the product.

Clean the apparatus and repeat the experiment but this time use $\sim$2·0M potassium cyanide. This gives a Co:CN ratio of 1:6·6 in the solution. Compare the products of the two experiments.

All the hydrocarbons required for this experiment can be obtained from Cambrian Chemicals, Bermondsey, London, S.E. 16.

Complementary work:

(1) How would you demonstrate that complex formation was occurring between hydrogen and the pentacyanocobaltate(II) ion?

(2) Suggest a possible mechanism for the hydrogenation reaction.

(3) Calculate ΔG^0 at 25°C for the reaction

$$C_4H_6 + H_2 = C_4H_8$$

when only *trans*-but-2-ene is produced and when only but-1-ene is produced. Comment.

Reference

Kwiatek, J., Mador, I. L. and Seyler, J. K., in *Reactions of Co-ordinated Ligands*, Advances in Chemistry Series, No. 37, American Chemical Society (1963), p. 201.

Kwiatek, J. and Seyler, J. K., in *Homogeneous Catalysis—Industrial Applications and Implications*, Advances in Chemistry Series, No. 70, American Chemical Society (1968), p. 207.

13 Chemistry in non-aqueous solvents

Introduction

Many chemical reactions require a suitable solvent. Water is the solvent of choice in inorganic chemistry, although in organic chemistry other solvents are more often used.

The choice of water as a solvent is due to a number of factors:

(a) It is cheap and readily available in a pure form.

(b) It is non-toxic and has a convenient liquid range.

(c) It is not very viscous and can be easily poured from one vessel to another. Operations such as crystallization and filtration can be readily carried out.

(d) It is a good solvent for a wide variety of solutes.

The use of water as a solvent has some disadvantages in certain cases:

(a) Reactions involving strong reducing agents cannot be carried out in water, since the water would be reduced, resulting in the evolution of hydrogen.

(b) Some compounds are hydrolysed by water and hence cannot be isolated in aqueous systems.

(c) Reactions at high temperatures ($>100°C$) cannot be carried out unless recourse is made to special equipment. Nor can reactions at low temperatures be conveniently studied.

The use of solvents other than water has therefore developed. The most studied non-aqueous solvents are: ammonia, sulphuric acid, hydrogen fluoride, certain liquid oxides, bromine trifluoride, and glacial acetic acid; of these only ammonia and dinitrogen tetroxide will be discussed here. For the use of other non-aqueous solvents in preparative chemistry see pp. 10, 147.

Ammonia

A comparison of some physical properties of liquid ammonia with the corresponding properties of water is given in Table 13.1.

Table 13.1

	Liquid Ammonia	Water
Melting point	$-77 \cdot 74°C$	$0 \cdot 0°C$
Boiling point	$-33 \cdot 35°C$	$100 \cdot 0°C$
Heat of fusion cal/mole	1352	1435
Heat of vaporization cal/mole	5581	9732
Dielectric constant	$26 \cdot 7$ at $-60°C$	80 at $0°C$
Density g/ml	$0 \cdot 677$ at $-33°C$	$0 \cdot 96$ at $100°C$

Liquid ammonia, like water, has an abnormally high boiling point; this is attributed to hydrogen bonding. Despite this, ammonia boils below room temperature, a property which may at first sight appear to present difficulties in the handling of liquid ammonia. However, due to the high heat of vaporization, liquid ammonia may be handled in ordinary apparatus without excessive boiling, although it is desirable to use vacuum jacketed vessels. Unsilvered Dewar vessels are suitable and have the advantage over the silvered variety of ease of observation of the contents.

Ammonia undergoes ionization in a manner similar to that of water

$$2NH_3 \rightleftharpoons NH_4{}^+ + NH_2{}^- \qquad K = 1 \cdot 9 \times 10^{-33} \text{ at } -50°C$$

$$\text{cf. } 2H_2O \rightleftharpoons H_3O^+ + OH^- \qquad K = 1 \cdot 0 \times 10^{-14} \text{ at } 25°C,$$

but the extent of ionization is much less than that of water. Any solute in liquid ammonia which produces NH_4^+ ions will behave as an acid, and any solute which produces NH_2^- ions will behave as a base. Just as neutralization reactions can be carried out in water between H_3O^+ and OH^- so can neutralization reactions be performed in liquid ammonia between NH_4^+ and NH_2^-.

One of the most interesting and characteristic properties of liquid ammonia is its ability to dissolve alkali, and alkaline earth metals with the formation of metal ions and solvated electrons; such solutions are intensely blue. A large number of reduction reactions involving metal-ammonia solutions are known, and these can be conveniently divided into three categories:

(1) Electron addition without bond cleavage

e.g.
$$e_{am}^- + O_2 = O_2^-$$

$$e_{am}^- + MnO_4^- = MnO_4^{2-}$$

(2) Bond cleavage by the addition of one electron

e.g.
$$e_{am}^- + NH_3 = NH_2^- + \tfrac{1}{2}H_2$$

(3) Bond cleavage by the addition of two electrons

e.g.
$$2e_{am}^- + Ge_2H_6 = 2GeH_3^-$$

Experiments

Ammonia is a toxic material and all operations involving its use must be carried out in a fume cupboard. An ammonia-type gas mask should be available in case of accident.

Ammonia is stored as a liquid under pressure in cylinders. Two types of cylinder are available. The most common type delivers ammonia gas when in an upright position, but liquid can be obtained by partially inverting the cylinder when, on opening the valve, liquid will be obtained. If it is inconvenient to invert the cylinder the ammonia gas may be condensed in a trap cooled to $-78°C$ in a solid carbon dioxide–acetone bath. The other type of cylinder which is available is equipped with a dip-pipe, which continues internally from the outlet valve to the bottom of the cylinder and delivers liquid ammonia when in an upright position.

Charge a large test tube with 50–100 ml of liquid ammonia by either of the two methods described above. Add several small pieces of freshly cut sodium to the ammonia in order to dry it. Close the vessel with a silica gel drying tube and store in a solid carbon dioxide–acetone bath. When the ammonia is dry, as indicated by the intense blue colour, set up the apparatus as shown in Figure 13.

Remove the cold bath surrounding the large test tube and place it round the smaller one. Allow about 5 ml of the dry liquid ammonia to condense into the smaller tube. Remove the B19 Drechsel head and fit the test tube with a silica gel drying tube. Repeat this procedure whenever a quantity of dry ammonia is required. It is convenient to have a selection of B19 test tubes and to be charging one with dry ammonia while another experiment is being carried out.

Store the tubes in a bath of melting chlorobenzene while carrying out the experiments described below. See p. 142 for a description of the preparation of such a bath.

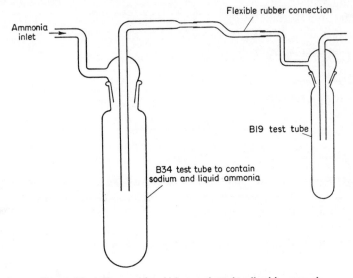

Figure 13. Apparatus for drying and storing liquid ammonia.

Experiment 1

To ~5 ml of dry ammonia add a small piece of freshly cut sodium about the size of a pin head. When the sodium has dissolved, add a crystal of iron(III) nitrate to the solution, note what happens and interpret your observations. To the solution so obtained add a few drops of phenolphthalein, and note the colour change. In a separate test tube prepare a solution of ammonium chloride in liquid ammonia, and add this solution slowly to the solution containing phenolphthalein. Comment on your observations.

Experiment 2

Prepare separate solutions of silver bromide and barium nitrate by dissolving small quantities of each in ~5 ml of liquid ammonia. Add the silver bromide solution to the barium nitrate solution. Comment.

Experiment 3

Dissolve a few crystals of potassium permanganate in ~5 ml of liquid ammonia. Prepare a solution of potassium amide by dissolving a small piece of potassium in $\sim$5 ml of liquid ammonia, add a crystal of iron(III) nitrate, and allow the blue solution to become colourless. Add slowly excess potassium amide solution to the potassium permanganate. Now add ammonium chloride to the mixture until in excess. Compare the results of these reactions with the analogous reactions in water.

Experiment 4

Dissolve a small piece of barium metal in $\sim$10 ml of liquid ammonia. Equip the test tube with a Drechsel head and bubble a slow stream of oxygen through the solution until the colour is discharged. There is no necessity to cool the solution during oxygenation. Add further quantities of ammonia if evaporation is excessive. When the colour of the solution is discharged allow the ammonia to evaporate.

To a sample of the product add 1–2 ml of 4M hydrochloric acid followed by 1–2 ml of dilute potassium permanganate solution. To a further sample of the product in hydrochloric acid add titanium(IV) sulphate solution. From your observations deduce the nature of the product. What are the likely impurities in the product? Compare this reaction with the reaction between barium metal and oxygen at high temperature, see p. 34.

The preparation of potassium tetracyanonickelate(II)

Materials required: Nickel(II) sulphate
Potassium cyanide

Exercise caution when using potassium cyanide. Wash your hands and the apparatus thoroughly after completing the reaction. Clean up any spillage immediately. Carry out the reaction in a fume cupboard.

Prepare solutions containing nickel(II) sulphate hexahydrate (6 g) in 20 ml of water, and potassium cyanide (3 g) in 7 ml of water. Add slowly, with stirring, the potassium cyanide solution to the nickel(II) sulphate solution at room temperature. Filter off the precipitate of nickel(II) cyanide and wash with water. Dissolve the paste-like precipitate in a solution of potassium cyanide (3 g) in 5 ml of water. Evaporate the red solution to about half its volume, cool, and filter off the orange-yellow crystals. Dry in a current of air on the filter.

Reference
Fernelius, W. C. and Burbage, J. J., *Inorg. Synth.*, **2**, 227.

The preparation of potassium tricyanonickelate(I)

Materials required: Potassium tetracyanonickelate(II)
                        Potassium metal

Prepare a saturated solution of potassium tetracyanonickelate(II) in ~ 5 ml of liquid ammonia. Add a small piece of clean potassium metal, and allow the tube to stand in the cold bath. Avoid addition of excess alkali metal. A red precipitate settles out. Wash by decantation with several 5 ml portions of liquid ammonia. The traces of ammonia remaining after the last washing may be removed by evaporation.

Complementary work:
   Add a little of the dry solid to
   (1) ~ 2 ml of water.
   (2) ~ 2 ml of 0·1M silver nitrate.
Comment on your observations.

Potassium tetracyanonickelate(0) may also be prepared by alkali metal reduction in liquid ammonia, but because of its instability in air it cannot be prepared in open tubes.

Reference
Eastes, J. W. and Burgess, W. M., *J. Amer. Chem. Soc.*, (1942), **64**, 1187.

Dinitrogen tetroxide

Dinitrogen tetroxide has a lower dielectric constant than ammonia. Consequently covalent compounds are more soluble than ionic compounds, and the degree of self-ionization is small. However, much of the chemistry in liquid dinitrogen tetroxide can be understood in terms of ionization to form a nitrosonium ion and a nitrate ion

$$N_2O_4 \rightleftharpoons NO^+ + NO_3^-$$

Dinitrogen tetroxide boils at 21·1°C and melts at −11·3°C; it thus has a useful liquid range, and from this point of view is convenient to use as a non-aqueous solvent. Because of its high toxicity, dinitrogen tetroxide must be handled in a fume cupboard, and care must be taken to avoid breathing the gas. Very few simple inorganic salts are soluble in liquid dinitrogen tetroxide, consequently acid-base reactions and metathetic reactions, as studied in liquid ammonia, are relatively unimportant in this solvent. When inorganic salts do dissolve in liquid dinitrogen tetroxide complex formation often occurs. For instance, zinc nitrate will dissolve in liquid dinitrogen tetroxide to form the adduct $Zn(NO_3)_2.2N_2O_4$, which can be isolated as a solid when excess solvent is removed by evaporation. The compound is not a solvate but a nitrosonium salt $(NO)_2 Zn (NO_3)_4$.

The usefulness of dinitrogen tetroxide as a solvent can be extended by mixing it with other co-solvents, when its properties are considerably modified. Solvents such as nitromethane, ether, and ethyl acetate are used for this purpose and are known to increase the self-ionization of the dinitrogen tetroxide. Nitromethane does this by virtue of having a high dielectric constant ($\varepsilon = 37$). Ether, and ethyl acetate do not have a high dielectric constant but function by complexing with nitrosonium ions to produce a significant increase in the self-ionization of dinitrogen tetroxide

$$a\,CH_3.COO.C_2H_5 + N_2O_4 \rightleftharpoons (CH_3.COO.C_2H_5)_a\,NO^+ + NO_3^-.$$

The reaction of copper metal with a mixture of ethyl acetate and dinitrogen tetroxide illustrates the usefulness of such solvent pairs. Copper reacts slowly with dinitrogen tetroxide and not at all with ethyl acetate. When copper is added to a mixture of the two solvents a vigorous reaction ensues and nitric oxide is liberated. Anhydrous copper(II) nitrate is formed and is isolated as the solvate $Cu(NO_3)_2 N_2O_4$. Other anhydrous transition metal nitrates have been prepared by analogous methods.

The preparation of dinitrogen tetroxide

Materials required: Lead nitrate
Salt

This experiment must be carried out in a fume cupboard. Dinitrogen tetroxide is a corrosive compound. Avoid breathing the vapour and wear protective gloves when handling apparatus containing the liquid.

Pulverize the lead nitrate and dry it in an oven at 110–120°C for 2–3 days. Place dry lead nitrate (~100 g) in a 250 ml round-bottomed long-necked, flask and assemble the apparatus as shown in Figure 14(*a*).

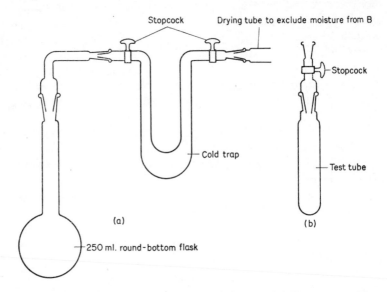

Figure 14 (a & b). Apparatus for the preparation of dinitrogen tetroxide.

Use silicone grease on the joints near the flask. Cool the U-tube in a mixture of ice and salt. Heat the flask with a bunsen burner until the lead nitrate begins to decompose and melts. Adjust the rate of heating so as to keep an even rate of decomposition. When the reaction is complete a solid residue remains in the flask.

Use the vacuum line (Figure 16, p. 137) to transfer the dinitrogen tetroxide into a tube (F) or (G) containing phosphorus pentoxide on glass wool to remove any traces of water from the product. Note that because dinitrogen tetroxide reacts with mercury, care must be taken to keep the vapour away from manometers during the transfer. When the product is dry transfer it to a weighed dry tube of the type shown in Figure 14(*b*). Weigh the product and calculate the percentage yield.

Complementary work:

(1) Why cannot calcium chloride be used to dry dinitrogen tetroxide?

(2) Pour a small amount of dinitrogen tetroxide on to a little crushed ice in a test tube. Comment on your observations.

(3) Reserve the remainder of the product for the preparation of anhydrous copper(II) nitrate.

The preparation of anhydrous copper(II) nitrate

Materials required: Copper foil
                        Dinitrogen tetroxide
                        Ethyl acetate

The initial stages of this experiment must be carried out in a fume cupboard. Set up the apparatus shown in Figure 15. Calibrate 20 ml of the B34 test tube in 10 ml divisions.

Place' strips of freshly abraded copper foil (~5 g) in the B34 test tube, and add dry ethyl acetate (10 ml), and dinitrogen tetroxide (10 ml), using the calibrations on the test tube for the volume measurement. *Immediately* attach the tube to the rest of the apparatus with screw-clip (H) open. A vigorous reaction commences and copious brown fumes are evolved. The reaction soon subsides but continues slowly for some time. Leave the reactants for 3–4 hours, or preferably overnight in order that the reaction shall proceed as near to completion as possible. Close screw-clip (H). Filter the solution from any unreacted copper by inverting the apparatus, connecting the tube (J) to the vacuum line (see p. 138), and opening screw-clip (G). If the adduct does not precipitate at this stage remove some of the solvent by evaporation *in vacuo*. This is easily done by allowing some of the solvent to condense into a cooled trap. When a precipitate forms, close the screw-clip (G), and remove the apparatus from the vacuum line. Filter by inverting the apparatus and applying suction at tube (K) with screw-clip (H) open. Close screw-clip (H). Fill the apparatus with nitrogen via tube (J), invert the apparatus, and shake the precipitate back into the flask. Replace the B14 cone at (A) with a drying tube containing phosphorus pentoxide. Wash the precipitate with dinitrogen tetroxide by pouring a few ml through the drying tube. Seal the end of the drying tube and filter the product as before, by applying suction at tube (K). Fill the apparatus with nitrogen via tube (K), remove the B34 test tube, and quickly apply a stopper to the B34 socket. When filling the apparatus with nitrogen a mercury-sealed lute must be incorporated into the inlet line. Remove the two-necked flask and quickly attach a test tube to the B24 cone. Evacuate the apparatus via tube (K).

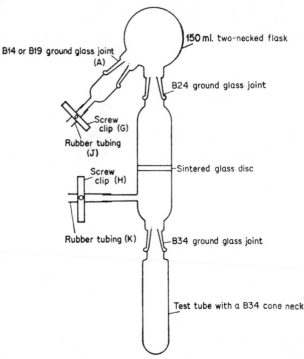

Figure 15. Apparatus for the preparation of anhydrous copper(II) nitrate.

The copper(II) nitrate-dinitrogen tetroxide adduct can now be broken down and the resulting anhydrous copper(II) nitrate purified by vacuum sublimation. Shake the product into the B24 test tube and place the end containing the solid in a silicone oil bath. Slowly raise the temperature of the oil bath while continuously evacuating the apparatus via tube (K). The adduct gives off dinitrogen tetroxide at about 160°C; at 200°C the anhydrous copper nitrate begins to sublime, and deposits on the cool parts of the tube. Continue the sublimation at 200–210°C. When complete, remove the oil bath and fill the apparatus with dry nitrogen. The B24 test tube containing the sublimed product can now be removed from the rest of the apparatus and is quickly stoppered to prevent the ingress of moist air. Any further manipulations of this material should be carried out in a dry box.

Complementary work:
  (1) Determine the copper content of the product.
  (2) What is the structure of anhydrous copper(II) nitrate? (See reference [3] below).
  (3) Use a dry box or dry bag (see p. 149) to prepare a sample of the product for infrared analysis [1] [2]. Consult references [1] and [2] for details of the infrared spectrum.

References
[1] Gatehouse, B. M., Livingstone, S. E. and Nyholm, R. S., *J. Soc.*, (1957), 4222.
[2] Addison, C. C. and Hathaway, B. J., *J. Chem. Soc.*, (1960), 1468.
[3] Wallwork, S. C., *Proc. Chem. Soc.*, (1959), 311.
[4] Addison, C. C. and Hathaway, B. J., *Proc. Chem. Soc.*, (1957), 19.

Bibliography

Fowles, G. W. A. and Nicholls, D., *Quart. Rev.* (1962), **16**, 19.
Holliday, A. K. and Massey, A. G., *Inorganic Chemistry in Non-aqueous Solvents*, Pergamon, (1965).
Sisler, H. H., *Chemistry in Non-aqueous Solvents*, Reinhold, New York, (1965).
Gould, R. F., *Free Radicals in Inorganic Chemistry*, American Chemical Society, Advances in Chemistry Series, No. 36, (1962).

14 Inorganic polymers

Introduction

Organic polymers have been known for a considerable time and include such compounds as polythene, polymethylmethacrylate ('Perspex'), polyvinyl chloride (P.V.C.), and nylon. In general terms a polymer is a compound with a high molecular weight which is made up from small repeating units. For instance, in polyvinyl chloride the repeating unit is —CH$_2$—CHCl—. Organic polymers of this type are limited in their applications, by their tendency to degrade in air below 250°C. Attempts have therefore been made to prepare thermally resistant polymers from inorganic starting materials, but with limited success as yet. Of the polymers so far studied the silicones are by far the most useful, although their discovery was accidental and the useful properties of silicone polymers went unnoticed for many years. A delay which is by no means uncommon!

Silicone polymers consist of chains or networks of alternating silicon and oxygen atoms with alkyl groups bonded to the silicon atom. Typical silicone polymers are poly(dimethylsiloxane)

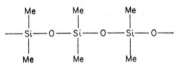

and hexaphenylcyclotrisiloxane

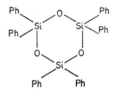

Silicone polymers of this type are prepared by the controlled hydrolysis of alkyl or aryl silicon halides. This hydrolysis is not unlike that of silicon tetrachloride (see p. 37) where the initial product is a hydrated form of silica. Silica may be thought of as a giant molecule containing silicon to oxygen bonds in a vast, three dimensional network. The substitution of one or more of the chlorine atoms in silicon tetrachloride with an alkyl or aryl group helps to control the hydrolysis so that a giant molecule (or polymer) of predetermined shape and size can be obtained. When two chlorine atoms are replaced by alkyl groups, hydrolysis and subsequent condensation can only occur at two centres, and hence a linear molecule is produced. The intermediates $R_2Si(OH)_2$, which arise from the initial hydrolysis reaction, are known as silanols. It is generally impossible to isolate the intermediate silanols, since they are so reactive that condensation follows immediately with the formation of a silicone polymer.

$$R_2SiCl_2 + 2H_2O = R_2Si(OH)_2 + 2HCl$$

$$2R_2Si(OH)_2 \rightarrow R_2Si(OH) - O - Si(OH)R_2 \rightarrow etc.$$

In certain cases, e.g. diphenyldichlorosilane, the initially formed silanols may be isolated, and demonstrated to undergo polymerization. If a third alkyl group is introduced into the silicon tetrachloride molecule polymerization can only proceed as far as the dimer

$$R_3SiCl + H_2O = R_3SiOH + HCl$$

$$2R_3SiOH = R_3Si - O - SiR_3 + H_2O$$

In the formation of long-chain polymers for silicone rubbers the purity of the monomer, dimethyldichlorosilane, is very important. A chain length of at least 8000 units is required for a useful rubber, and the presence of only 0·05% trimethylchlorosilane will reduce the desired chain length by about one half. The initially formed trimethylsilanol condenses with the growing polymer chain, effectively preventing any further polymerization at that point

$$- O - SiMe_2 - OH + HO - SiMe_3 \rightarrow - O - SiMe_2 - O - SiMe_3$$

Conversely, if a trifunctional unit as produced by the hydrolysis of methyltrichlorosilane is incorporated into the polymer chain, polymerization proceeds in three directions. This produces a cross-linked polymer and reduces the amount of purely linear polymerization

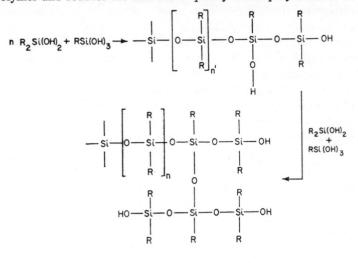

The preparation of cyclic and linear polysiloxanes

Materials required: Dimethyldichlorosilane

Add slowly, from a dropping funnel, dimethyldichlorosilane (25 ml) to well stirred water (100 ml) maintained at 15–20°C. The temperature is conveniently maintained by surrounding the reaction mixture with an ice bath. Extract the oily product with ether, separate from the aqueous layer, and dry the ethereal extract over magnesium sulphate. Filter off the magnesium sulphate, and remove the ether on a water bath. Distil the residual oil to obtain two fractions: (*a*) boiling range 170–175°C, mainly the cyclic trimer, and (*b*) boiling range 175–180°C, mainly the cyclic tetramer.

Complementary work:

To 2 ml of the tetramer add 4 ml of ether, and 0·5 ml of concentrated sulphuric acid. Shake the mixture for 6–10 hours. Remove the ether solution by means of a dropping pipette, and evaporate off the ether. Comment on any change in physical properties of the product compared with the starting material. Examine the infrared spectrum of the product and identify the bands due to the Si—O and Si—C linkages.

Reference
Bellamy, L. J., *The Infrared Spectra of Complex Molecules*, Methuen, 2nd edition, (1958).

The preparation of diphenylsilanediol

Materials required: Diphenyldichlorosilane
Toluene
tert-Amyl alcohol

Prepare a mixture of toluene (2 ml), *tert*-amyl alcohol (4 ml), and water (16 ml), and cool this to 20°C. To this mixture add slowly, with stirring, a mixture of toluene (2 ml) and diphenyldichlorosilane (4 ml). Keep the temperature below 25°C during the addition of the diphenyldichlorosilane. Continue the stirring for a further five minutes, and filter off the white solid by suction. Wash the product with water, until it is freed from organic solvent and hydrochloric acid, and dry at the pump. Record the yield, and measure the m.p.

Complementary work:
(1) Why is it possible to hydrolyse diphenyldichlorosilane whereas diphenyldichloromethane is stable to hydrolysis?
(2) To a refluxing solution of diphenylsilanediol (1 g) in 95% ethanol (10 ml) add one or two drops of 4M sodium hydroxide, within a few minutes crystals of octaphenylcyclotetrasiloxane separate. Continue the refluxing for 10 minutes, cool, filter off the tetramer, and dry at the pump. Measure the m.p. of the product.
(3) Reflux together diphenylsilanediol (1 g), ether (15 ml), and concentrated hydrochloric acid (0·5 ml) for three hours. Remove the ether solution, and dry it over magnesium sulphate. Filter, and evaporate off the ether until crystallization of the hexaphenyl-cyclotrisiloxane commences. Filter on a Hirsh funnel, dry the product in air, and measure the m.p.
(4) Measure the infrared spectra of the diphenylsilanediol and the two siloxanes. Identify the bands characteristic of the Si—Ph link, the monosubstituted aromatic ring, and the O—H bond.

Reference

Bellamy, L. J., *The Infrared Spectra of Complex Molecules*, Methuen, 2nd edition, (1958).

The preparation and polymerization of phosphonitrilic chloride

One of the problems associated with the synthesis of inorganic polymers is the tendency of many monomers to form four-, six-, or eight-membered rings, instead of linear molecules. The formation of siloxane trimers and tetramers has already been demonstrated. Cyclic trimeric and tetrameric phosphonitrilic chlorides may be readily obtained, and the pure trimer polymerized to a linear polymer with the structure $(- PCl_2 = N -)_n$.

The preparation of $(PNCl_2)_3$

Materials required: Phosphorus pentachloride

Ammonium chloride

sym—Tetrachloroethane

Add dry ammonium chloride (17·5 g) to a solution of phosphorus pentachloride (65 g) in dried *sym*-tetrachloroethane (150 ml), and reflux the suspension until the evolution of hydrogen chloride has ceased. Attach a calcium chloride tube to the open end of the condenser and cool the mixture. Remove excess ammonium chloride by filtration, and remove the solvent by distillation under reduced pressure. Do not allow the temperature to exceed 50–60°C. Transfer the residue to an open dish and allow it to cool. The oily material and traces of solvent are removed by suction on a funnel, and the product washed with 50% aqueous ethanol. The residual powder, which is almost entirely phosphonitrilic trimer, is recrystalized *three* times from benzene before polymerization. Measure the m.p. of the purified product.

Complementary work:

The polymerization of phosphonitrilic chloride: Place a sample of the purified trimer (5–10 g) in a Carius' tube, flush out the tube with nitrogen and seal. See p. 147 for a description of the construction and use of a Carius' tube. Heat the tube to 300°C for 4–6 hours in a suitable furnace. If a furnace is not available, a sand bath heated by a bunsen burner can be used *but a safety screen must be used to protect the operator*. When the tube is cool, cut it open and examine the product. Leave the product exposed to the atmosphere for a day or so, and note what happens.

Bibliography

Paddock, N. L., *Quart. Rev.*, (1964), **18**, 168.

Stone, F. G. A. and Graham, W. A. G., *Inorganic Polymers*, Academic Press, New York, (1962).

Sorenson, W. R. and Campbell, T. W., *Preparative Methods of Polymer Chemistry*, Interscience, New York, (1961).

Rochow, E. G., *Chemistry of the Silicones*, Wiley, New York, 2nd ed., (1951).

15 High vacuum techniques in chemistry

Introduction

The work described in this chapter is designed to introduce students to the use, advantages, and limitations of high vacuum techniques in chemistry.

The apparatus in which gases and volatile liquids are manipulated is referred to as a vacuum system and is usually constructed from Pyrex glass. Materials to be handled in such a system must have saturated vapour pressures of at least a few tenths of a millimetre at room temperature. In practice most compounds which are used have saturated vapour pressures considerably in excess of this.

The high vacuum technique for the manipulation of volatile condensable substances is based on the fact that when vapours are introduced into an evacuated space they rapidly diffuse throughout that space. The substance may then be moved quantitatively to any part of that system by cooling the appropriate part to a temperature at which the substance will exert a negligible vapour pressure. In addition to volatility limitations the substances manipulated must not react with glass, nor with stopcock lubricant where stopcocks are used.

Vacuum systems differ considerably from one to another depending upon the purpose for which they are designed. Despite this, every vacuum system has certain basic features.

These are:

(1) A pumping system consisting of an oil, or mercury, diffusion pump backed by a rotary oil pump.

(2) A main line to which ancillary parts of the system are connected.

136

(3) A means of measuring pressure in various parts of the system.
(4) A means of introducing gases into the system.
(5) A trap placed between the pumping system and the main line. This is always cooled with liquid nitrogen and prevents volatile material being carried into the pumping system.

The various parts of the vacuum system are interconnected with glass stopcocks. A simple high vacuum system is shown in Figure 16. *Evacuated glass vessels may implode. Therefore wear safety goggles when working with a vacuum line.*

Pressure measurement

The pressure in the storage bulbs is measured by means of mercury manometers which are placed adjacent to a reference manometer. The reference manometer shares the same mercury reservoir, and the space above the meniscus of the reference manometer, (M), is kept permanently evacuated. The pressure in the storage bulb is then indicated by the difference between the manometer attached to the bulb and the reference manometer. The McLeod type gauge attached to the main line measures the pressure down to 10^{-3}mm Hg and is used to check that a good vacuum has been obtained in the apparatus, and that no part of the system is leaking. This is done by evacuating the system, with the McLeod type gauge in position A, and measuring the pressure by turning the gauge to position B, see Figure 17. Return the gauge to position A, close tap 1, allow the system to stand for about 5–10 minutes, and measure the pressure again. If there is an increase in pressure within the system during this time examine all the stopcocks for signs of the grease streaking, and regrease where streaking occurs. Evacuate and test the system as before. If the system is still leaking it may be necessary to test the glass with a discharge leak detector, and the assistance of an experienced person must be sought.

The transfer of gases to and from the system

It is frequently necessary to introduce gases into the system for storage and measurement, and also to remove measured quantities into reaction vessels. Gases are usually obtained under pressure in metal cylinders or thick-walled glass containers. Both types of container are fitted with a control valve and a suitable outlet point. Before introducing a gas into the system place a Dewar vessel filled

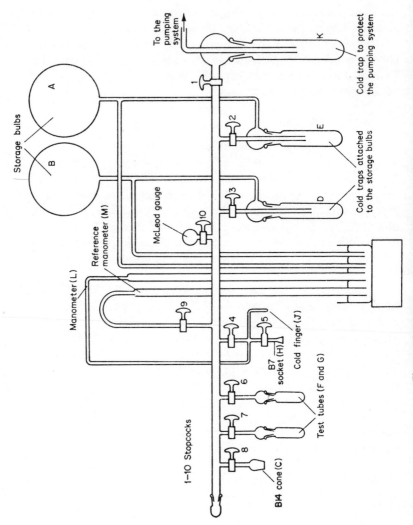

Figure 16. Diagram of a simple vacuum system.

Storage bulbs

A

B

To the pumping system

K

Cold trap to protect the pumping system

E

D

Cold traps attached to the storage bulbs

McLeod gauge

Reference manometer (M)

Manometer (L)

Cold finger (J)

B7 socket (H)

Test tubes (F and G)

B14 cone (C)

1–10 Stopcocks

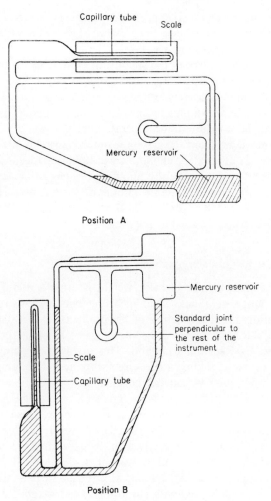

Figure 17. Diagram of a Mcleod-type gauge.

with liquid nitrogen around the cold trap (K) and evacuate the system and the bulb where the gas is to be stored. Attach the cylinder to the B14 cone, C, (Figure 16) on the vacuum line by means of rubber pressure tubing and a B14 socket. Evacuate the connector by opening stopcocks 8 and 1. Open stopcock 3 and close stopcock 1. The cylinder valve can now be opened gently when gas will enter the apparatus and fill bulb B. When sufficient gas has entered the bulb, as indicated by the pressure on the manometer, close the cylinder valve. Do not allow the pressure of gas in the vacuum system at this stage to exceed 60 cm Hg.

Cool in liquid nitrogen the small trap D attached to bulb B until the pressure in the apparatus is zero. Close stopcocks 3 and 8, and allow the solidified gas to warm up to room temperature. The amount of gas in the bulb can now be calculated, knowing the volume of the bulb and the pressure and temperature of the gas.

To remove gas from the system a suitable vessel is attached to the B14 cone, C, evacuated, and cooled in liquid nitrogen. Close stopcock 1, and open 3 carefully allowing the gas to condense in the cooled vessel. When a suitable amount of gas has been removed, as indicated by the fall of pressure in B, close stopcock 3. The measured quantity can now be used as required.

Molecular weight determination

The measurement of molecular weight is often a useful indication of the purity of a gas. Such measurements will also give some information about the nature of the products from a reaction.

Molecular weight measurements of gases are most conveniently measured by Regnault's method. This involves weighing a known volume of gas at a known pressure and temperature, and from this data the molecular weight can be calculated.

A glass bulb of 250 ml capacity (known accurately), equipped with a micro-tap and a B7 cone is used for the purpose. This is attached to the vacuum system at the B7 socket, H, (Figure 16) and is evacuated. Do not handle the bulb directly with the hands but protect it with a lintless cloth. When the bulb is evacuated, close stopcock 5, remove the bulb from the vacuum system, wipe the grease from the B7 cone, using a cloth moistened with chloroform, and weigh. Re-attach the bulb to the vacuum line, evacuate the connecting lines, and fill the bulb to a pressure of *ca*. 20 cm Hg with the gas under investigation. Record the pressure of the gas and the ambient temperature. Close the tap on the molecular weight bulb and condense the rest of the gas back into the storage bulb. Close taps 4 and 5, remove the bulb from the vacuum line, clean the B7 cone, and reweigh. The weight of a known volume of gas at a known pressure and temperature has now been determined and the molecular weight (the weight of 22·4 l of gas at S.T.P.) can be calculated.

When only a small volume of gas is available, condense it all into the cold finger J, close tap 4 and allow the gas to expand into the molecular weight bulb. Now proceed as above.

Spectroscopic measurements

A gas cell of the type shown in Figure 26 on p. 169 can be used for measuring both infrared, and visible or ultraviolet spectra. Sodium chloride windows are used for infrared work and silica windows for ultraviolet and visible spectroscopy. The windows are attached to the ground glass flange by means of silicone grease. The cell is filled with gas to a pressure of *ca.* 20 cm Hg in a similar way to that described for filling the molecular weight bulb. The cell is then placed in the beam of the spectrometer and the spectrum recorded. In order to resolve all the bands in the spectrum the pressure is reduced to *ca.* 2 cm Hg and the spectrum again recorded. Further reductions in pressure can be made if any bands still remain unresolved. See p. 169 for further details of spectroscopic measurements.

The measurement of vapour pressure—temperature data

The equilibrium vapour pressure of a material can be conveniently measured in a vacuum apparatus, and such a measurement is often a useful guide to the purity of the material. In addition, physical constants such as boiling point, Trouton constant, latent heat of vaporization, and latent heat of fusion, can be readily calculated from such vapour pressure data.

The apparatus used for this work is called an isoteniscope, and a simple form is shown in Figure 18.

The isoteniscope is attached to the vacuum line at H by means of the B7 cone, and a small amount of mercury is placed in bulb, B. Evacuate the isoteniscope by opening taps 4 and 5 (Figure 16). A small amount of the material under investigation is now condensed into the sample bulb, by cooling the latter in liquid nitrogen. The remaining material is returned to the storage bulb. The mercury in bulb B is now tipped into the apparatus to form a small manometer, and tap 4 is closed. A cold bath is now prepared by cooling a suitable solvent with powdered 'Drikold' to a temperature at which the material under investigation has a negligible vapour pressure. For temperatures below $-78°C$ the bath is further cooled with liquid nitrogen.

This cold bath is prepared in a Dewar vessel so that the low temperature can be maintained. *When preparing cold baths in this way take care not to use liquid nitrogen which has condensed oxygen from the atmosphere, since liquid oxygen and hydrocarbons can form dangerously explosive mixtures.*

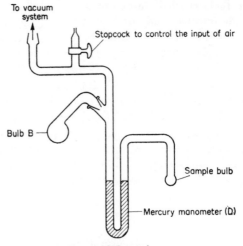

Figure 18. Isoteniscope.

A solvent used for a cold bath should, where possible, have a high flash point. Some suitable liquids for low-temperature baths are given in Table 15.1.

Table 15.1 *Low-temperature baths*

Bath liquid	m.p.
Chlorobenzene	$-45°C$
Chloroform	$-63·5°C$
Solid carbon dioxide in methylated spirits	$-78°C$
Toluene	$-96°C$
Liquid nitrogen	b.p. $-196°C$

The cold bath is equipped with a thermometer, and a stirrer and placed around the bulb containing the sample. Air is admitted to the apparatus via a stopcock so that the small manometer, D. maintains the null position (Figure 18). When there are no further fluctuations in the pressure of the sample, equilibrium has been attained, and the vapour pressure can be measured from the manometers (L) and (M). Temperature measurements are made immediately before and after the pressure measurement and should be identical. Temperature and pressure measurement to 0·2 of a unit (°C and mm) are satisfactory.

Practice in the techniques described above will be obtained by carrying out the experiments described below.

The reaction between boron trifluoride and ammonia

The boron atom in boron trihalides has six electrons in its outer shell. A consequence of this electron deficiency is that boron trihalides have a strong tendency to behave as acceptors (Lewis acids) and acquire a stable octet of electrons. Thus boron trihalides will react with molecules which can donate a pair of electrons (Lewis bases), e.g. ammonia, amines, carboxylic acids, and ethers. It should be noted that the relative strengths of the boron trihalides as Lewis acids are $BBr_3 \geqslant BCl_3 > BF_3$, which is not what would be expected from steric and electronegativity considerations. However, calculations indicate that boron-halogen π-bonding energies are in the order $BF_3 \gg BCl_3 > BBr_3$, and when an addition compound is formed this π-bonding is mainly lost. Therefore an addition compound, formed from a trihalide with the most π-bonding, will be the most destabilized by loss of π-bonding energy.

The acceptor properties of boron trihalides are illustrated by the reaction of boron trifluoride with ammonia. The product is physically and chemically quite different from the reactants, which is true of many of the adducts of boron trifluoride with Lewis bases.

Materials required: Boron oxide
Potassium borofluoride
Cylinder of ammonia

Prepare a mixture of boron oxide (7 g) and potassium borofluoride (13 g), pour this mixture into a vessel of the type shown in Figure 19 until a layer is obtained in the larger diameter tube.

Plug the narrow bore tube with glass wool near the B14 socket to prevent any solid material being carried into the vacuum line.

Attach this tube to the vacuum line by the B14 socket. Evacuate the tube, tapping it gently to dislodge any air trapped in the solid. Close the tap to the pumping system, warm the solid mixture gently, and discard the first 30–50 ml of gas produced. This ensures that

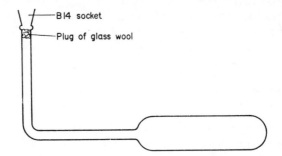

Figure 19. Tube used for preparing boron trifluoride.

any absorbed or occluded air is removed. Heat the solid mixture more strongly and allow the boron trifluoride evolved to expand into a suitable storage bulb, until about 100 ml of gas has been collected. Discontinue the heating, close the storage bulb and pump out the main line and the boron trifluoride generator until the latter stops evolving boron trifluoride. Transfer *ca* 100 ml of ammonia from a cylinder to a suitable storage bulb as previously described, see p. 137. Measure the molecular weight, infrared spectrum, and vapour pressure-temperature data of ammonia. Attach a test tube directly to the vacuum system and into this condense IN TURN 100 ml of ammonia and 100 ml of boron trifluoride. Do not allow the gases to mix in the vacuum system. Close the tap connecting the test tube to the main line, remove the liquid nitrogen surrounding the test tube, and allow the condensed gases to warm slowly. After a few minutes a white solid will suddenly form. When the tube has reached room temperature, pump off any unreacted gas, and remove the test tube from the vacuum line.

Complementary work:

(1) Test the solubility of the product in water and common organic solvents. What may be concluded about the nature of this material from these tests?

(2) Measure the infrared spectrum, identify the B–F and N–H absorptions. See p. 165 for further experimental details.

(3) Heat a sample of the boron trifluoride-ammonia adduct and identify the volatile product. Formulate an equation for the reaction.

(4) Determine the composition of the product. Ammonia may be determined by the Kheldahl technique and boron by dissolving a known weight of the product in a slight excess of dilute sodium hydroxide and titrating the solution by the mannitol method.

References

Greenwood, N. N. and Martin, R. L., *Quart. Rev.*, (1954), 8, 1.
Laubengayer, A. W. and Condike, G. F., *J. Amer. Chem. Soc.*, (1948), 70, 2274.

The preparation of nitrosonium hexachloroantimonate

A molecule of nitric oxide can readily lose its odd electron to give the nitrosonium ion NO^+. This easy loss of an electron can be explained in terms of the molecular orbital theory of valence since the odd electron is accommodated in an antibonding orbital, and the loss of this electron will confer additional stability on the resultant ion. The formation of the nitrosonium ion has been well demonstrated experimentally. For instance, the dissolution of the oxides N_2O_3 and N_2O_4 in sulphuric acid is best interpreted in terms of the formation of the nitrosonium ion:

$$N_2O_3 + 3H_2SO_4 = 2NO^+ + 3HSO_4^- + H_3O^+$$
$$N_2O_4 + 3H_2SO_4 = NO^+ + NO_2^+ + 3HSO_4^- + H_3O^+$$

The experiment described below illustrates the formation of a nitrosonium salt from a nitrosyl halide and a metal halide. This reaction is applicable to the formation of a number of salts such as $NOFeCl_4$, $NOAsF_6$, $NOSbCl_6$.

The preparation of nitrosyl chloride

Materials required: Hydrochloric acid
Sodium nitrite
Potassium chloride
Calcium chloride

Carry out the reaction in a fume cupboard. Equip a 500 ml three-necked flask with a dropping funnel, stirrer, and air condenser. The air condenser should have been packed previously with sodium nitrite, moist potassium chloride, and calcium chloride in three equal sections. Connect the outlet of the packed air condenser to a previously weighed trap which is subsequently cooled in a mixture of solid carbon dioxide and acetone. Attach a calcium chloride drying tube to the outlet of the trap.

Place concentrated hydrochloric acid (200 ml) in the flask and a solution of sodium nitrite (35 g in 50 ml of water) in the dropping funnel. Run the sodium nitrite solution dropwise into the well stirred hydrochloric acid. Nitrosyl chloride is evolved and collects in the cooled trap. When the reaction is complete, close the taps on the cooled trap and immediately dismantle the apparatus to prevent the glass joints sticking due to the attack of nitrosyl chloride on grease. The nitrosyl chloride so prepared may be used without further purification for the next part of the experiment.

The reaction of nitrosyl chloride with antimony pentachloride

---

Materials required: Nitrosyl chloride
                           Antimony pentachloride

Pour antimony pentachloride (1 ml) into a 25 ml round bottomed flask and evacuate the flask for about half a minute. The flask need not be cooled at this stage since antimony pentachloride has a low vapour pressure. Attach the trap containing the nitrosyl chloride to the vacuum system, cool the nitrosyl chloride in liquid nitrogen, and evacuate the trap. The nitrosyl chloride must now be 'degassed' by allowing the solid to melt, and pumping away uncondensable gases at the melting point. Uncondensable gases such as nitrogen and oxygen are least soluble at the melting point of the liquid and can easily be pumped off. Two or three such 'freeze-melt-pump' cycles will ensure complete removal of uncondensable gases. Allow the nitrosyl chloride to warm up, and the vapour to come into contact with the antimony pentachloride. Reaction is immediate and exothermic, and a solid product is formed. Freeze the nitrosyl chloride, and remove the tube and contents from the vacuum system. Fill the main line of the vacuum system with dry nitrogen. Remove the flask from the vacuum line, and quickly stopper it to prevent the ingress of moist air.

Complementary work:

(1) Measure the infrared spectrum using a fluorocarbon grease or oil as the mulling agent and 'Irtran' or arsenic sulphide plates. See p. 165 for further experimental details. Ideally the mull should be prepared in a dry atmosphere, as obtained in a conventional dry box, see p. 149. A satisfactory spectrum can be obtained in the atmosphere if the operations are carried out quickly. Identify the band(s) due to the nitrosonium ion, compare this with the N—O absorption in nitric oxide and comment.

(2) Why cannot sodium chloride plates be used when measuring the infrared spectrum?

References

Morton, J. R. and Wilcox, H. W., *Inorg. Synth.*, **4**, 48.
Sharp, D. W. A. and Thorley, J., *J. Chem. Soc.*, (1963), 3557.

The preparation of amidosulphuric acid

Materials required: Hydroxylamine sulphate
Sulphur dioxide
Carius' tube

A Carius' tube is a thick-walled (2–4 mm) glass tube (2–4 cm o.d.) used for reactions at pressures up to 10 atmospheres. One end of the tube is reduced to a narrower diameter (8–10 mm o.d.) and the other end is sealed. Once a tube is under pressure, handling must be kept to a minimum. When handling is necessary the tube is wrapped in a protective cloth. *During the course of a reaction the operator must be shielded from the tube by a blast screen.* A piece of 'Perspex' sheet (ca. 5 mm thick) makes a suitable screen. When opening a Carius, tube the contents of the tube must be cooled to a temperature at which they exert only a low vapour pressure. For reactions in which the nature of the products is unknown it is advisable to cool the tube in liquid nitrogen.

Calibrate a Carius' tube at a capacity of 20 ml and then by 5 ml divisions to a capacity of 35 ml. Prepare an aqueous solution of hydroxylamine sulphate (8 g in 20 ml of water) and pour this into the Carius' tube. Make a constriction in the narrow part of the Carius' tube and attach the tube to the vacuum system. Degas the solution by two or three 'freeze-melt-pump' cycles. Cool the tube and contents to −23°C using a carbon tetrachloride slush bath. Attach a cylinder of sulphur dioxide to the vacuum system and allow ca. 10 ml of sulphur dioxide to condense on to the hydroxylamine sulphate solution. Seal off the tube at the constriction, and allow the tube and contents to warm up to room temperature. Allow the reaction to proceed for 3–4 days when crystals of amidosulphuric acid will have formed.

To open the tube, cool it to −23°C and cut a small piece off the narrow part of the glass tubing. Leave the tube to warm in a fume cupboard when the bulk of the sulphur dioxide will boil off. Remove the dissolved sulphur dioxide by suction at a water pump. Filter off the amidosulphuric acid, washing out the tube with portions of alcohol. Wash the product with alcohol to remove any unreacted hydroxylamine sulphate, and dry the product at the pump.

Complementary work:

(1) Write an equation for the formation of amidosulphuric acid from hydroxylamine sulphate.

(2) Treat an aqueous solution of the product with barium chloride solution. Comment.

(3) Treat an aqueous solution of the product with sodium nitrite solution. Keep the solution cool during the addition of the nitrite. Try to identify the gas evolved. When no more gas is evolved on the addition of nitrite solution test the resultant solution with barium chloride. Write an equation for the reaction between amidosulphuric acid and sodium nitrite.

Bibliography

Sanderson, R. T., *Vacuum Manipulation of Volatile Compounds*, Reinhold, New York, (1948).

16 Inert atmosphere techniques

Introduction

The preparation and manipulation of certain inorganic compounds requires the use of an inert atmosphere. Inert often implies that the atmosphere is free from water and oxygen. The reactions are carried out in a dry nitrogen atmosphere. In other cases nitrogen must also be excluded and then an argon atmosphere is used. Such inert atmospheres are conveniently maintained in a glove box. Glove boxes are available in a variety of shapes and sizes, constructed from a variety of materials. They all possess the following basic features:

(1) A gas-tight box in which the experimental work is performed.
(2) A smaller gas-tight box fitted to the side of the main unit, which functions as an air-lock. All materials are introduced into the main unit through this lock.
(3) A transparent window in the front of the box through which the manipulations may be observed.
(4) A pair of arm-length rubber gloves sealed to two ports in the front of the box.
(5) A variety of tubes sealed through the wall of the main box, to supply standard services, e.g. water, gas.

Production of the inert atmosphere

The atmosphere in the glove box is displaced by nitrogen. This may be achieved by connecting a cylinder of nitrogen to one of the tubes in the wall of the glove box and purging the box for a number of hours. The displacement of all the air in the box in this way is very time consuming and the following procedure is recommended. Make a balloon from a polythene bag or polythene sheet, sealing the edges with a heated sealing wheel or plastic cement. A small opening is left in which to seal a short length of rubber tubing. The volume of the balloon when inflated should be more than sufficient to fill the glove box. Place the deflated balloon in the glove box, connect the rubber tubing to the nitrogen inlet stream and inflate the bag. This effectively displaces the air from the glove box. Remove the balloon from the nitrogen inlet while allowing the nitrogen flow to continue. Deflate the balloon in the glove box. Re-attach the balloon to the nitrogen inlet and inflate it again. Repeat this cycle of inflation and deflation three times to effectively displace the air from the glove box. A dry atmosphere is conveniently produced by using dry nitrogen. The nitrogen from the cylinder is passed through a column containing molecular sieve (Linde 5A) before entering the glove box. The molecular sieve may be regenerated by heating.

A pressure slightly in excess of atmospheric should be maintained in the glove box. This prevents ingress of air, due to the box not being completely air-tight. A suitable pressure head is maintained by having a continuous flow of dry nitrogen through the glove box. A slow flow rate is satisfactory when the box is not in use; the flow can be increased when carrying out experimental work. The nitrogen exit from the glove box is connected to a mercury float valve. The mercury in the float valve chamber provides the pressure head. Withdrawal of one's arms from the glove box causes a reduction in pressure in the box. The mercury float valve then seals the exit and prevents air from being drawn into the box.

Transfers to and from the glove box

The air-lock is used when transferring material to and from the glove box. The size of the lock is governed by the need to accommodate the equipment required, while keeping size to a minimum so that the purging and drying of the atmosphere in the lock is not too lengthy a procedure. In some glove boxes the air-lock can be purged by evacuating the lock, filling partially with inert gas and then evacuating again. The lock is then filled with inert gas to atmospheric pressure. Alternatively, an inert atmosphere can be obtained by streaming dry nitrogen through the air-lock for about half an hour.

When the glove box contains an intert atmosphere, materials which are to be introduced into the glove box are placed in the lock. The door is closed and an inert atmosphere produced in the lock by one of the above methods. The connecting door to the glove box is opened and all the material transferred. The connecting door is closed. To remove material from the glove box first ensure that the atmosphere in the lock is inert. Open the connecting door to the glove box, place the material in the lock, and close the connecting door. The material may now be removed from the lock. Two points should be remembered when using the lock:

(1) Once the lock has been opened to the laboratory it no longer contains an inert atmosphere.

(2) Always ensure that the lock contains an inert atmosphere before opening it to the glove box.

In view of the rather time consuming nature of transfers to and from the glove box, material requirements should be well considered before commencing any experimental work.

Manipulations within the glove box are performed while wearing the armlength rubber gloves fitted to the front of the glove box. Some discomfort may be experienced from perspiration, with some of the water vapour diffusing into the glove box. To reduce this problem sprinkle the hands and arms liberally with talc. Remember that the gloves are made of rubber and liable to damage by sharp or hot objects.

The interior of the glove box should be kept clean. Spillages must be cleared up immediately. To facilitate cleanliness within the box, a sheet of aluminium may be spread on the bottom of the glove box before starting the experimental work. The sheet can be folded and removed with any spillage at the end of the experiment. Apparatus used in the glove box may contain products which are unstable in the laboratory atmosphere. Care must be taken in removing and immediately cleaning out this apparatus.

When a rigid glove box is not available, inert atmosphere bags can be conveniently prepared from polythene sheets. Several models have been described [1, 2]. Some of the simpler manipulations can be carried out in these.

The following preparations give products whose further manipulation requires a glove box;

(1) The preparation of anhydrous copper(II) nitrate (p. 127).

(2) The preparation of nitrosonium hexachloroantimonate (p. 146).

The preparation of chromium(II) acetate may be carried out in a glove box, as an alternative to the procedure described on p. 205.

References

[1] Ocone, L. R., and Simkin, J., *J. Chem. Educ.*, (1962), **39**, 463.
[2] Shore, S. G., ibid., (1962), **39**, 465.

The preparation of organometallic compounds

Many compounds are known in which a direct metal to carbon bond exists. Some of these organometallic compounds react violently with oxygen or water, e.g. aluminium alkyls, whereas others are quite stable under similar conditions. Between these two extremes are many compounds which are hydrolytically and oxidatively unstable and where synthesis must be carried out in an atmosphere of dry nitrogen. An important group of such compounds is the lithium alkyls and aryls; these compounds are relatively easy to prepare and are of considerable use as intermediates in the synthesis of other organometallic compounds. In the examples described below, phenyllithium is prepared in an atmosphere of nitrogen and used for the synthesis of tetraphenyllead.

Cautionary Note

All lead compounds must be regarded as toxic and handled with care. Contact with the skin should be avoided since organolead compounds can be absorbed in this way. Should accidental contact with the skin occur, wash the affected parts with a petroleum fraction followed by complete washing with soap and water. Avoid inhaling volatile lead compounds. Carry out the experiments described below in a fume cupboard and wear rubber gloves when handling organolead compounds.

The preparation of phenyllithium

Materials required: Lithium
　　　　　　　　　　　Bromobenzene
　　　　　　　　　　　Ether

Dry the ether (400 ml) by standing it over sodium or molecular sieve 6A; use the dry ether for this and the following experiment.

Equip a three-necked flask with a stirrer, a double-surface reflux condenser, a dropping funnel, and an inlet for nitrogen. Fit the upper end of the condenser with a silica gel drying tube. Maintain a steady stream of nitrogen through the apparatus. Pour dry ether (150 ml) into the flask and add small pieces of freshly cut lithium (3 g). To the stirred suspension of lithium in ether, add slowly a solution of bromobenzene (20 ml) in ether (50 ml). The rate of addition of the bromobenzene solution should be such that the reaction mixture refluxes steadily during the reaction. When the reaction is complete, disconnect the ancilliary apparatus from the flask and stopper the three necks. This operation should be carried out quickly so as to minimize the entrance of moist air into the flask. Transfer the flask into a dry box. Allow the suspension to settle and decant the solution through glass wool into a dry graduated dropping funnel. Store the solution of phenyllithium until required for the next experiment.

Complementary work:
Pipette a 2 ml aliquot of the phenyllithium solution into a conical flask and remove it from the dry box. Add water to the 2 ml aliquot and titrate the solution with 0·05M sulphuric acid using phenolphthalein as indicator. Determine the phenyllithium content of the solution and hence calculate the yield for the reaction.

The concentration of phenyllithium solution must be known so that the volume of phenyllithium solution required in the following reaction can be calculated.

Reference
Gilman, H., Summers, L. and Leeper, R. W., *J. Org. Chem.*, (1952), **17**, 630.

The preparation of tetraphenyllead

Materials required: Phenyllithium (see the previous experiment)
Iodobenzene
Lead(II) chloride
Ether

Assemble the apparatus used for the preparation of phenyllithium but replace the dropping funnel with a stoppered dropping funnel containing the phenyllithium prepared in the previous experiment. The phenyllithium solution must be measured in a dry box and transferred to the apparatus in a stoppered dropping funnel. Place in the flask lead(II) chloride (12 g), iodobenzene (10 g), and dry ether (100 ml). Stir this suspension thoroughly so that no lead(II) chloride settles out. Add the phenyllithium solution (containing 0·14 moles of phenyllithium) at such a rate that the reaction mixture refluxes gently. When all the phenyllithium solution has been added reflux the reaction mixture for one hour. Cool the flask in ice and cautiously add water (100 ml) to the reaction mixture. Filter the white solid on a Buchner filter, air dry the solid product and extract it with chloroform (200 ml) in a soxlet extractor. When extraction is complete, filter off the tetraphenyllead from the chloroform suspension. Record the yield and measure the melting point. An equimolar amount of bromobenzene may be used in place of iodobenzene, but the yield of tetraphenyllead is reduced. Carry out one of the following preparations using tetraphenyllead.

(A) *The preparation of triphenyllead chloride*

Bubble hydrogen chloride into a refluxing solution of tetraphenyllead (5 g) in chloroform (80 ml). When shiny plates of diphenyllead dichloride begin to appear stop the flow of hydrogen chloride. If the tetraphenyllead is impure or the hydrogen chloride is introduced very rapidly, a flocculent precipitate may be formed. This may be ignored since the diphenyllead dichloride is easily recognized in the presence of the flocks. When the flow of hydrogen chloride has been stopped, reflux the solution to complete the reaction with dissolved hydrogen chloride. Distil off the chloroform on a water bath and extract the residue with two 50 ml portions of hot ethanol. Evaporate the alcohol until triphenyllead chloride begins to crystallize; cool the solution, filter by suction, and dry the product on the filter.

(B) *The preparation of diphenyllead dichloride*

Pass excess hydrogen chloride into a solution of tetraphenyllead (5 g) in benzene (50 ml) at *ca.* 50°C. When the reaction appears complete filter off the shiny plates of diphenyllead dichloride.

Complementary work:
(1) Identify each product from the infrared spectrum.
(2) Write an equation for the formation of tetraphenyllead.

References
Gilman, H. and Robinson, J. D., *J. Amer. Chem. Soc.*, (1929), **51**, 3112.

Gilman, H., Summers, L. and Leeper, R. W., *J. Org. Chem.*, (1952), **17**, 630.

The preparation of N-trimethylborazine

The reaction between diborane and ammonia at elevated temperatures gives a mixture of products, including borazine, $B_3N_3H_6$. This molecule has a planar cyclic structure containing alternating B—N linkages. The molecule is isoelectronic with benzene and has similar physical properties. However, the greater polarity of a B—N bond compared with a C—C bond results in marked differences in chemical behaviour. More recently syntheses of borazine and substituted borazines have been developed which do not require the use of diborane. This eliminates the problems associated with the handling of diborane. The reaction between sodium borohydride and ammonium chloride or an alkylammonium chloride in a high boiling solvent gives borazine or N-substituted borazines. Methylammonium chloride gives a higher yield of product than ammonium chloride, and the preparation of N-trimethylborazine is described below. The reaction must be carried out in an inert atmosphere to obtain a high yield of product.

The preparation of N-trimethylborazine

Materials required: Sodium borohydride
Methylammonium chloride
Triethylene glycol dimethyl ether

Mix together sodium borohydride (5·5 g) and methylammonium chloride (10 g) and place the mixture in a 1-litre three-necked flask. All further manipulations should be carried out in a dry box. Fit the flask with a dropping funnel, a stirrer, and a reflux condenser. Care must be exercised when using the reflux condenser, since a *dry* atmosphere must be preserved in the box. Place a dry condenser in the dry box. Use pressure tubing to attach the condenser to the water supply, and fasten the rubber tubing securely by means of circular clips. Leave the condenser connected in this way until all the experimental work is complete. Before disconnecting the condenser, drain out all the water and seal the rubber tubing with screw clips. Add triethylene glycol dimethyl ether (40 ml) from the dropping funnel and heat the flask on a heating mantle. Continue to heat the flask until the solvent is refluxing and hydrogen evolution has ceased. Evolution of hydrogen is essentially complete after about two hours. Allow the flask to cool and then distil the product (b.p. 134°C) from the mixture. Redistil the product. Prepare a sample for infrared analysis and place ~0·5 ml samples in four stoppered test tubes. Remove the infrared cell and the tubes from the dry box and carry out the reactions listed below.

In this preparation a considerable amount of hydrogen is evolved. This will be carried out of the dry box in the nitrogen stream. *As a precautionary measure the exit stream from the dry box must be led away to a fume cupboard or to an open window.*

Complementary work:

(1) Measure the infrared spectrum of the product [2].

(2) Investigate the reaction of the product with (*a*) water, (*b*) ethyl alcohol, (*c*) copper(II) sulphate solution, warm gently, and (*d*) bromine water. Comment on your observations. Compare the results with the behaviour of the corresponding aromatic carbon compound.

(3) How does the stability of boron-nitrogen ring compounds compare with the stability of analogous boron-phosphorus ring compounds?

References

[1] Haworth, D. T., and Hohnstedt, L. F., *Chem. and Ind.*, (1960), 559.

[2] Watanabe, H., Kuroda, Y. and Kubo, M., *Spectrochim. Acta*, (1961), **17**, 454.

[3] Sheldon, J. C. and Smith, B. C., *Quart. Rev.*, (1960), **14**, 200.

[4] *Borax to boranes*, p. 232. Advances in Chemistry Series, No. 32, American Chemical Society.

Bibliography

Jonassen, H. B. and Weissberger, A., *Technique of Inorganic Chemistry*, Vol. III, p. 259, Interscience, New York, (1963).

17 Spectroscopic techniques

Introduction

The application of spectroscopic techniques to the solution of chemical problems is now well established. The following account deals primarily with experimental procedure, which will enable the reader to carry out successfully the spectroscopic aspects of the experimental work described previously. The interpretation of results is discussed and an elementary theoretical treatment presented. This treatment, although not exhaustive, is introduced in order that the reader may more readily correlate theory with practice. Many advanced texts are available which deal with the basic theory of spectroscopy, and some are suitable for student use.

Spectroscopy is concerned with the study of energy transitions in atoms and molecules, and the interpretation of these transitions in terms of atomic and molecular structure. At room temperature most molecules and atoms exist in the lowest energy state, known as the ground state. When a molecule or atom interacts with electromagnetic radiation (e.g. light), energy is absorbed by the molecule or atom which is consequently raised to a higher energy state. This absorption of energy varies with the structure of the molecule and with the wavelength or frequency of the incident radiation. The way in which absorption varies with frequency or wavelength is referred to as an absorption spectrum, and a variety of instrumental techniques is available for observing and recording such a spectrum.

The various types of radiation available for energizing molecules are indicated in Figure 20 together with their wavelength range.

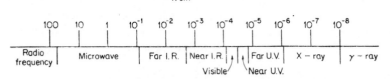

Figure. 20. Wavelength range of various types of radiation.

Units

Radiation may be described in terms of wavelength (λ) or frequency (ν). These two quantities are related by the equation

$$\nu = c/\lambda$$

where c = the velocity of light, cm sec^{-1}

ν = the frequency, sec^{-1}

λ = the wavelength, cm.

The units of frequency and wavelength as indicated above are not convenient for all types of radiation, and other units have been adopted. In particular, frequency is seldom used and is replaced by wave number. The relationship between wave number, wavelength, and frequency is shown by the following equation:

$$\text{Wave number } (\bar{\nu}) = \frac{1}{\text{wavelength } (\lambda) \text{ cm}} = \frac{\text{frequency } (\nu)}{\text{velocity of light } (c)}.$$

The unit of wave number is cm^{-1} which can be readily derived by writing the units in the above equation,

$$\text{Units of wave number} = \frac{1}{\text{cm}} = \frac{\text{sec}^{-1}}{\text{cm sec}^{-1}}.$$

The concept of wave number is also useful since it is a direct measure of energy. Consider the relation between energy (E) and frequency (ν).

$$E = h\nu, \quad \text{where } h = \text{Planck's constant.}$$

This may be rewritten

$$E = \frac{hc}{\lambda}$$

$$= hc\bar{\nu}$$

and since h and c are constants $\bar{\nu}$ must be an energy term.

Units of wavelength other than centimetres are often used, the most commonly encountered being microns, millimicrons, and Ångström units. These are given the symbols μ, $m\mu$ and Å respectively. They are related in the following way:

$$1\mu = 10^{-4}\text{cm}$$
$$1m\mu = 10^{-3}\mu = 10^{-7}\text{cm}$$
$$10^{-8}\text{cm} = 1\text{Å}.$$

Energy and transitions

The relationship between frequency (or wave number) and energy just discussed, shows quite clearly that the magnitude of a quantum of energy varies with the frequency of the radiation. Radiation of high frequency carries larger quanta of energy than radiation of lower frequency. Thus the energy sequence for the most commonly encountered forms of radiation is:

radio-frequency < microwave < infrared < visible < ultraviolet.

We shall be concerned in the main with spectra arising from the absorption of infrared, visible, and ultraviolet radiation by molecules.

A molecule possesses electronic, vibrational, and rotational energy and to a first approximation the total energy E of a molecule may be represented by

$$E = E_{\text{el.}} + E_{\text{vib.}} + E_{\text{rot.}}$$

where $E_{\text{el.}}$ = electronic energy

$E_{\text{vib.}}$ = vibrational energy

$E_{\text{rot.}}$ = rotational energy.

The rotational energy levels of a molecule are close together, of the order of 1–20 cm^{-1} apart, and hence only a small quantum of energy is required to effect a transition from a lower to a higher energy state. This is readily brought about by radiation in the far infrared and microwave region of the spectrum: Vibrational energy levels of a molecule are much further apart (*ca.* 100–4000 cm^{-1}) and so require larger quanta of energy to effect transitions between them. Infrared radiation (*ca.* 664–6000 cm^{-1}) is effective for this purpose and is a much used portion of the spectrum for analytical purposes.

Vibrational transitions are always accompanied by rotational transitions so that the spectrum does not appear as a series of lines but rather as a set of bands.

Each band represents a vibrational transition accompanied by transitions between rotational energy levels of the molecule. Figure 21 shows a typical infrared spectrum in the 2·5–15μ region. Visible

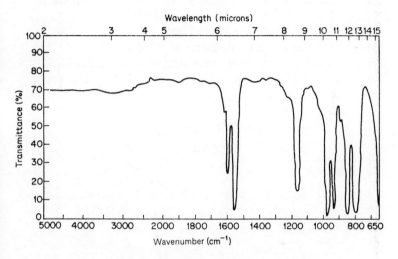

Figure 21. Infrared spectrum of hexachlorobutadiene.

and ultraviolet radiation is even more energetic than the infrared and is capable of promoting electrons in the molecule from a low energy to a higher energy orbital, thus giving rise to an electronic absorption spectrum. Electronic transitions are always accompanied by vibrational and rotational transitions, and hence a band spectrum results. Electronic spectra of atoms, which are usually observed in emission rather than absorption, are line spectra since vibrational and rotational transitions cannot occur.

Infrared spectroscopy

Introduction

A vibrating molecule, or group within a molecule, will only absorb infrared radiation if the vibration of that molecule or group produces a change in dipole moment. Vibrations of homonuclear diatomic molecules such as oxygen and nitrogen do not produce a change in dipole moment, and hence such molecules do not give rise to an infrared absorption spectrum. Heteronuclear diatomic molecules and groups, e.g. HCl, $>C=O$, give characteristic infrared absorption spectra, since vibrational motion along the bond axis results in a change in dipole moment.

The frequency at which a given group absorbs is governed by:

(a)   The masses of the vibrating atoms
(b)   The force constant of the bond
(c)   The molecular environment of the group.

Items (a) and (b) are of most importance in determining the absorption frequency of a group. This can be shown by considering a diatomic molecule AB and treating it as a simple harmonic oscillator, when the expression

$$\Delta E = \frac{h}{2\pi} \sqrt{\left(\frac{k}{\mu}\right)}$$

can be derived.

ΔE = the energy difference between two adjacent vibrational levels

k = the stretching force constant

μ = the reduced mass = $m_A m_B/(m_A + m_B)$

where m_A and m_B = the mass of atoms A and B respectively.

Since $E = h\nu$

Then $\nu = \frac{1}{2\pi} \sqrt{\left(\frac{k}{\mu}\right)}$.

Other factors such as mass, inductive, and conjugative effects of adjacent groups are much less important in fixing the absorption frequency of a band.

Group vibrations

It has been observed that many functional groups absorb in a characteristic portion of the spectrum regardless of the type of molecule which contains them. This is because the normal mode of vibration of that group is not influenced to any marked degree by other atoms in the molecule. The variations of group frequency which do occur are often no more than ± 150 cm^{-1} and are due to factors such as mass, inductive, and conjugative effects of adjacent groups.

This concept of typical group vibration is often useful in identifying functional groups in unknown compounds, and tables of typical group absorption frequencies have been compiled to make this task easier. The concept of typical group vibrations is a simplification which implies that the vibration of a particular group is independant of vibrations in the rest of the molecule. This is not necessarily the case. When the atoms in a molecule are of similar mass connected by bonds of similar force constant, the molecule as a whole will participate in the vibration. Such simultaneous vibration of more than one group is refered to as coupling of the group vibrational frequencies. This coupling is demonstrated by the molecule HCN. The absorption band attributed to the C–H stretch involves some C–N motion and vice versa. Further evidence of coupling is obtained from deuteration studies. The C–N absorption is seen to shift from 2089 cm^{-1} in HCN to 1906 cm^{-1} in DCN. If no coupling occurred, deuteration would have little or no effect on the C–N absorption frequency.

Therefore, when interpreting spectra of inorganic compounds due regard should be paid to the complexity of the molecule. The table of typical group frequencies (Table 17.1, p. 164), should be used with caution.

Instrumentation

Many commercial instruments are available for measuring infrared spectra and no attempt is made to describe them all in detail. Fortunately such instruments all have certain basic features in common and it is only in the design of these features that instruments differ.

Every instrument must have the following items:

(1) An energy source

(2) A means of splitting the radiation into its component wavelengths, e.g. a prism or grating.

(3) A suitable place for locating the sample under investigation.

(4) A means of measuring the amount of radiation absorbed by the sample and converting this to an electric signal. Most of the instruments at present available are double-beam instruments, that is, radiation from the source is split into two beams. One beam passes through the sample, and the other beam through a reference material (usually air). The degree of absorption is then

Table 17.1 *Infrared group absorption frequencies. Inorganic ions*

Group	Wave numbers	Microns	Intensity
$BF_4{}^-$	*ca.* 1,060	*ca.* 9·43	vs
$CO_3{}^{2-}$	1,450–1,410	6·90– 7·09	vs
	880–800	11·36–12·50	s
CN and CNO$^-$	2,200–2,000	4·55– 5·00	m
C—N in SCN(a)	2,086–2,120	4·72– 4·79	s
C—S in SCN(a)	696–706	14·16–14·37	w
C—N in NCS(a)	2,040–2,123	4·71– 4·90	s
C—S in NCS(a)	844–863	11·59–11·85	w
$NH_4{}^+$	3,335–3,030	3·00– 3·30	vs
$NO_2{}^-$	1,400–1,300	7·14– 7·69	s
	1,250–1,230	8·00– 8·13	w
	840–800	11·90–12·50	w
$NO_3{}^-$	1,410–1,340	7·09– 7·46	vs
	860–800	11·63–12·50	m
$NO_2{}^+$	1,410–1,370	7·09– 7·30	s
NO^+	2,370–2,230	4·22– 4·48	s
NO^+(a)	1,940–1,630	5·16– 6·14	s
NO^-(a)	1,170–1,045	8·55– 9·57	s
NO (nitrosyl halides)	1,850–1,790	5·41– 5·59	s
$SO_4{}^{2-}$	1,130–1,080	8·85– 9·26	vs
	680–610	14·71–16·40	vs
$HSO_4{}^-$	1,180–1,160	8·84– 9·26	vs
	1,080–1,000	9·26–10·00	s
	880–840	11·36–11·90	s
	Silicon compounds		
$Si(CH_3)_3$	1,250	8·00	vs
	840	11·90	vs
	755	13·25	vs
$Si(CH_3)_2$	1,259	7·94	vs
	814–800	12·27–12·50	vs
$SiCH_3$	1,259	7·94	vs
	800	12·50	vs
Si–Ph	1,430–1,425	6·99– 7·02	vs
	1,135–1,090	8·81– 9·17	vs
Si—O—Si in cyclic trimers	1,020–1,010	9·80– 9·90	
in cyclic tetramers	1,090–1,080	9·17– 9·26	
in higher rings	1,080–1,050	9·26– 9·52	
Si—O—Si	1,090–1,020	9·17– 9·80	vs
Si—O—C	2,300–2,100	4·35– 4·76	vs
	Boron compounds		
B—N	1,380–1,330	7·25– 7·52	s

vs = very strong; s = strong; m = medium; w = weak
a — coordination compounds.

determined by measuring the difference between the signal obtained from the sample and from the reference material.

Figure 22 is a simple line diagram of an infrared spectrophotometer.

Sample Preparation

(1) *General Remarks.* In order to measure an infrared spectrum, the sample, in a suitable form, must be contained in a vessel which is fitted with windows capable of transmitting infrared radiation. The most commonly used window material is sodium chloride; the window is well polished on both surfaces so that a high degree of transmission is obtained. These windows or plates may be purchased in a polished form, and commercial polishing kits are available, which lightens the task of repolishing to keep the plates up to standard. Sodium chloride is suitable for the wavelength range $2 \cdot 5$–$15 \cdot 0\mu$. Above $15 \cdot 0\mu$ other materials such as potassium or caesium bromide must be used, since sodium chloride begins to absorb infrared radiation above $15 \cdot 0\mu$. Windows used for infrared work are fragile and hygroscopic and must be manipulated with care. They must be stored in a dry atmosphere and not handled except when wearing gloves. Every care must be taken to ensure that samples for infrared spectroscopic examination are free from water. Recently, a new material has become available which is transparent to infrared radiation and is not affected by moisture. This is known as 'Irtran' and windows of this material are available from Eastman Kodak Co. (see *J. Chem. Educ.*, 1966, **43**, A54).

(2) *Solids.* Samples may be prepared (*a*) as a mull, (*b*) dispersed in an alkali halide (usually potassium bromide) disc, or (*c*) in solution.

Preparing a mull. A mull consists of a fine dispersion of solid in an inert mulling agent. Suitable mulling agents include Nujol (a high boiling petroleum fraction) and hexachlorobutadiene. Hexachlorobutadiene is used only when the sample may have bands which are obscured by Nujol absorption bands. The spectra of Nujol and hexachlorobutadiene are shown in Figures 23 and 21.

The sample (2–5 mg) is ground to a fine powder using an agate mortar and pestle. A drop of the mulling agent is added, and the grinding is continued until an even dispersion is obtained. The mull so obtained is transferred by means of a microspatula to a sodium

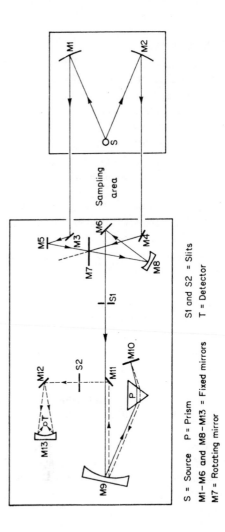

S = Source   P = Prism   S1 and S2 = Slits

M1–M6 and M8–M13 = Fixed mirrors   T = Detector

M7 = Rotating mirror

Figure 22. Simplified optical path of a typical infrared spectrophotometer.

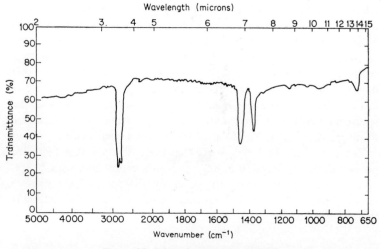

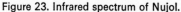

Figure 23. Infrared spectrum of Nujol.

chloride plate and covered with a second sodium chloride plate. Care must be taken to avoid trapping any air bubbles. The plates, contained in a suitable plate holder, are then placed in the sample beam path of the spectrophotometer and the spectrum measured. At this stage the spectrum must be examined to see if all the absorption bands have been resolved, that is the peak of the absorption band must be clearly defined, see Figure 24.

When unresolved bands are observed, two procedures may be followed. The spectrum is re-run using either a thinner layer of the mull, or a new mull is prepared using a smaller amount of sample.

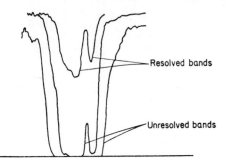

Figure 24. Portion of an infrared spectrum showing resolved and unresolved bands.

Alkali halide disc. This is prepared by thoroughly mixing a small amount of the finely ground sample with dry finely ground alkali halide and compressing the mix to a transparent disc. A 1% w/w mixture of sample with the alkali halide is suitable for materials of molecular weight up to *ca.* 200. The mix is compressed in a suitable device which may be a hand operated, or hydraulic press. The disc is removed from the press, placed in the sample beam, and the spectrum recorded in the usual way. The press must be washed free of all traces of alkali halide after the disc has been made.

The use of an alkali halide disc has the advantage that there are no extraneous absorption bands, such as are obtained with Nujol, and the absorption bands are generally sharper and show more detail. Heat is generated in the formation of a disc and the method is therefore unsuitable for heat sensitive compounds.

(3) *Liquids and solutions.* The spectrum of a liquid may be examined as a film between suitable plates. A drop of the liquid is placed on a plate and covered with a second plate, care being taken to avoid the inclusion of air bubbles. The spectrum may also be observed using specially constructed cells of a known path length; a typical cell of fixed path length is illustrated in Figure 25. The liquid is introduced

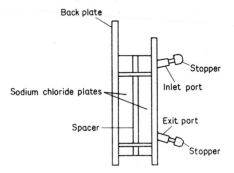

Figure 25. Infrared liquid cell of fixed path length (side view).

into the cell via the inlet port using a glass dropper. When the cell is full, plastic stoppers are placed at the end of the inlet and outlet ports. After use the cell is washed out with a suitable solvent and dried with a current of dry air.

The measurement of solution spectra is usually done in cells of known path length as described above for liquids. The most frequently used solvents are chloroform, carbon tetrachloride, or carbon disulphide. When measuring solution spectra a compensating cell is often used; that is a cell of identical path length to the sample cell is filled with pure solvent, and placed in the reference beam. The recorded spectrum is then that of solution minus solvent, i.e. the solute, except in those regions where the solvent absorbs strongly.

(4) *Gases*. Although commercially produced gas cells are available, a simple glass cell can be readily constructed and is shown in Figure 26.

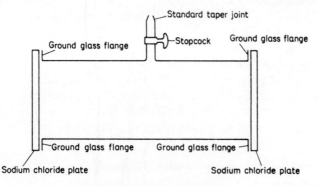

Figure 26. Infrared gas cell.

This consists of a length of glass tubing, the ends of which are fashioned into ground glass flanges, giving an overall length of 10 cm. The sodium chloride plates are attached to these flanges by means of silicone grease. The cell may be attached to a vacuum system for evacuation. A known pressure of gas for spectrum measurement can then be admitted, and the cell sealed by closing the attached stopcock, see p. 141. The cell is placed in the sample beam path of a spectrophotometer and the spectrum measured in the usual way.

Experiments
The complex $Ni(CN)_2(NH_3)$ and its clathrate with benzene have been prepared and some indication of clathrate formation has been obtained from the figures for nickel analyses, see p. 63. Confirmation may be obtained by studying the infrared spectra of the two materials.

Prepare a mull in Nujol of each of the compounds and measure the infrared spectrum. Any differences between the two spectra should be noted and checked against an authentic spectrum of benzene. From the correlation tables provided, (see p. 164), identify the bands due to C≡N and N—H absorption.

The following experiments also provide compounds which can be analysed by infrared spectroscopy:

The preparation of nitro- and nitrito-pentamminecobalt(III) chloride p. 105
The preparation of dithiocyanatobis(triphenylarsine)-palladium(II) p. 106
The products from the cobalt(II) bromide catalysed oxidation of *p*-xylene p. 109
The product from the pentacyanocobaltate(II) ion catalysed hydrogenation of buta-1,3-diene p. 115
The preparation of a boron trifluoride-ammonia adduct p. 143
The preparation of nitrosonium hexachloroantimonate p. 146
The preparation of silicone polymers p. 132
The preparation of tetrakis(thiourea)platinum(II) chloride p. 96

Electronic spectra of coordination compounds

Introduction

The colour of coordination compounds of the transition elements is one of their characteristic properties. These colours are due to the absorption and subsequent emission of light in the visible part of the spectrum. Light in this region of the spectrum causes promotion of *d* electrons from a lower to a higher energy level. The spectra which result are generally referred to as Electronic Spectra. Note that electronic transitions may also be effected by ultraviolet light. Because of the size of the quanta involved, electronic transitions in molecules are always accompanied by vibrational and rotational changes, and hence a band spectrum is observed. In general, the bands which arise are much broader than bands in an infrared spectrum and are little used for identification purposes.

The crystal field theory of bonding in transition metal complexes has helped appreciably to rationalize many of the physical properties of such complexes. The student must have a knowledge of this theory before proceeding further. Much of the data required for crystal field theory calculations is obtained from a study of the absorption spectra of transition metal complexes. It is instructive, therefore, to consider what data can be obtained from the measurement of such spectra.

Consider the simplest possible case, namely a complex in which there is one electron in a d level, as in the ion $[Ti(H_2O)_6]^{3+}$. The origin of the spectrum can be readily explained. The spectrum appears as a single absorption band at 20,000 cm^{-1}. The water ligands have split the degeneracy of the free gaseous ion into two: the t_{2g} and e_g levels, and in the ground state the electron occupies the t_{2g} level. Irradiation of the complex with light of an appropriate frequency results in excitation of the electron in the lower t_{2g} level to the higher e_g level. Knowing that light of frequency 20,000 cm^{-1} is required the crystal field splitting energy for a d^1 system in an octahedral field of water ligands can be calculated.

The interpretation of spectra of complexes in which the central metal ion has more than one but less than nine d electrons is more complicated, and requires the use of an energy-level diagram. The Russell-Saunders states of a free ion when placed in a crystal field are split into different energy states. The energy level diagram shows how the magnitude of this splitting is affected by the crystal field splitting energy, Δ_o. Since Δ_o varies with the nature of the ligands in the complex, the energy level diagram is simply a way of showing how the Russell-Saunders states of the free ion vary with the nature of the ligands in the complex. The crystal field states are referred to by their Mulliken symbols. Mulliken symbols originate in group theory but we will regard them as a convenient label for a particular energy state or level. The energy level diagram for a d^2 ion is shown in Figure 27. The Mulliken states are shown on the extreme right of the diagram. A typical d^2 ion is $[V(H_2O)_6]^{3+}$, the spectrum of which is given in Figure 28. The spectrum shows three absorption bands at 17,200, 25,000, and 38,000 cm^{-1}.

A complete explanation of the spectrum can only be given in the light of certain selection rules indicating which electronic transitions give rise to optical absorption and which do not.

In a free atom, transitions which involve the redistribution of electrons within a quantum shell are forbidden. The strict operation of this rule would mean that no absorption due to transitions within the d shell would be observed. When the ion forms part of a compound, the ion need not have a centre of symmetry and the d and p orbitals of the ion may become mixed together to some extent. An electronic transition now involves some transfer from a d orbital to a

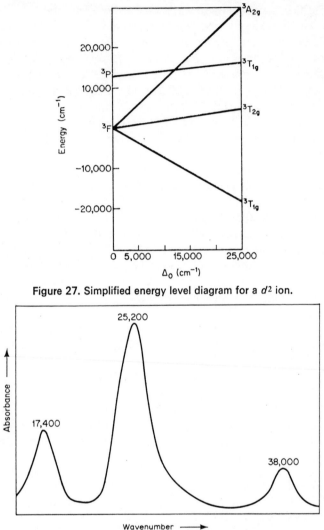

Figure 27. Simplified energy level diagram for a d^2 ion.

Figure 28. Electronic spectrum of the $[V(H_2O)_6]^{3+}$ ion.

p orbital, this is allowed, and hence a low intensity absorption band is observed.

If, in a compound the transition metal ion is at a centre of symmetry, mixing of the d and p orbitals cannot occur. However, during the course of molecular vibration the ion spends part of the time away from the equilibrium position and d and p orbitals can now mix together.

There is also a selection rule which prohibits transitions between states of different spin multiplicity (actually some multiplicity-forbidden transitions do occur but the resultant absorption is so weak that they are not ordinarily observed). Therefore, in the d^2 case only transitions from the ground state, $^3T_1(F)$ to the three excited states $^3T_2$, $^3A_2$, and $^3T_1(P)$ can occur. Consider the energy diagram in Figure 27. A position on the x axis can be selected where the magnitude of these transitions corresponds (or nearly so) with the frequency of the absorption bands quoted above. In this case a Δ_0 value of 21,500 cm^{-1} would be expected to give three transitions at 17,300, 25,500, and 38,600 cm^{-1}. This is in close agreement with the bands actually observed.

The spectrochemical series

The magnitude of the d orbital splittings for a particular metal ion varies with the nature of the ligands coordinated around that metal. Extensive study of the spectra of a large number of complexes has shown that ligands may be arranged in order of their ability to cause d orbital splittings. For the most common ligands the order is

$$CN^- > NO_2^- > NH_2 \cdot CH_2 \cdot CH_2 \cdot NH_2 > NH_3 > NCS^- > H_2O \sim C_2O_4{}^{2-}$$
$$> OH^- > F^- > Cl^- > Br^- > I^-.$$

Consideration of this series enables one to predict the relative frequencies of absorption bands of complexes of a given metal ion with different ligands.

Instrumentation

A large number of instruments is available for the measurement of visible, and ultraviolet spectra. The basic features of these instruments are similar to those which were enumerated when discussing infrared spectrometers, with suitable modifications to accommodate a different region of the spectrum. The energy source usually consists of two lamps, a tungsten filament lamp for the visible region of the spectrum, and a hydrogen discharge lamp for the ultraviolet. These lamps effectively cover the wavelength region 15,000–50,000 cm^{-1}, and can be switched in and out as required. The optics of the instrument are constructed of quartz as are the cells used for containing the sample to be studied. Where only a visible spectrum is to be measured, Pyrex cells may be used.

Light from the source is reflected, by an arrangement of mirrors, into the monochromator where it is dispersed by a quartz prism. A narrow bandwidth of this light is then selected by a suitably placed slit. This narrow beam of monochromatic light then passes through the sample and is allowed to impinge on a suitable detector. Rotation of the prism results in light of different wavelength passing through the sample, and hence the spectrum is scanned. The detector is a device for converting light energy into electrical energy. It may be a photocell, in which case two are required, each being sensitive to a different region of the spectrum; or a photomultiplier tube may be employed. Whichever method of detection is used, a measure of the amount of light absorbed by the sample can be obtained from the magnitude of the electrical signal produced in the detector. The signal from the detector is amplified and displayed in some convenient way. The method of display varies from instrument to instrument, and may consist of a percentage transmittance scale on a calibrated dial in the case of the manually operated instruments, or a completely drawn out spectrum in the case of the fully automatic machines.

Sample preparation

Ultraviolet and visible spectra of solids and liquids are usually measured in solution; in the present work aqueous solutions are used exclusively. The cells which contain the sample have the two light-transmitting faces polished. Care must be taken to avoid scratching, or touching these faces with ones hands.

Prior to use, wash the cell with distilled water and then wash it several times with the solution to be examined. Fill the cell with this solution, wipe the polished faces dry with lens tissue, and place the cell in the sample beam of the instrument. Follow the manufacturers' instructions with regard to the operation of the particular instrument in use. After the spectrum has been measured wash the cell thoroughly with distilled water to remove all traces of the sample solution.

The determination of Δ_0 for the ion $[Ti(H_2O)_6]^{3+}$

Materials required: Titanium(III) chloride

Titanium(III) chloride may be prepared by the electrolytic reduction of titanium(IV) chloride, (see p. 86), or purchased as an aqueous solution. Measure the spectrum of the aqueous solution using a 1 cm cell. A $\sim$3% solution gives a band of suitable intensity.

Complementary work:

(1) Determine the position of maximum absorption and hence calculate the crystal field splitting energy for a d^1 system in an octahedral environment of water ligands.

(2) What is the probable geometric structure of the excited ion?

(3) What effect does this have on the absorption band?

The determination of Δ_0 for certain ligands, and construction of part of the spectrochemical series

---

Materials required: (1) Tris(ethylenediamine)chromium(III) sulphate. (See p. 93)

(2) Potassium trioxalatochromate(III). (See p. 56)

(3) Chloropentaquochromium(III) chloride. (See p. 102).

(4) Potassium chromium(III) sulphate (chrome alum)

(5) Dichlorotetraquochromium(III) chloride

The synthesis of compounds (1)–(3) in the above list has been described in the text (page references are indicated above) and compounds (4) and (5) are available commercially. Measure the spectra of these compounds in aqueous solution over the range 350–750 mμ; in the case of the hexaquo complex it is desirable to measure the spectrum over the range 200–750 mμ in order to include all the absorption bands.

The recommended approximate concentrations and cell path lengths are given in Table 17.2. Note that by using a fairly strong solution a band due to a low-intensity, spin-forbidden transition may be observed in the high wavelength region of the spectrum of the tris(ethylenediamine)chromium(III) ion.

Use the spectra so obtained to determine the positions of the maxima and from the energy level diagram given in Figure 29 determine Δ_0 for the ligands; water, ethylenediamine, and oxalate.

Table 17.2 *Recommended concentrations*

Compound	Concentration	Path length (cm)
$[Cr\,en_3]_2\,(SO_4)_3$	(1) 0·25 g in 10 ml (Soln. A)	4
	(2) Dilute 5 ml of A to 100 ml	4
$K_3[Cr(C_2O_4)_3]\cdot3H_2O$	(1) 0·15 g in 10 ml (Soln. B)	4
	(2) Dilute 1 ml of B to 10 ml	4
$K_2SO_4\cdot Cr_2\,(SO_4)_3\cdot24H_2O$	0·1 g in 10 ml	1
$[Cr(H_2O)_4Cl_2]\,Cl\cdot2H_2O$	0·11 g in 10 ml	1
$[Cr(H_2O)_5Cl]\,Cl_2\cdot H_2O$	0·13 g in 10 ml	1

Examine qualitatively the spectra of the two chloroaquo-isomers and hence decide which of the two ligands, water or chloride, produces the greater *d* orbital splitting. An abbreviated spectrochemical series can now be constructed for the four ligands considered.

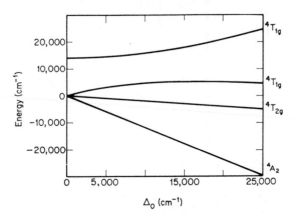

Figure 29. Simplified energy level diagram for a d^3 ion.

Colorimetry

Introduction

In the spectrophotometric work carried out so far, little emphasis has been placed upon the intensity of absorption bands in either infrared, visible, or ultraviolet spectra. It will have been noticed from the work done on the spectra of coordination compounds that by increasing the concentration of the solute the intensity of the

absorption band(s) is increased. In other words, the more concentrated a solution the more light is absorbed by the solution at a
particular wavelength. Conversely, less light is transmitted by that
solution.

The relationship between the concentration of a solute in solution
and the light transmitted by that solution was first recognized by
Beer, and a quantitative relationship established. Beer found that
the intensity of a transmitted beam of monochromatic light decreases
exponentially as the concentration of the absorbing substance increases arithmetically. This relationship may be expressed in the form

$$I_t = I_o.e^{-kc}$$

where I_o = the intensity of the incident light

I_t = the intensity of the transmitted light

c = the concentration

k = is a constant.

Transposing to base 10 gives the equation

$$I_t = I_o. 10^{-0.4343\,kc} = I_o. 10^{-Kc}$$

where K is a constant.

A similar law obtains between the thickness of the solution and
the intensity of the emitted light. This is known as Lambert's law
and states: the intensity of the transmitted light decreases exponentially as the thickness of the absorbing medium increases arithmetically. This relationship may also be expressed in the form

$$I_t = I_o. e^{-k^1 l} = I_o. 10^{-0.4343\,k^1 l} = I_o. 10^{-K^1 l}$$

where k^1 and K^1 are constants

l = the thickness of the solution in cm.

The two laws may be combined to give the equation,

$$I_t = I_o . 10^{-\varepsilon cl}$$

or $$\log \frac{I_o}{I_t} = \varepsilon cl$$

which is often referred to as the Beer-Lambert law. If c is expressed
in g moles/litre and l in centimetres then ε is the molecular extinction
coefficient.

Two other terms are in common use in colorimetry, these are;

optical density D, and transmission T. Optical density is defined as the logarithmic ratio of the intensity of the incident light to that of the transmitted light, which in a mathematical form is written

$$D = \log\left(\frac{I_o}{I_t}\right). \qquad (17.1)$$

Transmission is defined as the ratio of the intensity of the transmitted light to that of the incident light, that is

$$T = \frac{I_t}{I_o}. \qquad (17.2)$$

By combining equations (17.1) and (17.2) it can be seen that the relationship between optical density and transmission is given by

$$D = -\log T.$$

It is important to distinguish clearly between optical density and transmission, since spectrophotometers are frequently calibrated in both units.

Beer's law will apply over a wide range of concentration, provided the structure of the solute does not change with concentration. Deviations from the law occur when the solute associates, or dissociates in solution, since the nature of the light-absorbing species is then changing with concentration. The validity of Beer's law for a particular system can be readily checked by plotting a graph of optical density against concentration. A straight line will result if Beer's law is obeyed.

When using colorimetric techniques for quantitative analysis two operations must first be carried out:

(1) Determine the absorption spectrum of the species to be measured. Select a region in the spectrum where the species absorbs strongly and use this region for subsequent measurements.

(2) Using the region of the spectrum determined above measure the variation of optical density with concentration, and plot the results graphically.

The concentration of an unknown solution of the solute can now be determined by measuring the optical density, and reading off the concentration from the graph. In the work to be described below a colorimetric technique will be used to follow a reaction rate.

An investigation of the rate of isomerization of *trans*-potassium dioxalatodiaquochromate(III) to the *cis* isomer

Materials required: Cis- and *trans*-potassium dioxalatodiaquochro-mate(III). (The preparation of these two compounds is described on p. 91)
Perchloric acid.

Measure the absorption spectrum of each isomer in aqueous solution over the range 300–600 mμ. A solution containing 1·5–2·0 g/l will be found satisfactory. When measuring the spectrum of the *trans* isomer dissolve the compound in ice-cold water in order to minimize isomerization to the *cis* isomer while the spectrum is being measured. Plot a graph of optical density against wavelength, and from this determine the wavelength at which to study the isomerization; that is the wavelength at which there is the maximum difference in absorption between the two isomers.

The kinetic measurements
Dissolve the *trans* isomer (0·07–0·1 g) in 50 ml of 10^{-4}M perchloric acid in a graduated flask and allow this solution to stand for about two hours at 25°C until isomerization is virtually complete. A sample of this solution is then placed in a 1 cm cell in the cell carriage of a suitable spectrometer. A second sample, equal in weight to the first is also dissolved in 50 ml of 10^{-4}M perchloric acid which has been kept at 25°C. A 1 cm cell is quickly filled with this solution and placed in the cell carriage. If possible, use a thermostatted cell holder. The difference in optical density between the two solutions is then measured, initially at 2-minute intervals. As the reaction slows down, the time intervals may be increased.

Theory
The optical density D of a solution containing two absorbing species A and B is given by

$$D_t = l\{\varepsilon_A[A]_t + \varepsilon_B[B]_t\} \qquad (17.3)$$

If A and B are reactant and product respectively in a first-order reaction the rate law is given by the expression

$$\frac{d[A]}{dt} = -k[A] \qquad (17.4)$$

by integration $[A]_t = [A]_o e^{-kt}$ $\qquad$ (17.5)

where $\qquad$ $[A]_t$ = the concentration of A at time t

$\qquad\qquad$ $[A]_o$ = the initial concentration of A.

Therefore the concentration of B after time t is given by the expression

$$[B]_t = [A]_o - [A]_o e^{-kt}. \qquad (17.6)$$

Substituting for $[A]_t$ and $[B]_t$ in equation (17.3) gives

$$D_t = l\{\varepsilon_A[A]_o e^{-kt} + \varepsilon_B[A]_o - \varepsilon_B[A_o] e^{-kt}\}$$

therefore $\qquad \dfrac{D_t}{l[A]_o} = \{\varepsilon_A - \varepsilon_B\} e^{-kt} + \varepsilon_B$

therefore $\qquad \dfrac{D_t}{l[A]_o} - \varepsilon_B = \{\varepsilon_A - \varepsilon_B\} e^{-kt}. \qquad (17.7)$

Therefore by plotting the logarithm of the left-hand side of equation (17.7) against time, a straight line of slope $-k$ results. To make such a plot requires a knowledge of ε_B and $[A]_o$. In the present work ε_B is unknown and hence a somewhat different approach is followed.

The quantity measured is the difference between the optical density of the isomerizing *trans* isomer solution and the optical density of an exactly similar solution which has undergone virtually complete isomerization. The absorption spectrum of the isomerized *trans* isomer is identical with that of the *cis* isomer.

Let $\qquad$ D_T = the optical density of the *trans* isomer in solution

and $\qquad$ D_c = the optical density of the *cis* isomer in solution

$\qquad$ D_1, D_2, D_3 = the optical densities of isomerizing solution at time $t_1, t_2, t_3 \ldots$

$\qquad$ D_1^i, D_2^i, D_3^i = the optical densities of the isomerizing solution at time $t_1 + \Delta t, t_2 + \Delta t, t_3 + \Delta t \ldots$

where Δt = a constant time interval = the time elapsing between making up the two solutions.

Now $\qquad\qquad (D_c - D_1) = (D_c - D_T) e^{-kt_1}. \qquad (17.8)$

This follows from the first-order rate equation (17.5) since $(D_c - D_T)$ is a measure of the initial concentration of the solution containing the *trans* isomer, and $(D_c - D_1)$ is a measure of the *trans* isomer remaining in solution after time t_1.

Similarly

$$D_c - D_1^i = (D_c - D_T) e^{-k(t_1 + \Delta t)}. \qquad (17.9)$$

Subtracting equation (17.9) from equation (17.8) gives

$$(D_1^i - D_1) = (D_c - D_T) \{e^{-kt_1} - e^{-k(t_1 + \Delta t)}\}$$

therefore $(D_1^i - D_1) = (D_c - D_T) \{e^{-kt_1} (1 - e^{-k\Delta t})\}$

therefore $\qquad \dfrac{(D_1^i - D_1)}{(D_c - D_T)} e^{kt_1} = 1 - e^{-k\Delta t}$

therefore $\qquad e^{kt_1} = \dfrac{(1 - e^{-k\Delta t}) (D_c - D_T)}{(D_1^i - D_1)}.$

Taking logarithms

$$kt_1 = \ln(1 - e^{-k\Delta t}) (D_c - D_T) - \ln(D_1^i - D_1).$$

Similarly

$$kt_2 = \ln(1 - e^{-k\Delta t}) (D_c - D_T) - \ln(D_2^i - D_2)$$

and in general

$$kt = \text{constant} - \ln D$$
$$= \text{constant} - 2 \cdot 303 \log_{10} D$$

where $D =$ the difference in optical density between the two solutions at time t.

Therefore by plotting $\log_{10} D$ against time in seconds a straight line should result, showing that the reaction is first order. From the plot determine the velocity constant k for the isomerization.

The reaction rate may be determined at temperatures up to 35°C provided a thermostatted cell holder is available. Different members of a class could determine the reaction rate at different temperatures and hence sufficient data obtained to calculate the activation energy and frequency factor for the reaction.

References
King, E. L., *J. Amer. Chem. Soc.*, (1952), **74**, 563.
Hamm, R. E., *J. Amer. Chem. Soc.*, (1953), **75**, 609.
Ashley, K. R. and Hamm, R. E., *Inorg. Chem.* (1965), **4**, 1120.

The determination of the composition of complex ions in solution by a spectrophotometric method

The formation of a complex in solution is often accompanied by the appearance of a colour. Measurement of the optical density of such a solution will afford a measure of the amount of complex ion in solution (see p. 176). For a reaction of the type,

$$M^{n+} + yL \rightleftharpoons [ML_y]^{n+} \qquad (17.10)$$

the amount of complex ion in solution can be determined colorimetrically for various ratios of $[M^{n+}]$ to $[L]$; the *total* concentration of metal ion and ligand is kept constant. Measurements of optical density at a suitable wavelength will show a maximum when the ratio of ligand to metal is equal to that in the complex. The method is known as 'Job's Method', after the originator, and is often referred to as 'The Method of Continuous Variation.' Measurements may be made at any wavelength where the complex shows appreciable absorption. A position of maximum absorption is preferred.

If the measurements are made at only one wavelength then the system must be such that only one complex is formed. This may be verified by making measurements at a number of wavelengths within the absorption spectrum of the complex(es). If measurements at all wavelengths give the same result it may be concluded that only a single compound is formed. Note that concurrent formation of a colourless compound may be overlooked by this method.

Theory
The discussion will be confined to the case where only one complex species is formed. Consider reaction (17.10), above.

Let c_1, c_2, and $c_3 = $ the concentration of M^{n+}, L, and $[ML_y]^{n+}$, respectively. Mixtures of L and M^{n+} are prepared by mixing solution of a moles/l in the ratio $x:(1 - x)$ by volume. Thus keeping the total concentration constant.

$$c_1 = a(1 - x) - c_3 \qquad (17.11)$$

$$c_2 = ax - yc_3 \qquad (17.12)$$

$$c_1 c_2{}^y = Kc_3 \qquad (17.13)$$

where K = the equilibrium constant of reaction (17.10). The condition for a maximum in the plot of c_3 against x is that

$$dc_3/dx = 0$$

Differentiating equations, (17.11), (17.12) and (17.13),

$$\frac{dc_1}{dx} = -a - \frac{dc_3}{dx} \qquad (17.14)$$

$$\frac{dc_2}{dx} = a - y\frac{dc_3}{dx} \qquad (17.15)$$

$$c_2{}^y \frac{dc_1}{dx} + yc_1 c_2{}^{(y-1)} \frac{dc_2}{dx} = K\frac{dc_3}{dx}. \qquad (17.16)$$

When

$$dc_3/dx = 0$$

$$c_2{}^y \frac{dc_1}{dx} + yc_1 c_2{}^{(y-1)} \frac{dc_2}{dx} = 0. \qquad (17.17)$$

Dividing equation (17.17) by $c_2{}^{(y-1)}$ gives

$$c_2 \frac{dc_1}{dx} + y^{c_1} \frac{dc_2}{dx} = 0.$$

Substituting for dc_1/dx and dc_2/dx from eqns. (17.14) and (17.15), and taking into account the condition $dc_3/dx = 0$, then

$$- c_2 a + yc_1 a = 0$$

therefore

$$c_2 = yc_1.$$

Substituting $c_1 y$ for c_2 in eqn. (17.12) gives:

$$yc_1 = ax - yc_3. \qquad (17.18)$$

Multiplying equation (17.11) by y gives:

$$yc_1 = ay(1 - x) - c_3 y. \qquad (17.19)$$

Subtracting (17.19) from (17.18) gives:

$$0 = ay(1 - x) - ax$$

therefore

$$y = \frac{ax}{a(1 - x)} = \frac{x}{1 - x}. \qquad (17.20)$$

Therefore by determining the value of x for which c_3 is a maximum, y can be calculated.

To determine the composition of the Fe^{III}—salicylic acid complex

Materials required: Ammonium iron(III) sulphate
                       Salicylic acid

Prepare 500 ml of 2×10^{-3}M solutions of ammonium iron(III) sulphate and 500 ml of a 2×10^{-3}M solution of salicylic acid each in M/500 hydrochloric acid. Prepare a series of mixtures of these two solutions differing by increments of 0·1 in the mole fraction of each component, as indicated below,

ml Fe^{III} solution = 2·5; 5·0; 7·5; . . . 22·5

ml salicylic acid
        solution = 22·5; 20·0; 17·5; . . . 2·5.

Use a suitable spectrometer to measure the spectrum of one of these mixtures and the two original solutions over the range 350–700 mμ, and hence determine the most suitable wavelength for measuring the optical density. For each prepared solution determine the optical density D at the selected wavelength. Plot D against x. From this preliminary plot estimate the approximate value of x at the maximum D. Prepare other solutions in this region of molar proportion. Optical density measurements of these solutions will enable the maximum in the plot of D against x to be more accurately determined.

Note that these plots give a sharp maxima when a single stable complex is the predominant species. When a less stable complex is formed these maxima are broadened and are usually of smaller magnitude.

References
Job, P., *Ann. Chim.*, (1928), **9**, 113.
Vosburgh, W. C. and Cooper, G. R., *J. Amer. Chem. Soc.*, (1941), **63**, 437.

Moore, R. L. and Anderson, R. C., *J. Amer. Chem. Soc.*, (1945), **67**, 167.

Foley, R. T. and Anderson, R. C., *J. Amer. Chem. Soc.*, (1948), **70**, 1195.

Bibliography

Drago, R. S., *Physical Methods in Inorganic Chemistry*, Reinhold, New York, (1965).

Bellamy, L. J., *The Infrared Spectra of Complex Molecules*, Methuen, 2nd Ed., (1958).

Orgel, L. E., *Transition Metal Chemistry*, Methuen, 2nd Ed , (1966).

18 Conductance measurements

Introduction

The conductance of a solution is a measure of the ability of that solution to carry a current. The transfer of electricity through the solution results from the movement of ions. The specific conductance (γ) of a solution may be defined as the current passing across unit area under unit potential gradient. Specific conductance of a solution varies with the number of ions in solution, i.e. with concentration. In order to compare conductances of different compounds some account must be taken of concentration.

Molar conductance, μ, is defined by the expression

$$\mu = \gamma V = \gamma/c \text{ ohm}^{-1} \text{ cm}^2$$

where V = the volume in ml containing 1 mole of solute

c = the concentration, in moles of solute/ml.

Consider equimolar solutions of sodium chloride and barium chloride. The concentration of chloride ions in the solution of barium chloride is double the concentration of chloride ions in the solution of sodium chloride. The amount of charge carried by one barium ion is double the amount of charge carried by a sodium ion. Molar conductance will therefore change with the number of ions produced per mole of solute. A study of molar conductance will provide information as to the number of ions produced per mole of a given solute.

Equivalent conductance allows for this difference in number and charge of ions in equimolar solutions. Equivalent conductance, Λ is defined by the expression

$$\Lambda = \gamma V_e = \gamma/c_e$$

where V_e = the volume in ml containing 1 equivalent of solute

c_e = the concentration in equivalents of solute/ml.

The term equivalent in this context refers to the quantity of solute associated with the transfer of 96,500 coulombs of electricity, when a current is passed. Therefore 1 equivalent = 1 mole/($n.z.$)

where z = the valence of the cation (or anion)

n = the number of cations (or anions) produced per molecule

Conductance measurements on a variety of solutions show that the molar and equivalent conductances increase with decreasing concentration, and approach a constant value in very dilute solution. When determining conductance it is advisable to use very dilute solutions. For very precise work measurements should be made at several concentrations and the values obtained extrapolated to infinite dilution.

Conductance measurements are of assistance in determining solubilities of relatively insoluble salts, measuring salt hydrolysis, titrimetry, and determining the structure of transition metal complexes. Only the last topic will be considered.

Measurement of conductance

The conductance of an electrolyte is measured by placing the solution under investigation, in a suitable container, in one arm of a Wheatstone bridge network. The bridge is balanced and hence the resistance of the solution determined. Although simple in principle, careful attention must be paid to certain experimental details. A high frequency alternating current must be employed. If a direct current is used the electrochemical action at the electrodes of the conductivity cell would give rise to erratic results. Alternating currents in the audio range (1000–4000 Hz) are suitable; they effectively eliminate electrochemical action, and reproducible results can be obtained.

The conductivity cells used for conductance measurements may be of various designs, but all have certain features in common. They are constructed of an insoluble glass such as borosilicate or silica. The electrodes, which are made from stout platinum, are rigidly mounted so that they cannot bend, and their position relative to each other is fixed.

The cell constant

Conductance measurements require a knowledge of the area (A) of the electrodes and the distance (l) between them. The quotient l/A is known as the cell constant, and although it may be determined by direct measurement, it is more usual to measure the conductance of a solution of accurately known equivalent conductance and to determine the cell constant from this. Potassium chloride solutions are invariably used for this purpose.

Preparation of the electrodes

Clean the cell and electrodes with chromic acid, rinse well with distilled water, and fill the cell with platinizing solution. Platinizing solution is 2% in platinum(IV) chloride and 0·02% in lead acetate. Connect both the electrodes to the cathode of a 4-volt battery. Connect the anode of the battery to a piece of platinum wire via a variable resistance. The platinum wire is dipped into the platinizing solution and the variable resistance adjusted until there is a brisk, but not violent, evolution of gas. When the electrodes have acquired a thick velvety layer of platinum black the electrolysis is stopped, the cell and electrodes washed thoroughly with distilled water, and finally with conductance water. Conductance water may be obtained by redistilling distilled or deionized water to which a little potassium permanganate has been added. Use hard glass apparatus. The main impurity in water produced in this way is carbon dioxide dissolved from the air. Keep the electrodes in water when not in use. If the electrodes are already blacked they may be used as they stand, although the best results are obtained by giving the plates a light coating of black on the old one.

The determination of the cell constant

Prepare a 0·0005M solution of potassium chloride using conductance water. Wash the cell out several times with this solution before filling it with the solution. Place the cell and the rest of the solution in a thermostat bath at 25°C. Connect the cell to a suitable conductance bridge and measure the conductance of the solution. Repeat the measurement with other samples of the same solution until concordant results are obtained. Given that the molar conductance of a 0·0005M solution of potassium chloride is 147·8 ohms⁻¹ at 25°C, calculate the cell constant.

Conductance bridges are available which are easy to operate and are accurate to 0·25%. Instruments of this type use an audible method of determining when the bridge is balanced. A pair of head-phones is connected across the bridge and the variable resistors in the bridge are adjusted until no sound can be heard in the headphones. The value of the conductance can then be obtained directly from a calibrated dial.

The preparation of trinitrotriamminecobalt(III)

Materials required: Cobalt(II) acetate
Sodium nitrite
6% Hydrogen peroxide (20 volume)
Aqueous ammonia (S.G. 0·88)
Charcoal

Dissolve sodium nitrite (15 g) in 70 ml of aqueous ammonia (S.G. 0·88); and to this add cobalt(II) acetate (10 g) dissolved in 50 ml of water. Cool the solution in ice, keep the solution at 10°C or below, and add slowly, with constant stirring, 20 ml of 6% hydrogen peroxide. Leave the mixture in the ice bath for a further 20 minutes. Add charcoal (0·5 g) and heat the solution for about ¾ hour. *This operation must be carried out in a fume cupboard since a considerable amount of ammonia is evolved.* Maintain the original volume of solution by adding water as necessary. The end of the reaction is indicated by the separation of a yellow solid, although the colour of the solid may be difficult to discern in the presence of charcoal. Cool the solution in ice, filter off the precipitated product, wash it with ice-cold water, and ethanol. Dry in air.

Recrystallization
Dissolve the crude product in 25 × its own weight of boiling water which has been acidified with a few drops of acetic acid. Filter hot to remove the charcoal. Cool the filtrate in ice, filter off the precipitated product, wash it with ice-cold water, and ethanol. Dry in air, and record the yield.

Complementary work:

(1) Use cerium(IV) sulphate as an oxidant to determine the nitro content of the complex.

(2) Prepare a complex of empirical formula $Co(NH_3)_3$ Cl_3 H_2O by the procedure described below.

(3) Reserve a sample for conductivity measurement.

The preparation of the compound $Co(NH_3)_3Cl_3H_2O$

Materials required: Trinitrotriamminecobalt(III)
                       Urea
                       Concentrated sulphuric and hydrochloric acids

Prepare a solution of mixed acids by adding *slowly, and carefully* 10 ml of concentrated sulphuric acid to 20 ml of ice-cold concentrated hydrochloric acid. Dissolve urea (1 g) in 25 ml of the mixed acids, and cool in ice. A large boiling-tube makes a convenient reaction vessel. Add trinitrotriamminecobalt(III) (1 g), and stir the mixture thoroughly. Allow the mixture to warm to room temperature while continuing to stir; a series of colour changes terminating in green will be observed. With the development of the green colour, warm the mixture to 35–40°C, when nitrogen is evolved. After the evolution of nitrogen has slowed, warm the mixture to 50–60°C and maintain this temperature until the evolution of nitrogen has ceased. Cool the mixture, and add slowly 20 ml of ethanol. Filter the green product so obtained, and wash with ethanol, and acetone. Record the yield.

Conductivity measurements on the compounds $[Co(NH_3)_3(NO_2)_3]$ and $Co(NH_3)_3Cl_3H_2O$

Prepare a 0·0005M solution of the compound $Co(NH_3)_3Cl_3H_2O$ at 0°C and measure the conductance at 0°C. Care must be taken to keep all solutions at 0°C. Determine the molar conductance at 0°C. Prepare 0·0005M solutions of both the compounds under investigation at 25°C and determine their molar conductances.

Comment on the results and on the structure of the two compounds.

Reference

Bailar, J. C., (ed.), *The Chemistry of Coordination Compounds*, Reinhold, New York, (1956), pp. 113–118.

Bibliography

MacInnes, D. A., *The Principles of Electrochemistry*, Dover, New York, (1961).

19 Gas chromatography

Introduction

Gas chromatography is one of a wide range of chromatographic techniques which are used for the separation and analysis of mixtures of gases, liquids, and solids. All chromatographic techniques utilize a two-phase system, one stationary and one mobile. Separation of the components of a mixture is achieved by the different degree of partition of the components between the two phases.

The stationary phase may be a solid, or a liquid supported on an inert solid. The mobile phase may be a gas or a liquid. Accordingly several types of chromatographic procedures are recognized:

(1) Gas-solid chromatography.

(2) Gas-liquid chromatography.

(3) Liquid-liquid chromatography, a special case of which is known as paper chromatography. In paper chromatography the stationary phase is water supported by the cellulose of the paper.

(4) Liquid-solid chromatography. In this system the solid, such as alumina or silica gel, is in the form of a column, or thin layer coated on a glass plate.

In all forms of chromatography the mixture to be separated is placed at one end of the stationary phase, and the mobile phase or eluent is allowed to flow through the mixture and the rest of the stationary phase. This procedure is known as elution. During elution the components of the mixture become resolved due to differences in partition between the two phases. The identity and quantity of each component can then be established by methods which vary, depending upon the type of chromatography employed.

Instrumentation for gas chromatography

Numerous instruments are available for carrying out gas chromatographic analysis. These vary in design and complexity, but all have certain features in common. The basic requirements for a satisfactory analysis are:

(1) A column containing the solid, or liquid supported on a solid.

(2) A source of carrier gas.

(3) A means of measuring the rate of flow of the gas.

(4) Facilities for injecting the sample to be analysed on to the column.

(5) A means of detecting and measuring the components of the mixture as they are eluted from the column.

An additional desirable feature, although not essential, is an oven, to contain the column, injection point, and detector. In this way the temperature may be controlled. Temperatures up to 250°C are usually adequate for most work. Without this facility analyses can only be performed on gases and very volatile liquids.

These five features will now be discussed briefly. A flow diagram is shown in Figure 30.

(1) *The Column* is constructed from glass or metal tubing and can take almost any shape. The most usual shape is a helix wound from $\frac{1}{4}$ in. o.d. metal tubing. The length is varied depending upon the stationary phase used and the mixture to be analysed.

The column packing for gas-liquid chromatography is prepared from an inert solid such as 'Celite' or brick dust and a suitable liquid stationary phase. Liquids in common use include dinonyl phthalate, silicone oils, squalane, 'Apiezon' greases, and fluorocarbon oils and greases. Note that liquids which make satisfactory stationary phases usually have a low vapour pressure. This is desirable since the tendency for the stationary phase to be stripped off the column when working at elevated temperatures is much reduced. To prepare the column packing the liquid is dissolved in a volatile solvent such as diethyl ether, and the inert support stirred into this solution. Evaporation of the ether then leaves a coating of the stationary phase on the solid support. The resulting solid is a free-running powder and can easily be poured into the column. The metal tubing is packed before it is coiled. Plug one end of the tube with glass wool and pour the packing in a little at a time. Tap the metal tubing during this

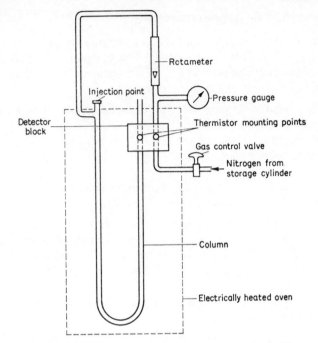

Figure 30. Schematic diagram of a gas liquid chromatographic apparatus.

process to ensure that the packing settles down evenly. It is essential that an even packing is obtained, otherwise channelling of the mobile phase may occur, with consequent lowering of the efficiency of the column. When the column is full the packing is kept in place with a small plug of glass wool.

(2) *The carrier gas* may be either hydrogen, helium, argon, or nitrogen. Nitrogen is favoured for most work since it is inexpensive and readily available. The flow of gas is controlled by a valve on the storage cylinder and by a valve built in to the gas-chromatrographic apparatus.

(3) *The gas flow* may be measured either with a rotameter or a soap-film meter. A rotameter is a short length of calibrated glass tubing containing a closely-fitting conical float. The rate of flow is indicated by the height to which the float rises in the tube. Rotameters are usually connected at the input to the column as shown in Figure 30,

and may be conveniently calibrated against a soap-film meter. When a soap-film meter is used it is attached to the exit of the column. The construction and operation of a soap-film meter has been described elsewhere, see p. 113.

(4) *Injection of the sample* to be analysed is at a point near the beginning of the column. The injection point consists of a small rubber diaphragm which is incorporated into the apparatus. Facilities are provided to heat the apparatus at the point of injection so as to ensure immediate volatilization of the whole of the sample. A glass hypodermic syringe is used for the injection of both liquid and gas samples. Sample sizes of the order of 2–20 μl for liquids and 1–5 ml for gases are usually adequate.

(5) *Methods of detecting* the components of a mixture as they are eluted from the column make use of a difference in a physical property of the pure carrier gas, compared with carrier gas containing an eluted component of the original mixture.

Properties that have been exploited include:

Thermal conductivity
Density
Ease of ionization
Thermal capacity

Instruments have been constructed which can measure small differences in these properties and relate them to a change in an electrical property such as reistance. In the case of a thermal conductivity detector, the sensing element, one type of which is a thermistor, is mounted in the gas stream at the output end of the column. A second, exactly similar thermistor is mounted in such a position that it is in contact with carrier gas only. This is conveniently done by allowing the carrier gas to flow through this part of the apparatus before entering the column. These two thermistors form two arms of a Wheatstone bridge circuit, which is completed by resistors R_1 and R_2, see Figure 31.

The current passing through these thermistors causes them to heat up. The temperature of the thermistor and hence its resistance depends upon the amount of heat conducted away by the surrounding gas stream. When both thermistors are surrounded by carrier gas their temperatures, and hence resistances, will be constant and the Wheatstone bridge circuit can be adjusted by using R_1 so that there is no

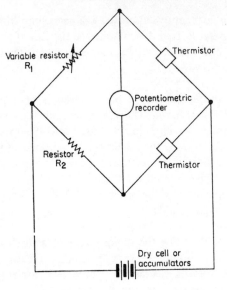

Figure 31. A Wheatstone bridge circuit.

output signal. When a sample is eluted from the column the conductivity of the gas surrounding the sensing thermistor changes. The temperature and the resistance of the thermistor will also change. This change in resistance will unbalance the Wheatstone bridge so that an output signal is produced which can be amplified and displayed. The display usually takes the form of a peak on a recording potentiometer. Figure 32 shows a potentiometric trace produced

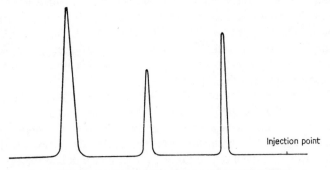

Figure 32. Chromatogram of a three-component system.

when analysing a three-component mixture; such a trace is known as a chromatogram.

The time required for a given compound to be eluted from the column is typical of that compound for a given set of operating conditions. The conditions which affect this time are:

(1) Flow rate, and type of carrier gas used.
(2) Temperature of the column.
(3) Length, and diameter of the column.
(4) Type, and amount of stationary phase.

The time required for a compound to be eluted is known as the retention time. A more fundamental parameter is the retention volume which is the volume of carrier gas required just to elute a compound from the column. Retention volume is the product of the retention time and the flow rate.

Qualitative analysis is carried out by comparing the retention times of the components of a mixture with the retention times of known compounds. Some knowledge of the source of the sample and the possible compounds present is useful in making this interpretation. Further confirmation of the identity of a component may be obtained by adding a small amount of the suspected compound to the unknown mixture, and comparing the chromatogram produced by this mixture with that of the original mixture. If the added compound was present in the original mixture one of the peaks of the chromatogram will increase in size. If the added compound was not present an extra peak will appear on the chromatogram.

An approximate quantitative analysis may be made by measuring the area under each peak of the chromatogram. By estimating each as a fraction of the total peak area the molar fractions of the components in the original mixture can be estimated. For a more accurate quantitative analysis peak areas must be calibrated against the component composition of various known mixtures. By comparing the peak areas of the unknown mixture with the calibrated areas, an estimate of the percentage composition of the mixture can be obtained.

Experiments

The preparations listed below give products which may be analysed by gas chromatography:

The preparation of a sulphur dioxide–quinol clathrate   (p. 61)

Bibliography

Keulemans, A. I. M., *Gas Chromatography*, Reinhold, New York, 2nd ed., (1959).

20 Magnetic measurements

Introduction

The study of materials placed in a magnetic field reveals two types of behaviour. Substances which tend to move from a stronger to a weaker part of the applied field, are referred to as diamagnetic. Substances which tend to move in the reverse sense are known as paramagnetic.

Paramagnetism arises as a result of the presence of unpaired electrons in a substance. Both the spin and the orbital motion of the electrons contribute to the total paramagnetism, although the former has the greater magnitude. When a paramagnetic substance is placed in a magnetic field the atomic, or molecular permanent magnets align themselves in the same direction as the applied field and are thus attracted to it. This alignment of magnetic moments will be opposed by thermal motion and hence the effectiveness of a magnetic field will decrease with increasing temperature. Diamagnetism arises as a result of the interaction of the applied field with a closed shell of electrons, inducing a magnetic moment which must therefore oppose the applied field. Since the direction of the induced magnetic moment is dependent only on the direction of the applied field, diamagnetism is independent of temperature. The measurement of paramagnetic susceptibilities enables the number of unpaired electrons to be determined. In the case of coordination compounds this determination then enables predictions to be made regarding the oxidation state, bond type, and stereochemistry of the metal atom.

When a substance is placed in a magnetic field the relationship

199

between field intensity within the substance, and the applied field is given by

$$B = H + 4\pi I \qquad (20.1)$$

where B = the intensity of the field in the substance, known as the magnetic induction

H = the intensity of the field *in vacuo*

I = the intensity of magnetization.

Dividing the expression (20.1) throughout by H gives

$$\frac{B}{H} = 1 + 4\pi\frac{I}{H}. \qquad (20.2)$$

The quotient B/H is known as the magnetic permeability, and I/H the volume susceptibility. The latter is the quantity determined experimentally and is usually given the symbol κ. Other expressions in use are the susceptibility per unit mass (χ), and the molar susceptibility (χ_M), which are related to κ in the following way

$$\chi = \frac{\kappa}{\rho} \quad \text{and} \quad \chi_M = \chi M$$

where M = the molecular weight

ρ = the density.

When determined experimentally, χ_M includes any diamagnetic contributions due to other ions and atoms present in the sample. To obtain a true value of the paramagnetic susceptibility (χ_M^{corr}), corrections must be *added* to the measured value for all diamagnetic species present. Table 20.1 (p. 204) gives these values.

The magnetic moment (μ) of a compound, resulting from the presence of unpaired electrons is given by

$$\mu = \sqrt{[n(n + 2)]} \qquad \text{Bohr magnetons (BM)}$$

where n = the number of unpaired electrons.

This is known as the spin-only formula, and ignores any contribution to the magnetic moment made by orbital motion of the electron. The Bohr magneton is the unit of magnetic moment

$$1 \text{ BM} = eh/4\pi mc = 9{\cdot}27 \times 10^{-21} \text{ erg/gauss.}$$

It can be shown that molar susceptibility and magnetic moment are related by the expression

$$\chi_M = \frac{N^2\mu^2}{3RT}.$$ (20.3)

Therefore from a susceptibility measurement the number of unpaired electrons may be determined. The temperature term arises as a result of thermal motion tending to randomize the molecular magnets, whereas the applied magnetic field tends to orient the molecular magnets. The expression (20.3) neglects any diamagnetic contribution to the magnetic susceptibility. Therefore when calculating μ use a corrected susceptibility value (χ_M^{corr}).

The determination of magnetic susceptibilities

The most commonly used method for the determination of magnetic susceptibilities is that due to Gouy. The apparatus, shown diagramatically in Figure 33, consists of an electromagnet, between the

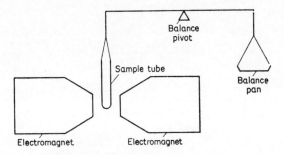

Figure 33. Diagram of a Gouy balance.

poles of which is suspended a cylindrical sample of the compound under investigation. The magnet is so designed that the lower end of the sample is in the pole gap, i.e. a region of high field strength, whereas the other end of the sample is in a region of negligible field strength. The sample is suspended from one beam of a suitable balance so that when the current to the electromagnet is switched on, the apparent change in mass of the sample can be measured.

The force (F) acting on a sample of volume susceptibility κ is given by the expression

$$F = \tfrac{1}{2}\kappa H^2 A$$ (20.4)

where H = the applied field strength

A = the cross-sectional area of the sample.

Equation (20.4) assumes that the atmosphere displaced by the sample has a negligible volume susceptibility. This is true for an atmosphere such as nitrogen and hydrogen but if a paramagnetic atmosphere, e.g. oxygen, is present the equation becomes

$$F = \tfrac{1}{2} \left(\kappa - \kappa_0 \right) H^2 A \qquad (20.5)$$

where κ_0 = the volume susceptibility of the atmosphere.

The force (F) is determined by measuring the apparent change in mass when the magnetic field is switched on, then

$$F = g\Delta w = \tfrac{1}{2}(\kappa - \kappa_0)H^2 A \qquad (20.6)$$

where Δw = the apparent change in mass

g = the acceleration due to gravity.

If V and W are the volume and mass of the sample respectively then

$$\chi = \frac{\kappa V}{W}$$

therefore
$$\kappa = \frac{\chi W}{V}. \qquad (20.7)$$

Substituting (20.7) in (20.6) gives

$$\frac{2g\,\Delta w}{H^2 A} = \frac{\chi W}{V} - \kappa_0$$

or
$$\chi = \left(\frac{2g\,\Delta w}{H^2 A} + \kappa_0 \right) \frac{V}{W}. \qquad (20.8)$$

Therefore, in order to determine χ; H, A, V, W, and κ_0 must be known. Equation (20.8) may be rewritten in the form

$$\chi = \frac{a\Delta w}{W} + \frac{\kappa_0 V}{W} \qquad (20.9)$$

where
$$a = \frac{2g\,V}{H^2 A}.$$

The term $\kappa_0 V/W$ makes allowance for the volume of air which has been replaced by the sample; κ_0 is the volume susceptibility of air.

By calibrating a sample tube with a substance of known susceptibility the constant a can be determined, and separate determinations of H and A need not be made.

Calibration of the sample tube and the determination of χ for an unknown material

The sample tube is a cylindrical glass container with a reference mark near the open end. Calibrate the tube with finely powdered 'Analar' copper(II) sulphate pentahydrate. Allowance must be made for the susceptibility of the glass tube.

The tube is calibrated in the following way:

(1) Weigh the tube empty with the magnet off W_1.

(2) Weigh the tube empty with the magnet on W_2.

(3) Fill the tube to the reference mark with the finely powdered copper(II) sulphate. This must be done in small portions, each occupying about a 2mm depth of the tube. Tap the tube after each addition.

(4) Weigh the tube and contents with the magnet off W_3.

(5) Weigh the tube and contents with the magnet on W_4.

(6) Remove the copper(II) sulphate, fill the tube to the reference mark with water, and weigh with the magnet off W_5.

This last weighing, coupled with W_1 gives the volume of the tube occupied by the copper(II) sulphate.

Repeat steps (1) and (2) until a constant value ($\pm$ 0·05 mg) for $W_1 - W_2$ is obtained. Repeat steps (4) and (5) until a constant value ($\pm$ 0·05 mg) for $W_4 - W_3$ is obtained.

Now $$\Delta w = (W_4 - W_3) + (W_1 - W_2).$$

The factor $(W_1 - W_2)$ makes allowance for the diamagnetism of the glass tube and is therefore added to $(W_4 - W_3)$.

$$\text{The weight of sample } W = W_3 - W_1.$$

Repeat steps (3), (4), and (5) until a constant value ($\pm 1\%$) for $\Delta w/W$ is obtained.

Now κ_0 = the volume susceptibility of air $= 0·029 \times 10^{-6}$ per g.atom,

$$V = W_5 - W_1,$$

χ = the gram susceptibility for copper(II) sulphate pentahydrate

$$= 5·92 \times \frac{293}{T} \times 10^{-6}$$

and W and Δw have been measured. Therefore, a can be determined from eqn. (20·9) above. The tube is now filled with the material whose susceptibility is to be determined and operations (4) and (5) carried out. Refill the tube and repeat steps (4) and (5) until a constant value ($\pm 1\%$) for $\Delta w/W$ is obtained. The gram susceptibility, and hence the molar susceptibility (χ_M) can then be calculated from eqn. (20.9) above. To determine the true value of molar paramagnetic susceptibility (χ_M^{corr}), χ_M must be corrected for diamagnetic constituents, values of which are given in Table 20.1.

Table 20.1. *Diamagnetic susceptibilities per g. ion* $\times 10^{-6}$

Na^+	1·0	F^-	9·1	H		2·93	F	6·3
K^+	14·9	Cl^-	23·4	C		6·00	Cl	20·1
NH_4^+	13·3	Br^-	34·6	N ring		4·61	Br	30·6
Cu^{2+}	12·8	I^-	50·6	N open chain		5·57	I	44·6
Co^{2+}	12·8	NO_3^-	18·9	N diamide, imide		2·11	S	15·0
Ni^{2+}	12·8	CN^-	13·0				As^v	43·0
Mn^{2+}	14·0	CNS^-	31·0	O ether, alcohol		4·61	As^{III}	20·9
Cr^{2+}	15·0	SO_4^{2-}	40·1				H_2O	13
Co^{3+}	10·0	CO_3^{2-}	29·5	O ketone, aldehyde		$-1·73$		
Mn^{3+}	10·0	OH^-	12·0					
		ClO_4^-	32·0	O carboxyl		3·36		

When making diamagnetic corrections, an addition to the measured value is made for each atom present in the molecule, e.g., $K_2[CuCl_4]2H_2O$ has a measured molar susceptibility of 1375×10^{-6}. The diamagnetic correction for K, Cl, and H_2O is obtained as:

$$
\begin{array}{lll}
K & 2 \times 14·9 & = 29·8 \times 10^{-6} \\
Cu^{2+} & 1 \times 12·8 & = 12·8 \times 10^{-6} \\
Cl & 4 \times 20·1 & = 80·4 \times 10^{-6} \\
H_2O & 2 \times 13 & = 26·0 \times 10^{-6} \\
\hline
\text{Total:} & & 149 \quad \times 10^{-6}
\end{array}
$$

therefore $\chi_M^{\text{corr}} = (1375 + 149) \times 10^{-6} = 1524 \times 10^{-6}$

The corrected value χ_M^{corr} is now substituted in eqn. (20.3) to determine μ and hence the number of unpaired electrons in the molecule.

Products suitable for magnetic susceptibility measurements are obtained from the following experiments:

The preparation of hexamminecobalt(III) chloride, p. 77.
The preparation of manganese(II) chloride, p. 49.
The preparation of tris(acetylacetonato)manganese(III) p. 51.

The magnetic moment of each of the above compounds can be explained in terms of high or low spin states of the metal ion. The magnetic moment of chromium(II) acetate is unusual for a d^4 ion, cf. Mn^{III} above, and can not be interpreted in such simple terms. The anomalous magnetic moment of chromium(II) acetate can be explained in terms of the structure of the compound.

The preparation of chromium(II) acetate

The qualitative reactions of chromium described on p. 41 have shown that the chromium(II) oxidation state is readily oxidized by atmospheric oxygen to chromium(III). Therefore all chromium(II) salts must be prepared in an inert atmosphere. Such conditions can be produced in a dry box, where one is available, see p. 149. Alternatively, by careful consideration of all the manipulations involved in the preparation of an air-sensitive compound, it may be possible to devise a simple apparatus in which an inert atmosphere is always maintained over the reactants and products. The preparation of chromium(II) chloride and chromium(II) acetate can be treated in this way.

Two filter tubes of the type shown in Figure 34 are required. Nitrogen gas is passed in through the side arm. For filtration steps the water pump may be attached either to the side arm or the delivery tube. All joints are ground glass and standard so that the two filter tubes may be easily connected together. The maintenance of the nitrogen atmosphere is greatly simplified if the open end of the filter tube is connected to a Drechsel bottle, containing paraffin oil. A steady flow of nitrogen, judged by the rate of bubbling through the oil, must be maintained at all stages of the preparation.

Materials required: Chromium(III) chloride hexahydrate
Granulated zinc
Nitrogen

All reaction vessels must be purged with nitrogen immediately before use.

Place granulated zinc (10 g) in a 250 ml dropping funnel and add carefully a solution of chromium(III) chloride hexahydrate (10 g) in 40 ml of hydrochloric acid (25 ml of concentrated hydrochloric acid and 15 ml of water). Pass a slow stream of nitrogen into the neck of the funnel until reaction is complete and a pale blue solution is obtained. Run the solution into the filter tube which is being purged

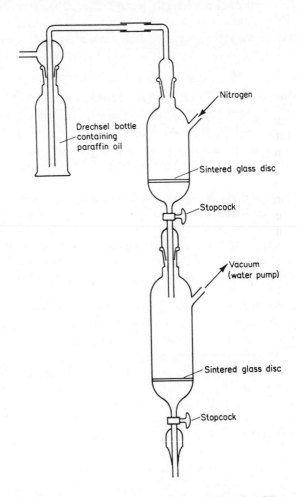

Figure 34. Apparatus for the preparation of chromium(II) acetate.

by a stream of nitrogen through the side arm. In a second identical filter tube place a solution of sodium acetate (15 g) in 20 ml of water. The water used to prepare this solution should have been boiled and cooled in a stream of nitrogen. Purge with nitrogen the filter tube containing sodium acetate and connect the two filter tubes together, with the chromium(II) chloride solution uppermost. Attach a water pump to the side arm of the lower filter tube and draw the chromium-(II) chloride through the sinter and into the sodium acetate solution. Ensure that a nitrogen flow is maintained through the side arm of the upper filter tube.

When filtration is complete, and a thick red precipitate has been obtained in the lower filter tube, quickly disconnect the water pump, remove the upper filter tube, and connect the nitrogen to the side arm of the filter tube containing the chromium(II) acetate. Filter the red precipitate with suction, maintaining the nitrogen flow over the solution. Wash with a little cold water, alcohol, and ether. Dry on the sinter in a nitrogen atmosphere. When dry the solid may be removed and kept in a stoppered container, previously flushed with nitrogen.

Complementary work:

(1) Measure the magnetic susceptibility of the product. Explain the result in terms of the structure of chromium(II) acetate.

(2) Determine the percentage of chromium in the product.

(3) Use a volumetric method to determine the equivalent weight of the product. Show that the results from (2) and (3) agree with the oxidation state of chromium(II) in the product.

Bibliography

Selwood, P. W., *Magnetochemistry*, Interscience, New York, (1956).

Figgis, B. N. and Lewis, J., in *Modern Coordination Chemistry*, Editors, Lewis, J. and Wilkins, R. G., Interscience, New York, (1960).

Earnshaw, A., *Introduction to Magnetochemistry*, Academic Press, London and New York, (1968).

21 Potentiometric titrations

Introduction

Visual methods for the determination of end points in volumetric analysis are not always satisfactory and in some cases cannot be used at all. This may be due to a variety of causes such as:

(a) Coloured solutions may mask the colour change of an indicator.

(b) The use of dilute solutions may mean that the end point of a titration cannot be accurately located.

(c) The available indicators may not undergo a colour change at the required point of reaction.

(d) It is not always possible to follow a reaction having a succession of end points by indicator techniques.

(e) A colour-blind worker may be unable to use the conventional indicators.

In such cases the measurement of the potential of a suitable electrode immersed in a solution can indicate when the end point of a titration is reached. Such potentiometric titrations can often give results of increased accuracy compared with established indicator methods. The only condition is that the potential of the electrode should vary with the addition or removal of some ion in the reactants. Since the potential of a single electrode cannot be measured directly, a second electrode of known and constant potential must also be present in the titrated solution, against which the potential of the indicator electrode may be measured.

The standard hydrogen electrode is accepted as the absolute reference electrode and is assigned a value of zero. The standard hydrogen electrode consists of hydrogen at 1 atm pressure in contact with a solution of hydrogen ions of unit activity; this is unsuitable for

routine work and consequently several secondary electrodes have
been devised. The most common is the calomel electrode which
consists of mercury in contact with a solution of potassium chloride
saturated with mercury(I) chloride (calomel). Electric contact with
the mercury is made by means of platinum wire. Contact with the
solution is made by an asbestos fibre projecting through the glass
container, or by contact at a loose glass joint. The potential of the
calomel electrode depends upon the concentration of the potassium
chloride solution, thus:

$$\left.\begin{array}{lll} 0{\cdot}1\text{M KCl} & -0{\cdot}334 \text{ volts} \\ 1{\cdot}0\text{M KCl} & -0{\cdot}280 \text{ volts} \\ \text{Saturated KCl} & -0{\cdot}246 \text{ volts} \end{array}\right\} \text{ at } 25°\text{C}$$

A frequently used hydrogen-ion responsive electrode is the glass
electrode. The working part of this electrode consists of a bulb or
membrane of pH-responsive glass which is sealed to a stem of a
harder, high-resistance glass such as Pyrex. The inside of this electrode contains an electrode of constant potential such as a platinum
wire, inserted into a buffer solution, which thus establishes electrical
contact with the pH-responsive membrane.

A variety of other electrodes such as the silver-silver chloride,
the quinhydrone, and the antimony electrode are also available but
a complete description of all available electrodes is out of place in a
text of this type.

Practical considerations

The apparatus for a potentiometric titration consists of a beaker
equipped with a stirrer, an indicator electrode, a reference electrode,
a potentiometer to measure the potential difference between the
two electrodes, and a burette for the delivery of titrant. The choice
of electrodes will depend upon the particular determination to be
carried out. A glass electrode as indicator and a calomel electrode
as reference are suitable for an acid-base titration but unsuitable
for a silver nitrate-halide titration. The choice of a potentiometer is
to some extent governed by the electrode assembly employed. Most
electrodes have a low resistance and the e.m.f. may be measured
with any type of potentiometer. However, the resistance of a glass
electrode is high, of the order of 100 megohms. When a glass
electrode is employed a vacuum tube voltmeter must be used to

measure the e.m.f. of the electrode assembly. Such a voltmeter is used in commercially produced pH meters, and so when using a glass electrode the titration should be followed using a pH meter. For most titrations the actual value of pH or e.m.f. need not be known; only the rate of change of pH or e.m.f. with added titrant is required. In some cases titration to a specific pH may be required, in which case the pH meter must be calibrated before use with standard buffer solutions. The composition and pH at 25°C of some buffer solutions is given in Table 21.1. Fluctuations of pH with temperature are not large, being of the order of 0·001 pH unit/°C. Consult the makers' handbook and/or obtain instruction in the operation of the potentiometer or pH meter available before commencing work.

Table 21.1. *Values of* pH *at* 25°C *for some buffer solutions*

Compound	Concentration	pH
Potassium hydrogen tetroxalate	0·05M	1·68
Potassium hydrogen phthalate	0·05M	4·01
Potassium hydrogen tartrate	Saturated	3·56
Potassium dihydrogen phosphate and disodium hydrogen phosphate, each 0·025M		6·86
Borax	0·01M	9·18

Pipette a suitable volume of the solution to be titrated into a beaker, and add distilled water until the beaker is about half full. Adjust the electrodes so that they dip into the solution to a depth of at least 1 cm. Where a calomel electrode is used, make sure that the level of liquid in the electrode is above the level of the liquid in the beaker. Take care that the electrodes will not be struck by the stirrer when the latter is rotating. Switch on the stirrer and adjust the rate of stirring to give efficient mixing of the added titrant. Record the burette reading and the e.m.f. across the electrodes. Add an increment of titrant, and record the e.m.f. across the electrodes when a steady value is reached. Repeat this process and plot a graph of e.m.f. against the volume of titrant added. The approach of the end point is indicated by a bending upwards or downwards of the titration curve; in other words the e.m.f. is changing more rapidly with the addition of titrant. In the vicinity of the end point add the titrant in small increments, 0·02–0·10 ml. Inspection of the titration curve will indicate where the rate of change of e.m.f. is greatest and this is taken as the end point for the reaction. In some cases, as in the titration of a di- or tribasic acid, more than one point of inflection will be observed and thus the position at which a part of the reaction is complete can be determined.

Potentiometric methods of following a titration are now well established and have been developed to such an extent that a titration can be carried out automatically. A variety of automatic titrimeters is now available but all have the same basic features. The e.m.f. of the electrode system is amplified and used to actuate an electromagnetic valve which controls the flow of titrant. In the early stages of a titration the titrant flows without interruption but when the e.m.f. of the electrode system begins to change rapidly, automatic operation commences, and the end point is approached slowly with progressively smaller increments of titrant added until an exact equivalence point is reached. The operator presets an e.m.f. on the instrument in use, at which equivalence occurs.

The titration of phosphoric acid with a base

Materials required: 0·1M Phosphoric acid
0·3M Sodium hydroxide
pH meter
Stirrer
Glass and calomel electrodes

Titrate aliquots of phosphoric acid with the standard sodium hydroxide solution. Demonstrate the tribasic nature of phosphoric acid by plotting the results graphically. Determine the pH at which each stage of the neutralization is complete.

The determination of the tripolyphosphate content of sodium tripolyphosphate

Materials required: Sodium tripolyphosphate (see p. 22)
Sodium hydroxide 0·1M
Hydrochloric acid 0·2M

Materials required: Zinc sulphate solution
(12·5% of zinc sulphate heptahydrate adjusted to pH 3·8)
Bromophenol blue, 0·04% solution.
pH meter
Titration assembly
Stirrer
Glass and calomel electrodes

Approximately 0·5 g of the sodium tripolyphosphate is accurately weighed and dissolved in 50 ml of water. Add sodium hydroxide solution until pH 7 is reached. Add sufficient indicator to give a definite blue colour to the solution, and add 0·2M hydrochloric acid until there is a definite yellow colour in the solution. Make up the volume of the solution to 100 ml and add 0·1M sodium hydroxide until the pH is exactly 3·8. Add 70 ml of the zinc sulphate reagent, stir for one or two minutes, and then titrate the solution to pH 3·8 with 0·1M sodium hydroxide.

Equations for the reactions:

$$Na_5P_3O_{10} + 2HCl = Na_3H_2P_3O_{10} + 2NaCl \text{ (adjusting pH to 3·8)}$$

$$Na_3H_2P_3O_{10} + ZnSO_4 = Na_3ZnP_3O_{10} + H_2SO_4$$

$$H_2SO_4 + 2NaOH = Na_2SO_4 + 2H_2O.$$

As a large excess of zinc sulphate is present a further reaction is possible,

$$Na_3ZnP_3O_{10} + ZnSO_4 = NaZn_2P_3O_{10} + Na_2SO_4.$$

However, unless the solution is heated, seeded or allowed to stand for several hours this reaction does not occur.

Reference
Bell, R. N., *Analyt. Chem.*, (1947), **19**, 97.

Bibliography

Willard, H. H., Merritt, L. L. and Dean, J. A., *Instrumental Methods of Analysis*, Van Nostrand, New York, 4th ed., (1965).
Vogel, A. I., *Textbook of Quantitative Inorganic Analysis*, Longmans, 3rd ed., (1961).

22 Polarimetry

The measurement of the change of orientation of plane polarized light when it interacts with optically active materials is known as polarimetry. It is one of the oldest instrumental methods used in the study of coordination compounds. The detection of the existence of optical activity in an isomer of a compound, as mentioned previously, see p. 97, often gives useful information as to the structure of that isomer.

The nature of polarized light

Most of the unreflected light that is usually observed is not polarized, that is the electromagnetic vibrations are in all possible orientations around the direction of propagation of the light. Plane polarized light consists of electromagnetic vibrations in one plane only, all others are excluded from the light beam. Since a ray of light consists of an electric and a magnetic component vibrating at right angles to each other the term 'plane' is not strictly accurate. However, by noting only the direction of the electric component the term plane polarized may be used. When making measurements on optically active materials a source of plane polarized light is required, and the presence of optical activity is determined by observing a change in the orientation of the plane of polarization.

In circularly polarized light the electric component, and therefore the magnetic component, spirals around the direction of propagation of the ray, either clockwise or anticlockwise. Plane polarized light may, for many purposes, be represented as the vector sum of two circularly polarized rays, one polarized in a clockwise sense, the other in an anticlockwise sense, both having the same amplitude of vibration. Consider Figure 35. While the clockwise polarized ray may rotate from A to B via C, the anticlockwise polarized ray will also have rotated from A to B via D, and the vectoral sum of the electric components will be the plane polarized ray AB. If the two

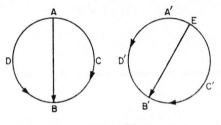

Figure 35.

rays pass through a medium which slows down the anticlockwise polarized ray, then while the clockwise polarized ray travels from A′ to B′ via C′ the anticlockwise polarized ray will travel from A′ to B′ via D′. The vectoral sum will now be represented by a plane polarized ray B′E, where the plane of polarization has been rotated from its original position.

Instrumentation for polarimetry

The essential features of any polarimeter are: a light source, a polarizer, an analyser, a graduated scale to measure the amount of rotation, and a sample tube. See Figure 36 for a schematic diagram

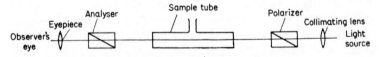

Figure 36. Schematic diagram of a polarimeter.

of a polarimeter. In all but the simplest instruments a half-shade device is also incorporated to facilitate the measurement of rotation of the plane of polarization.

The light source may be a sodium vapour lamp, in which case a filter of 7% potassium dichromate solution, 6 cm thick, is used to eliminate the continuous background from the wavelengths 5890, and 5896Å. An alternative light source is a mercury lamp which emits light mainly at wavelengths, 4358, 4916, 5461, 5770, and 5791 Å. Light of a particular wavelength may be obtained by employing suitable filters.

The polarizer and analyser both consist of a pair of calcite prisms cut in such a way that the emergent light is plane polarized. The other components of the light are totally reflected. The light entering the prism must be parallel in order to avoid the transmission of unpolarized light.

The sample tube is constructed from glass, the ends of which are flat and parallel. It is also important that these end plates are free from strain otherwise they will themselves produce partial polarization of the light. Sample tubes are nominally 10 cm long although the length will, of course, vary with temperature. This length may be determined precisely by measuring the rotation of a known strongly rotating solution at a definite temperature.

The half shade device. It might at first sight be thought that a polarimetric measurement could be made by rotating the analyser until light of minimum intensity emerges from the eyepiece of the instrument in the absence of a sample, and repeating the process wth a sample present. The difference in these two readings would then give the amount of rotation produced by the sample. In practice this is a difficult operation and assistance is obtained by introducing a half shade device. A simple form of a half shade device is constructed as shown in Figure 37. A polarizing prism is cut in half along the polarizing direction AB, a portion of one of the halves is ground down to BC, and the halves cemented together as shown in Figure 37c. When such a prism is used to polarize the light, the two halves of the prism will produce polarized light beams tilted at a slight angle to each other. Rotation of the analyser will result in complete extinction, first of one half of the field then of the other. The null position is obtained when both halves of the field appear of equal intensity. The analyser will then be at the same angle to each of the two polarized light beams. Such a state is relatively easy to determine visually.

Experimental procedure

To make a measurement of optical rotation set up the polarimeter and the light source according to the manufacturers' instructions. Determine the null point with an empty sample tube in the light path, by adjusting the analyser until the two halves of the field of view are of equal intensity. Note the reading on the scale. Prepare a solution of the compound to be studied, place this in the sample tube, and re-adjust the analyser until the two halves of the field of view again have the same intensity. The difference between this reading

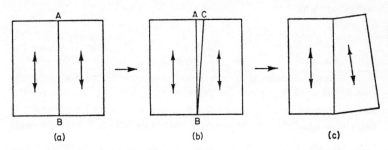

Figure 37. Diagram illustrating the formation of a half-shade device. The
(a, b & c)   symbol $\updownarrow$ indicates the direction of polarization.

and the null point gives the angle of rotation for the particular solution used. Repeat the determination until concordant results are obtained. Record the temperature of the solution at which the measurement was made. Suitable solution concentrations vary from compound to compound. In the case of intensely coloured compounds dilute solutions may have to be used in order that sufficient light is transmitted to make the measurement possible. Use a solution which gives a reading of several degrees, when possible. Determine the specific rotation from the measured angle, using the equation given on p. 98.

Optically active materials suitable for polarimetric measurements are produced by:

The resolution of *cis*-dichlorobis(ethylenediamine)chromium(III) chloride   p. 99

The preparation and resolution of the tris(ethylenediamine)-cobalt(III) ion   p. 100

Bibliography

Weissberger, A., *Technique of Organic Chemistry*, Vol. I, Interscience, New York, (1959).

Willard, H. H., Merritt, L. L. and Dean, J. A., *Instrumental Methods of Analysis*, Van Nostrand, New York, 4th ed., (1965).

General bibliography

The following references contain much information which is relevant to the complementary work given after each experiment. The use of a selection of these references, in addition to the references given at the end of specific chapters, is strongly recommended.

Belcher, R. and Nutten, A. J., *Quantitative Inorganic Analysis*, Butterworths, 2nd ed., (1960).

Brauer, G., *Handbook of Preparative Inorganic Chemistry*, 2 vols., Academic Press, New York, (1963).

Cotton, F. A. and Wilkinson, G., *Advanced Inorganic Chemistry*, Interscience, New York, 2nd ed., (1966).

Emeleus, H. J. and Anderson, J. S., *Modern Aspects of Inorganic Chemistry*, Routledge & Kegan Paul, 3rd ed., (1960).

Emeleus, H. J. and Sharpe, A. G. (Editors), *Advances in Inorganic Chemistry* and *Radiochemistry*, Academic Press, New York. *Inorganic Syntheses*, McGraw Hill, New York. Editions vary from year to year.

Heslop, R. B. and Robinson, P. L., *Inorganic Chemistry*, Elsevier, London, (1960).

Moeller, T., *Inorganic Chemistry*, Wiley, New York, (1952).

Palmer, W. G., *Experimental Inorganic Chemistry*, Cambridge Univ. Press, (1954).

Phillips, C. S. G. and Williams, R. J. P., *Inorganic Chemistry*, Clarendon Press, Oxford, (1966).

Vogel, A. I., *Quantitative Inorganic Analysis*, Longmans, 3rd ed., (1961).

Wells, A. F., *Structural Inorganic Chemistry*, Clarendon Press, Oxford, (1962).

Appendix — SI Units

SI is the abbreviation in many languages for Système International d'Unités, it is an extension and refinement of the traditional metric system. Non-SI units which are in current use are to be replaced eventually by SI units. The aim of this appendix is to assist with the introduction and use of the new units in course work.

To this end tables of SI units together with conversion factors are given below. Where further amplification is necessary this is given under chapter headings below. For further information the reader is referred to:

(a) The Royal Society Conference of Editors, *Metrication in Scientific Journals*. This is an 8-page pamphlet published by the Royal Society (1968) and available from the Executive Secretary, 6 Carlton House Terrace, London S.W.1, England.

(b) *Changing to the Metric System, Conversion Factors, Symbols and Definitions*. H.M.S.O., 1967.

(c) *Physico-chemical Quantities and Units* by M. L. McGlashan, R.I.C. Monograph for Teachers No. 15, July 1968.

Chapter 3
The calorie is replaced in the SI by the Joule. The following equations illustrate the change from calories to Joules.

Page 29	$Si(s) + 2Cl_2(g) = SiCl_4(g)$		
Entropy at 25°C and 101·325 kN m^{-2} in J°K^{-1}	18·7	223·0	331·4
	$\Delta S = 331·4 - (18·7 + 2 \times 223·0) = -133·3$ J°K^{-1}		

Page 30	$CaCO_3(s) = CaO(s) + CO_2(g)$		
Entropy at 25°C and 101·325 kN m^{-2} in J°K^{-1}	88·7	39·8	213·7
	$\Delta S = (39·8 + 213·7) - 88·7 = 164·7$ J°K^{-1}		

Page 31. At 700°C $\Delta G° = 0.66$ kcal becomes $\Delta G° = 2.76$ kJ
Reactants are each added at a pressure of 303.975 kN m^{-2} and products removed each at a partial pressure of 101.325 kN m^{-2}

then $J_p = \dfrac{1 \times 1}{3 \times 3} = 0.1111$

therefore $RT\ln J_p = 8.314 \times 973 \times 2.303 \times (-0.9643)$

$$= -17960 \text{ J} = -17.96 \text{ kJ}$$

Chapter 11

The term 'specific rotation', $\{a\}$ is replaced by 'specific optical rotatory power', a_m. It is defined by the equation

$$a_m = \frac{aV}{ml} \text{ rad m}^2 \text{ kg}^{-1}$$

Where $a =$ the measured angular rotation, radians

$m =$ the mass of solute, kg

$V =$ the volume of solution, m^3

$l =$ the length of the column of solution, m.

Suppose we have a solution containing 1 kg m^{-3} giving a rotation of 1 radian for a column of solution of 1 m

Then $a_m = \dfrac{1 \times 1}{1 \times 1} = 1$ rad m^2 kg^{-1}

On the CGS system the rotation will be $360/2\pi$ deg, the column of solution 10 dm and the concentration 0.1g/100 ml

$$\{a\} = \frac{100a}{cl}$$

$$= 100 \times \frac{360}{2\pi} \times \frac{1}{0.1} \times \frac{1}{10}$$

$$= \frac{36}{2\pi} \times 10^3 = 5.73 \times 10^3 \text{ deg ml g}^{-1} \text{ dm}^{-1}$$

Therefore values of $\{a\}$ must be multiplied by 1.75×10^{-4} to give values of a_m.

The term 'molecular rotation', $\{M\}$ is replaced by molar 'optical rotatory power', a_n. It is defined by the equation

$$a_n = \frac{a}{cl} \text{ rad m}^2 \text{ mol}^{-1}$$

where c = the concentration in mol m^{-3}

Chapter 13

Table 13.1.A.

	Liquid Ammonia	Water
Heat of fusion, kJ mol^{-1}	5·66	6·00
Heat of vaporization, kJ mol^{-1}	33·35	40·72
Density, kg m^{-3}	677 at –33°C	960 at 100°C

Chapter 17

The recommended unit of length is the metre. The widely used units centimetre, micron, millimicron and Ångström are not recommended under the SI. Fortunately, conversion to SI units is a simple matter, see Table A.

Colorimetry

The term 'transmission' is replaced by 'transmittance'. The term 'optical density' is replaced by 'decadic absorbance' with the recommended symbol A.

In the Beer–Lambert law

$$\log \frac{I_0}{I_t} = \epsilon cl$$

the concentration (c) is expressed in mol m^{-3} and the thickness of the absorbing solution in metres. Therefore the extinction coefficient (ϵ) is expressed in mol^{-1} m^2. Extinction coefficients on the CGS system must be multiplied by 10^{-1} to give the value in SI units.

Chapter 18

The term 'specific conductance' is replaced by 'electrolytic conductivity'. Electrolytic conductivity is defined as the current passing across unit area under unit potential gradient, and has the units Ω^{-1} m^{-1}. The recommended symbol is κ. Thus

$$\kappa = j/E \ \Omega^{-1} \ m^{-1}$$

j = electric current density, A m^{-2}.

E = electric field strength, V m^{-1}.

Values of the conductivity in CGS units must be multiplied by 10^2 to give the corresponding value in SI units.

Molar conductivity Λ is defined by the expression

$$\Lambda = \frac{\kappa}{c} \ \ \Omega^{-1} \ m^2 \ mol^{-1}$$

where c = concentration, mol m^{-3}.

Values of molar conductivity on the CGS scale must be multiplied by 10^{-4} to give the corresponding value in SI units.

Chapter 20

When a substance is placed in a magnetic field the relationship between field intensity within the substance, and the applied field is given by

$$\frac{B}{\mu_0} = H + M \tag{20.1.A}$$

where B = the magnetic flux density or magnetic induction, Wb m^{-2}

H = magnetic field strength, A m^{-1}

μ_0 = permeability of a vacuum, H m^{-1}

M = the magnetization, A m^{-1}.

Dividing the expression (20.1.A) throughout by H gives

$$\frac{B}{\mu_0 H} = 1 + \frac{M}{H} \tag{20.2.A}$$

The quotient M/H is known as the volume susceptibility, and is given the symbol χ.

On the CGS system

$$\frac{B}{H} = 1 + 4\pi \frac{I}{H} \quad \text{eqn. 20.2, } p. \ 200.$$

Suppose that $B = x$ gauss and $H = y$ oersteds

Then x gauss $= x \times 10^{-4}$ Wb m^{-2}

and y oersteds $= y \times \dfrac{1}{4\pi} \times 10^3$ A m^{-1}

On the SI

$$\frac{B}{\mu_0 H} = \frac{x \times 10^{-4}}{(4\pi \times 10^{-7})\, y \times \dfrac{1}{4\pi} \times 10^3} = \frac{x}{y} = 1 + \chi$$

On the CGS system

$$\frac{x}{y} = 1 + 4\pi\kappa$$

where $\kappa =$ the CGS symbol for volume susceptibility.
Comparing the volume susceptibilities on the two systems

$$\therefore \chi = 4\pi\kappa.$$

Other expressions in use are the mass susceptibility, χ_m and the molar susceptibility, χ_M, which are related to χ in the following way

$$\chi_m = \frac{\chi}{\rho} \text{ m}^3 \text{ kg}^{-1}; \quad \chi_M = \frac{10^{-3}\chi M}{\rho} \text{ m}^3 \text{ mol}^{-1}$$

where $M =$ the molecular weight, g
$\rho\ =$ the density, kg m^{-3}

To convert values of mass susceptibility on the CGS system to the SI multiply by $4\pi \times 10^{-3}$, and to convert values of molar susceptibility from CGS to SI multiply by $4\pi \times 10^{-6}$. When determined experimentally, χ_M includes any diamagnetic contributions due to other ions and atoms present in the sample. To obtain a true value of the paramagnetic susceptibility ($\chi_M{}^{\text{corr}}$), corrections must be added to the measured value for all diamagnetic species present. Table 20.1 (*p. 204*) gives these values.

The magnetic moment (μ) of a compound resulting from the presence of unpaired electrons is given by

$$\mu = g\beta\sqrt{S(S+1)}$$

where $g =$ the spectroscopic splitting factor, often referred to simply as the 'g-factor'

$\beta =$ the Bohr magneton $= eh/4\pi m = 9{\cdot}273 \times 10^{-24}$ A m^2
$S =$ the total spin quantum number.

This is known as the spin only formula and ignores any contribution to the magnetic moment made by orbital motion of the electron. The corresponding equation on the CGS system differs only in the value of the Bohr magneton, which on the CGS system is $9 \cdot 27 \times 10^{-21}$ erg gauss^{-1}. Therefore to convert values of magnetic moment from CGS to SI multiply by 10^{-3}.

It can be shown that molar susceptibility and magnetic moment are related by the expression

$$\chi_M = \frac{\mu_0 N \mu^2}{3kT} \text{ m}^3 \text{ mol}^{-1} \qquad (20.3.\text{A})$$

where μ_0 = the permeability of a vacuum
       = $4\pi \times 10^{-6}$ H m^{-1}
N = the Avogadro constant = $6 \cdot 023 \times 10^{23}$ mol^{-1}
k = the Boltzmann constant = $1 \cdot 381 \times 10^{-23}$ J K^{-1}
T = the temperature, °K
μ = the magnetic moment, A m^2.

The Determination of Magnetic Susceptibilities

The force (F) acting on a sample of volume susceptibility χ is given by the expression

$$F = \tfrac{1}{2} \mu_0 \chi H^2 A \quad \text{newtons} \qquad (20.4.\text{A})$$

where A = cross sectional area of the sample, m^2.
Equation 20.5 now becomes

$$F = \tfrac{1}{2} \mu_0 (\chi - \chi_0) H^2 A \quad \text{newtons} \qquad (20.5.\text{A})$$

where χ_0 = volume susceptibility of the atmosphere.
Equation 20.6 now becomes

$$F = g \, \Delta w = \tfrac{1}{2} \mu_0 \chi (\chi - \chi_0) H^2 A \qquad (20.6.\text{A})$$

If V and W are the volume (m^3) and the mass (kg) of the sample respectively, then

$$\chi_m = \frac{\chi V}{W} \text{ m}^3 \text{ kg}^{-1}$$

where χ_m = mass susceptibility

$$\therefore \chi = \frac{\chi_m W}{V} \qquad (20.7.\text{A})$$

Substituting equation 20.7.A in 20.6.A gives

$$\frac{2g\,\Delta w}{\mu_0 H^2 A} = \frac{X_m W}{V} - X_0$$

$$\text{or } X_m = \left(\frac{2g\,\Delta w}{\mu_0 H^2 A} + X_0\right)\frac{V}{W} \text{ m}^3 \text{ kg}^{-1} \tag{20.8.A}$$

On the CGS system $F = \frac{1}{2}XAH^2$ dynes. If a sample of $A = 1$ cm^2. exerts a force of 4·97 dynes in a field of 4000 oersteds then $4\cdot97 = \frac{1}{2}.X.4000^2$

$$\therefore X = 0\cdot621 \times 10^{-6}$$

On the SI $F = \frac{1}{2}\mu_0 X A H^2$ newtons. Taking the example used above

$$F = 4\cdot97 \times 10^{-5} \text{ Newtons}, \quad A = 10^{-4} \text{ m}^2,$$

and

$$H = \frac{4000}{4\pi \times 10^{-3}} = \frac{10^6}{\pi} \text{ A m}^{-1}$$

$$\therefore X = \frac{2 \times 4\cdot97 \times 10^{-5}}{4\pi \times 10^{-7} \times 10^{-4} \times (10^6/\pi)^2}$$

$$= 4\pi \times 0\cdot621 \times 10^{-6}$$

Therefore to convert volume susceptibilities on the CGS system to the SI the CGS value should be multiplied by 4π.

Table A: Units and Unit Symbols for some Physical Quantities

Physical quantity	Non-SI			SI			Equivalent
	Symbol for phys. quant.	Unit	Symbol for unit	Symbol for phys. quant.	Unit	Symbol for unit	
length	l	foot	ft	l	metre	m	1 ft = 0·3048 m
		inch	in				1 in = 0·0254 m
		micron	μ		micrometre	μm	$1\,\mu = 1\,\mu m = 10^{-6}$ m
		millimicron	mμ		nanometre	nm	$1\,m\mu = 1\,nm = 10^{-9}$ m
		Ångström	Å		nanometre	nm	$1\,Å = 10^{-1}\,nm = 10^{-10}$ m
energy	E	calorie	cal	E	joule	$J = kg\,m^2 s^{-2}$	1 cal = 4·184 J
pressure	P	atmosphere, atm millimetres of mercury	mm Hg	P	newton per square metre	$N\,m^{-2} =$ $Kg\,m^{-1}\,s^{-2}$	1 atm = 101·325 kN m^{-2} 1 mm Hg = 133·3 N m^{-2}
concentration	c	mole per litre	mol l^{-1} M	c	mole per cubic metre	mol m^{-3}	1 mol l^{-1} = 10^3 mol m^{-3}
frequency	ν	cycles per second	cps	ν	Hertz	Hz	1 cps = 1 Hz
density	ρ	gramme per millilitre	g ml^{-1}	ρ	kilogramme per cubic metre	kg m^{-3}	1 g ml^{-1} = 10^3 kg m^{-3}

Physical quantity	Non-SI			SI			Equivalent
	Symbol for phys. quant.	Unit	Symbol for unit	Symbol for phys. quant.	Unit	Symbol for unit	
specific rotation, renamed specific optical rotatory power in SI	$\{\alpha\}$	Degrees millilitres per gramme per decimetre	deg ml g⁻¹ dm⁻¹	α_m	radians square metres per kilogramme	rad m² kg⁻¹	1 deg ml g⁻¹ dm⁻¹ = 1·75 × 10⁻⁴ rad m² kg⁻¹
molecular rotation, renamed molar optical rotatory power in SI	$\{M\}$	Degrees millilitres per mole per decimetre	degml mol⁻¹ dm⁻¹	α_n	radians square metres per mole	rad m² mol⁻¹	1 deg ml mol⁻¹ dm⁻¹ = 1·75 × 10⁻⁵ rad m² mol⁻¹
magnetic flux density	B	gauss	G	B	Tesla	T $= \text{kg s}^{-2}\,\text{A}^{-1}$ $= \text{V s m}^{-2}$	1 G = 10⁻⁴ T
magnetic field strength	H	oersted	Oe	H	ampere per metre	A m⁻¹	$1\,\text{Oe} = \dfrac{1}{4\pi} \times 10^3\,\text{A m}^{-1}$
intensity of magnetization	I	electromagnetic units	emu	M	ampere per metre	A m⁻¹	1 emu = 10³ A m⁻¹
volume susceptibility	κ	no unit	—	χ	no unit	—	$4\pi\kappa = \chi$
mass susceptibility	χ_m	millilitres per gramme	ml g⁻¹	χ_m	cubic metres per kilogramme	m³ kg⁻¹	1 ml g⁻¹ = 10⁻³ m³ kg⁻¹
molar susceptibility	χ_M	millilitres per mole	ml mol⁻¹	χ_M	cubic metres per mole	m³ mol⁻¹	1 ml mol⁻¹ = 10⁻⁶ m³ mol⁻¹

Table B: *Recommended Values of Physical Constants*

Physical Constant	Symbol	Value
permeability of a vacuum	μ_o	$4\pi \times 10^{-7} \, \text{kg m s}^{-2} \text{A}^{-2}$
		$= 4\pi \times 10^{-7} \, \text{H m}^{-1}$
Boltzmann constant	k	$1\cdot380 \times 10^{-23} \, \text{J} \, {}^{\circ}\text{K}^{-1}$
Planck constant	h	$6\cdot625 \times 10^{-34} \, \text{J s}$
Bohr magneton	μ_B	$9\cdot273 \times 10^{-24} \, \text{A m}^2$
Avogadro constant	L, N_A	$6\cdot022 \times 10^{23} \, \text{mol}^{-1}$
Gas constant	$R = Lk$	$8\cdot314 \, \text{J} \, {}^{\circ}\text{K}^{-1} \text{mol}^{-1}$

Index

Periodic table of the elements

I	II												III	IV	V	VI	VII	0
H 1																		He 2
Li 3	Be 4												B 5	C 6	N 7	O 8	F 9	Ne 10
Na 11	Mg 12												Al 13	Si 14	P 15	S 16	Cl 17	Ar 18
K 19	Ca 20	Sc 21	Ti 22	V 23	Cr 24	Mn 25	Fe 26	Co 27	Ni 28	Cu 29	Zn 30		Ga 31	Ge 32	As 33	Se 34	Br 35	Kr 36
Rb 37	Sr 38	Y 39	Zr 40	Nb 41	Mo 42	Tc 43	Ru 44	Rh 45	Pd 46	Ag 47	Cd 48		In 49	Sn 50	Sb 51	Te 52	I 53	Xe 54
Cs 55	Ba 56	La^x	Hf 72	Ta 73	W 74	Re 75	Os 76	Ir 77	Pt 78	Au 79	Hg 80		Tl 81	Pb 82	Bi 83	Po 84	At 85	Rn 86
Fr 87	Ra 88	Ac†																

x Lanthanides

La 57	Ce 58	Pr 59	Nd 60	Pm 61	Sm 62	Eu 63	Gd 64	Tb 65	Dy 66	Ho 67	Er 68	Tm 69	Yb 70	Lu 71

† Actinides

Ac 89	Th 90	Pa 91	U 92	Np 93	Pu 94	Am 95	Cm 96	Bk 97	Cf 98	Es 99	Fm 100	Md 101	102	Lw 103